A	B	C	D	E	F	G	H
A4	B79		27	73	54	90	
						926	
						9172	

I	J	K	L	M	N	P	Q
82		KT62	60	mp20			07
				RT28			

THE GREAT WESTERN BEACH

A Memoir of a Cornish Childhood between the Wars

Emma Smith

BBC
LARGE
PRINT

First published 2008
by Bloomsbury Publishing
This Large Print edition published 2008
by BBC Audiobooks Ltd
by arrangement with
Bloomsbury Publishing Plc

Hardcover ISBN: 978 1 408 41419 4
Softcover ISBN: 978 1 408 41420 0

British Library Cataloguing in Publication Data available

Printed and bound in Great Britain by
CPI Antony Rowe, Chippenham, Wiltshire

When I set out on this recollection of my childhood it was with the idea of interesting, perhaps, and perhaps amusing, my three grandsons:

LUKE, and HUGO, and JOE.

But in writing it I came to realise that, first and foremost, I have to dedicate it to my sister:

PAM;

the companion who shared with me, more closely than my brothers could, those early long-ago years in Newquay, Cornwall.

To all of them, therefore, and, of course, to my own two children,

BARNEY and ROSIE,

as well as to all of my nieces, nephews, great-nieces and great-nephews, these pages of memories—which will cause, I hope, offence to no one—are offered, with my love.

PHOTOGRAPHS

mother, Harvey and the rather unlovable Aunt Margaret. Jack the Beachman is stacking deckchairs in the background

109. Sir Oliver Lodge's island retreat, above the Towan Beach (a photograph taken some years after we left Newquay)

162. Capt. Guthrie Hallsmith, my father, 1918

221. On a picnic, possibly in Porth. I am sitting between Pam, sporting pigtails, and Jim (*front*). My mother is pouring tea for Cousin Mildred Martin

260. Jim, Pam, me and Harvey sliding down a sand dune

296. At last! The new baby has arrived. Harvey, my mother, Pam and me

306. Tea at the Tennis Club. My mother (who has obviously been playing tennis!) on the extreme left, my father on the extreme right. Mr Cooper is sitting next to him. Mrs Vidal-Rowe is smiling at the camera

310. My father in front of Newquay Lawn Tennis Club's pavilion; 'Our Mr Lodge' behind him, to the right

341. The Hallsmiths of our grandparents' generation: Martin (killed in the Great War), my father (a schoolboy), Mary *née* Martin (our Granny), Harvey (who died in the 'flu epidemic, 1918), Dorothy, Mr Harvey Hallsmith (our Grandpa) and Rosemary (*front*), c. 1911 (before the old chap went bankrupt!)

344. My mother as a young woman

354. On our way back from lessons with Miss Howard, snapped by a street photographer: me,

Pam and Ada Møeller

357. Rex and Eve Dyer (Mrs Mulroney's grandchildren), with me, Jim, Harvey and Pam

361. Crossing the dunes, Holywell Beach: Jim and Pam transporting Harvey in the litter invented by our father

405. The last Newquay summer, 1935. Cousin Christine Pearce (*left, back*), who was staying with us, me, Pam, Jim, Robert Langley (who was killed early on in World War II), my mother and Harvey

424. Summer, 1935. Newquay Lawn Tennis Club: my partner, the hotel visitor, Graham, and I having won the Under-14s section of the Junior Tennis Tournament

440. Low tide between the Great Western Beach and the Towan Beach: me in the foreground, the Atlantic Hotel in the background, and very faintly visible further off, the Hewers' Hut

442. My father and mother in what appears to be the early happy days of their marriage, with the fairly newborn twins, *c.* late 1920. Pam is on my father's knee, Jim on my mother's

FOREWORD

My darling grandsons—Luke, Hugo and Joe, I've been told I should write my autobiography—that is to say, the story of my life—because, if for no other reason, it would be interesting for you, one day, to read it. But would it? I wonder. I've no idea what you might find interesting in my life, or whether it would have any interest at all for you. How can I tell? In any case, I couldn't possibly expose the story of my life on paper—not in full, and truthfully. I don't believe anyone can, and I don't believe anyone ever really does. Most people's lives are full of secrets—other people's secrets as well as their own. I've never felt any compulsion to air secrets, mine or anyone else's. All sorts of moments are private, and should remain so. And a great many thoughts are private, sometimes very private, and could be harmful if you let them out. I think privacy is extremely important: a source of understanding to be guarded as valuable for being exactly what it is—unshared, the ultimate sanctum.

You have, of course, to be strictly honest within yourself about yourself, as well as about other people; if not, how will you make sense of the puzzles, the whys and the wherefores of anything? I've never been able to prevent myself from finding out, even sometimes unwillingly, more and more of what has seemed to me to be the truth about people's characters and motivations, including the characters and motivations of those people I love (perhaps especially of those I love): what they are really like, which is often quite different from what they think they are like. But there is no need to tell them of your discoveries. Better not. In fact, much better not, even though your own feelings and behaviour may depend on, or alter, according to what you discover. You can keep quiet about it.

So any autobiography I chose to write would have had to be one with a lot missing: it would have had to be fragmentary, made up of selected glimpses, bits and pieces, and not, perhaps, worth anyone's while to read. I've therefore decided to try to put on record for you simply and only an account of my very early existence, from 1923 to 1935, by which time I had reached the age of twelve, and we left the seaside behind us and moved away, inland, to the fringes of Dartmoor in Devonshire. Nothing was the same, afterwards: everything changed. But that is another tale entirely, and not one I mean to embark upon telling.

If it bores you, this following little memoir of mine, please feel free to skip it. My advice is, never read anything that bores you. Reading *must* be a pleasure. For me it has always been one of the greatest of all the many pleasures of life; wonderful life!

I
The Bungalow

Where ought I to start?

I suppose by describing what I first remember.

I remember the cover on my cot, an eiderdown with a pattern of large dark-green and dark-red roses: beautiful. The room is a small one, crowded to its limits by my parents' big double bed, and my cot, and a wardrobe. My mother bends over the cot to say goodnight. She and my father are going out for the evening. Her head is swathed in a cloud of very soft pale pink and green silky material.

This is Newquay, Cornwall, 1924. We live in a house called, apparently, The Bungalow, even though it has a staircase and a floor above. It stands at the summit, or very nearly the summit, of Trenance Hill, the highest point of the long ridge that separates the town, with its network of shops, and its harbour, and its cliffs and beaches beyond, from lush buttercup and cowslip fields, a surprisingly countrified landscape sloping down to the tidal estuary of the River Gannel. On the seaward, or town side of the ridge, a bit lower than its actual crest but still commandingly high, runs a road called Mount Wise, a road leading on and on, perfectly straight, until it passes the few modestly inconspicuous hotels, the nursing home, the houses, and then continues on past the fields and the tall stone hedge that supports a line of mysteriously humming telegraph poles, to peter out eventually in the rabbity rough uptilting commonland of Pentire Head, off the rocky end of which, in the deep cold waters and unceasing swells of the Atlantic Ocean, lives a colony of seals.

Some fifty yards beyond our Bungalow, the top

3

of Trenance Hill flattens to accommodate on its windy plateau the half-dozen or so grass courts and the creosote-smelling pavilion of Newquay's only private Tennis Club. Skirting round the club's exclusive perimeter, the public road plunges precipitously down, down, sunk between over-arching trees, twisting and turning to reach the bottom where the Gannel meanders calmly out into its wide sandy estuary.

Our Bungalow's front door opens directly above a dangerously steep flight of concrete steps. These steps have to be negotiated with care, so as to be sure of arriving safely on the pavement below. The steps are flanked by masses of little bright white flowers in cushions of silvery-grey foliage: a sight worth staring at since they are all that the Bungalow offers in the way of a garden.

A fence, back and front, divides our property and our neighbour's property. The name of our neighbour is Mr Wright. He is a small man, smaller than my father, and he has an anaemic pinched ill-looking face. What a strange name, I think: for I have already learned that there is *right* and there is *wrong*.

Opposite to our house live the two elderly thin Misses Willisford together with their even older mother; and, next door to them, untidy fattish apron-clad Mrs Clements and her big orange cat. Why my brother Jim should have nightmares about Mrs Clements' big stripey orange cat, I do not know, nor ever will, but he does have nightmares about it. He fears and hates her orange cat, and continues to hate all cats, obsessively, till the day he dies, a long lifetime later.

This, then, is the immediate surrounding

geography of my first world, the world in which every scarlet pillar box, every gate and bush and tree, every face and flower, is new, and equally fascinating.

*   *   *

The earliest dress of my own that I can remember has been knitted by hand from a thick silk yarn, so that my dress is soft to touch, and slithery. But what teases the very edge of memory is its colour. That colour!—the strong pure sugary pink—it ravishes my senses. Even after eighty years I can recall the shock of pleasure at the delicious pinkness of my miniature silk dress.

I am still, though, not much more than a baby. I lie in my cot and chatter aloud of Starland. I can see hundreds and thousands, millions of stars. But where? Inside my head? They laugh at me. 'Listen!' they call to each other, bending close to hear this nonsense I'm prattling. But I don't laugh. Starland is my land. I know it well. That's where I've come from.

And now I'm older, and it's winter: cold. Lucy is buttoning on my gaiters, with a buttonhook. The buttons are in a row, each side of each leg, from knee to ankle. So many buttons! Then she hoists herself to her feet and fastens the hood of my coat under my chin with a safety pin. I don't much like her doing this. I'm afraid the pin may go by mistake through the skin of my neck, which would be a terrible thing to happen. But I'm only a little worried. I know I'm safe with Lucy. I trust her. She will take care of me.

And then one day she disappears. Why does she

5

disappear? There is something disgraceful about her going, but what it is I don't know. I'm not told, but I'm aware of lowered voices. It can have no connection with stealing. Lucy Coles's greatest virtue for my parents—they often declare it—is her absolute honesty; a virtue—they, as often, declare—that makes up for various other deficiencies. So what, then? Did she presume, in some way? Take a liberty? Answer back? Be rude? Unthinkable, surely. Something, though, must have gone dreadfully wrong, for Lucy has been banished. The Bungalow, without her, is hollow. I am bereft.

We drive into the country, to a muddy farm, and fetch home a young girl to take the place of Lucy Coles. But the young girl is frightened, and uses the corner of her bedroom for a lavatory, not knowing how to manage in urban conditions. The smell is appalling, so that her disgusting behaviour is very soon revealed and brings to an end this brief experiment of hiring a girl from the sticks. Lucy— oh joy!—returns. Whatever the fault for which the family slave, our domestic maid-of-all-works, had been dismissed, she is now, presumably, forgiven— severely reprimanded, no doubt—and reinstated. It has become clear that we can't, as a family, get along without Lucy. She is our Treasure. She is, most certainly, mine.

Lucy Coles has a completely round face, like a pudding, rather pock-marked and of a curious yellowish tinge which is due, she says, to her having had jaundice as a child. Her eyes are a pale blue and she has a meagre amount of hair, very blonde and straight, of a fine, dull texture, screwed into a tight bun. She's not exactly fat, but plumpish, and slow in her movements, deliberate—my parents use the word *sluggish*—with a frequent apologetic conversational laugh. I have never known her to be angry, or even cross. Lucy is very fond of me, and I love her dearly, but I keep this to myself.

*   *   *

Sitting in my high chair at one end of the dining-room table I can see through the window, beyond the steep steps, and into the road. Everyone else has finished breakfast and left me. I'm alone. I shall have to stay here—so they've told me—until I've been a good girl and drunk up all the milk in my mug. The inside of the mug is a chocolatey-brown colour, and on the outside is a picture of a

7

cock-a-doodle-doo, crowing. I like this mug, and I study it with interest, but I won't drink my milk. I sit there for a long time, uncomplainingly. It doesn't feel like a punishment. It's a nice place to sit. And finally I'm lifted down by Lucy; as I knew I should be.

For meals the dining-room table is covered by a stiff white cloth, of the same stiff whiteness as Lucy's apron. But beneath this cloth is another, made of a green velvety material which comes low down on all four sides of the table, with a fringe of bobbles that swing. When I crawl in underneath I'm completely hidden. Someone is reading aloud to the Twins, Pam and Jim, a very disturbing story about people who aren't proper people, but half men and half horses. I don't understand the story. It fills me with dread, but also with excitement. I'm afraid to listen, but I want to hear. I don't say a word. The green chenille and the bobbles protect me.

And of course there are other dangers even worse, because more possible, than mythological centaurs: tigers, for instance. The thought of these fearsome creatures keeps me awake in the dark. I can't sleep. I descend the stairs in my nightdress, slowly, step by step, while my parents are having their supper. My father lifts me on to his knee and tells me that I have no need to worry about being eaten by tigers. They live, he says, in Africa, far away across the sea; and the country we live in is an island—it has water all round it—and tigers can't swim. Then he carries me back upstairs, and tucks me into bed again.

*　　　*　　　*

I remember clearly this particular act of kindness and understanding on the part of my father because it was unusual. Although, to be sure, I was lucky regarding his occasional and always unexpected kindnesses—infinitely luckier than were my unfortunate older brother and sister. For there is no doubt that of his unwanted children it was me, the third, who was his favourite and who benefited accordingly, even if the favouritism might be manifested only sporadically. I daresay by the time I was born, three years after the Twins, our father had realised, and to some extent at least become accustomed to the dire consequences of the trap he had sprung so imprudently and ineluctably upon himself in 1919, almost immediately after his release from a German prisoner-of-war camp. Not that he was ever reconciled to the captivity of marriage, and all the encumbrances a poverty-stricken marriage entailed—quite the contrary: with every year that passed his frustration and his passionate desire to break free increased; and with it increased, as by a law of logic, the suffering he inflicted on his unhappy wife and on us, his children.

*   *   *

My mother stretches her hand across the table towards my father. It's her way of saying she's sorry to him for something; I don't know what. I sit in my high chair and watch. Her hand lies on the tablecloth, palm upwards, open. She wants him to take it, but he lets it lie there. She speaks his name, her special shortened version of it: 'Guth!' She

9

doesn't say *'Please'*, but she's pleading, I know. Then at last he does put out his hand and allows her to take it, but I see the look in his eyes and because it's a terrible look, I remember it. Later, much later, I learn the word that describes the look: it is *hate*.

My mother is tall, a little taller than my father. He maintains that he is the taller of the two. In these early days her long streaky auburn-golden hair is wound in a heavy bun at the nape of her neck, with a small cluster of short curls on either side of her face, covering her ears. She calls these clusters her 'bits'. And since her hair is naturally straight, these 'bits' have to be curled with tongs which are heated in the blue and yellow gas flame jetting up from some kind of apparatus attached to one of the kitchen walls.

First the hair has to be wrapped in strips of torn newspaper. Then the paper-clad 'bits' are gripped by the hot tongs, rolled over and over, tightly, held for a moment, and released. There is a strong smell of singed newspaper and sometimes, if the tongs are too hot, of singed hair as well. My mother laughs and shakes her head, so that the curly 'bits' bob up and down like springs. But I am too much alarmed by the hissing flame, the hot iron, the brown burnt paper, the smell, to join in her laughter. And when she offers, for fun, to give me curly 'bits' also, and the hot tongs touch, just touch for an instant, my ear, it's what I had feared and I cry out in horror. But it's my own fault. If I'd only stood still, quite still, it wouldn't have happened.

And then one day there is the teatime accident, an unforseen drama, when my mother trips over a

10

mat and empties on to me the whole contents of the silver-plated hot-water jug. I stand on the scrubbed kitchen table, naked, while she and Lucy smear my arms and legs and shoulders and bottom and stomach with butter. This is supposed to be the treatment for burns. I suffer no permanent scars from the scalding, nor, in this instance, do I remember any pain, but only the strangeness of standing high up on the kitchen table, stripped of clothes, and having butter, which is meant to be eaten on slices of bread, or possibly on scones, rubbed over every square inch of my body, from top to toe.

There is one other episode I remember involving nakedness, but—unlike the incident of the hot-water jug—this involves resentment too, and humiliation.

Our parents having gone away for the weekend—up to London, wherever that is—we three children find ourselves put in the charge of a stranger-woman, stout Mrs Brown, who doesn't know how we do things or how to behave with us. To my indignant astonishment, and much against my will, she stands me up, not on the kitchen table, but in the china bowl of a fixed bathroom hand-basin, and sponges me down roughly with cold water, unsmiling, and grumbling under her breath for no reason I can understand. We don't like this person at all. How long will she stay? Not long: as soon as our parents return she departs, and we don't see her again.

Horrid Mrs Brown must, I think, have been engaged in an emergency, to fill a gap; during, perhaps, the awful emptiness of Lucy's absence. Lucy would never have washed me, or let anyone else wash me, in freezing cold water, standing precariously balanced in a hand-basin. Goodness gracious, no! When Lucy gives me a bath it's in a tub, as it should be, and the water is nice and warm, and I don't have to hurry. Lucy is never rough.

The Twins and I play an exciting game where one of us, blindfolded, whirls about in the middle of the room with arms outstretched to catch hold of whoever is brave enough to try to rush past. I crook my finger, beckoning. This enticing gesture and the accompanying whisper—'Puss, Puss'—is the signal for either Pam or Jim to risk exchanging with me our safe opposite corners in a reckless dash from side to side across the intervening space, avoiding if possible the flailing arms of the Catcher. The room being small, this is not easy. Nor is the spoken signal easy. Pam, three years my senior, is impatient. 'You're not saying it properly, Ellie.' I know I'm not. I try harder. '*Puth*, PUTH ...' It's the best I can do.

There are two big armchairs in the sitting-room, covered in corduroy, the colour of cream-toffee: one for our mother, one for our father. They are too big for me to sit in with comfort. When I attempt it my legs stick stiffly out in front of me. My sister pushes me backwards and holds a cushion over my face. I can't see anything. It's black. I can't breathe. I struggle, kicking my legs in desperation. Pam takes the cushion away. Was she trying to smother me? To get rid of this new child who is treated more kindly by our father than she is? It would not be surprising. Our father—since my arrival, at any rate—appears to view his older daughter with a dislike that degenerates, as time

12

goes by, into actual cruelty. How can she defend herself against such bewildering unfairness and worse—far worse—than unfairness? She turns, bitterly, against her mother, and sometimes—although not often—against me.

On the fifth of November, Guy Fawkes Day, we have the special treat of our own firework display on the patch of earth and rubble behind the Bungalow; an area dishearteningly unchanged, it would seem, since whenever it was the builders packed up and left. Although not deserving the description of a back garden, it provides a perfectly adequate arena for fireworks. We have Golden Rain and Roman Candles and Catherine Wheels and sparklers and a few rockets. I'm allowed to watch them from indoors, with Lucy, through the scullery window. This is because, while the sparks and crimson smoke and whizzing Catherine Wheels are the stuff of magic, the bangs appal me. They hurt my eardrums. For years to come the thrill of children's parties is as good as ruined for me by the dread of crackers being pulled, balloons being burst. But I have, if I can, to hide this dread (which I never outgrow), for I am ashamed of it: no one, except me, is afraid of bangs.

Our firework display is quickly over, since fireworks, we know, cost money, and we three children, from a very early age, are made aware that money is a commodity of which we have wretchedly little. We also know that we mustn't speak of this. Our poverty, like my fear of explosions, is something to be ashamed of, and so to be concealed from the world outside the family. One day my mother, throwing a handful of scrumpled-up rubbish on the fire, notices with

13

horror that amongst the rubbish is a ten-shilling note. Ten shillings is a fortune! Too late! It's gone for ever in a lick of flame. Kneeling on the hearthrug, she bursts into tears. This is the first, but not the last time I behold my mother weeping.

In these early days we own a motor car, called—very curiously, I think—an ABC. It is a small grey two-seater with a folding canvas hood and a dickey-seat at the back into which are fitted, side by side, the Twins, like a couple of peas in a pod. I sit in front on my mother's knee. On Sundays we go for outings in our ABC to beaches beyond the boundaries of Newquay. We go to Porth, and to Perranporth, and Holywell Bay and Zennor Cove, and sometimes daringly head off into the hinterland of Bodmin and Indian Queens, traversing Cornwall to investigate Fowey on the south coast, Polperro and Mevagissey. My father, unsmiling at the wheel, presents an heroic and intimidating figure, and our outings, never jolly, are fraught with the anxious possibility of upsetting him and causing angry scenes. Instant and unquestioning obedience will usually enable us to steer clear of danger, but it is not an absolute guarantee.

The longest excursion we ever undertake is a visit to one of our father's two older half-brothers, both of whom are doctors. Uncle Ralph lives with his wife and family at so immense a distance that we are obliged to stay the night en route with Aunt Christine, our mother's younger sister, who inhabits Crewkerne Vicarage in the county of Dorset. This vicarage is a building of enormous proportions compared to our Bungalow, with huge stretches of uncarpeted floorboards in rooms almost bare of furniture, but pervaded by a delicious smell of stored apples. I go to sleep, and wake up in the morning, smelling apples, and seeing through the big uncurtained windows the leafy greenness of overgrown trees. Aunt Christine and Uncle Charnock and their children are as impoverished, apparently, as we ourselves are, but they don't seem to be ashamed of, or mind about it; and the scent of apples and the shining floorboards and leafy branches combine with Aunt Christine's blue eyes and her smile of welcome to make it a pleasant and comfortable stopping-off place on our journey. And this in spite of the awesome appearance of our elderly, toweringly tall Uncle Charnock who has only one blue eye as well as only one arm that operates, and who wears a funny vicar's collar without a tie. They have a maid, the equivalent of our Lucy Coles, a stoutish

15

middle-aged reassuring presence with a country accent. Her name is Selina.

We do visit, once, the other doctor-uncle, who lives with his wife, Lilian, I don't know exactly where, but also a long way off. I sit on Uncle Malcolm's capacious knee and he holds earphones to each of my ears and bids me listen to voices faintly, scratchily speaking. I listen dutifully to these tiny tickly voices. What they are saying is incomprehensible. I'm hearing, for the first time, the wizardry of wireless.

Our motor-car excursions, however, are brought to a dramatic conclusion one weekend on the very steep hill that winds up, up from Mevagissey harbour. Halfway up it the ABC's overtaxed engine splutters and stops, and then erupts into flames. The horror of this disaster is greatly increased when my brother Jim's left foot becomes jammed as he is being wrenched free of the dickey-seat by our father—our enraged father: enraged, unhappy man, at the consequences of too much family overloading fatally his prized possession, his precious ABC. It would have to happen to Jim, of course. Everything awful always happens to Jim. Eventually my poor terrified brother is extricated from his predicament with both feet intact. The only lasting loss sustained is of our motor car. No more outings.

*   *   *

The Twins attend a nursery school situated a little way along Mount Wise. One day, there being for some reason no one at home to look after me, I am required to accompany Pam and Jim inside this

16

establishment. I'm going to be spending the whole morning at school, just like a big girl. This alarming experience is represented to me as a very special treat, which I will undoubtedly enjoy. A teacher-woman takes charge of me, leads me inside, sits me at a low desk, and places in front of me an open exercise book with ruled lines and a capital A pencilled up in the top left-hand corner. This A I am to copy. She may also have told me I'm to do it very carefully and slowly; if so, it's an instruction I fail to hear. I think that what I have to do is to copy the A as many times and as fast as I possibly can. The teacher returns and is cross with me. Look what a dreadful mess I've made of that nice clean page, covering it with big untidy scrawls! And the next page; and the next! What a waste of paper! She scolds me. I had expected her to praise me. I don't like school at all. I don't want ever to have to come again.

My sister Pam is a far better teacher. I don't know how she manages it, but she does succeed in teaching me, at a very early age, to read, and later to write. She and I form an association of two that excludes our brother Jim. He is a boy and we are girls. Is this why we don't include him in our games?

Jim was born, the second of the Twins, with a double hernia. He wears a truss, a strange and repellent piece of equipment. He is permanently unhappy and frightened. He turns his feet out, like flippers. He hangs his head and picks at his eyelashes, which are fair and crusted. He stammers. Our father shouts at him to turn his feet in, to stand up straight, to look him in the eye when he answers.

17

Generally my father doesn't shout. He speaks—when he speaks—in a quiet voice. But he isn't a talkative man. It is my mother who is the gifted conversationalist. My father says nothing. He watches her, in silence, while she entertains an admiring audience. He walks quietly too, making no sound, wearing gym shoes about the house. His hair is dark brown and glossy. He has brown eyes, a smallish head, a rather fleshy, slightly aquiline nose, a clipped moustache. He stands in front of a mirror and gazes at his reflection; and as he gazes dreamily at himself he rubs the back of his thumbnail to and fro, to and fro, across the bristles of his moustache. What is he thinking? Of how handsome he is? Or that things were meant to be entirely different? He was to have been, not a miserable undervalued, underpaid bank clerk, with the burden of a family to maintain, but a painter, young, free, and, above all, famous. He yearns to be famous. And so he paints himself again and again, recording his face, as he sees it looking out at him from the mirror. And his angry eyes proclaim: I could have been, should have been, a painter of worldwide renown, with a picture accepted and hung on the line every year by the Royal Academy of Arts in London. This is the height of his ambition, doggedly pursued; never achieved.

From time to time the elusive dream seems capable of becoming reality, to be almost within reach: as when Admiral Cunningham actually commissions our father to paint a portrait of him in full rig, brass buttons, medals, gold epaulettes, the lot. At last! The whole Bungalow throbs with a current of anticipatory excitement. Daddy is going

18

to make our fortune. We are going to be rich. And he—our father—will have his heart's desire and be *famous*.

Weekend after weekend he disappears. The mysterious invisible house of the Admiral, somewhere in the miles of dark unlit unknown countryside surrounding Newquay, swallows him out of our sight. We wait, in confident expectation of glory.

But alas for hope! All too soon the sunny skies darken, the storm clouds gather. We dare not ask our father what has gone wrong. We only know that every Sunday evening his homecoming mood grows gloomier and gloomier. And then one despairing night he carries the finished portrait of Admiral Cunningham up the steps and into the Bungalow and props it, without saying a word, against the sitting-room wall. There, in full view, are the gold buttons, the gold epaulettes, the medals, the braid, and above them the Admiral himself, eyeing us coldly from the picture he wasn't pleased with, didn't appreciate, refused to accept or pay for. It is, I feel sure, a living likeness of the red-faced old gentleman; but why, I wonder, does he have a smaller face in the painting, a smaller chest and shoulders, than he really must have, as though he had shrunk in the wash? Is this the reason he didn't care for it?—the reason he caused an unforgiveable scene, our father tells us now, with rude words flying between them? Doesn't Admiral Cunningham realise that canvases are expensive, and the bigger they are the more money they cost? But it is too late—much too late—in any case to set things right. Our father won't apologise; he never does. And so that dream is dead. The picture, which wasn't big enough to satisfy the client, takes up far too much space in our overcrowded little Bungalow. Furthermore, for as long as Admiral Cunningham stays propped up, unwanted, against a wall, he serves the artist, our father, as a bitter reminder of failure.

*   *   *

On warm spring days, before the Tennis-Club season has begun, my sister and I are allowed to go hand in hand, unescorted, the few yards on beyond the Bungalow to the top of the hill. A rough rutted lane, the Tennis Club's boundary on that side, leads off to the right. At the junction of hill and lane is a little white-painted wicket gate, which Pam unlatches, and then together we trot down the short sloping stretch of concrete path to settle ourselves for the morning on the low single step running from end to end along the front of the pavilion. We are quite alone here except for the tall gaunt figure of Wilton, the groundsman, who is occupied in preparing for the summer months ahead: mowing the grass, marking out the courts with chalky white lines, carrying great unwieldy bundles of stringy netting from the interior of the tool shed away in the distance; going slowly, methodically, in silence, about his business. He doesn't pay any attention to us, but we know without being told that it is only because Wilton is there that we are permitted to push open the gate of the Tennis Club, which is private, and to sit by ourselves in the sunshine on the splintery creosote-smelling step of the pavilion and assemble daisy-chains and play at tea parties. He doesn't smile, or speak, or take any notice of us, but with Wilton there we are perfectly safe, we know, just as we would be with Lucy. So he counts as a friend.

Our father and Wilton are different in every particular except for being, both of them, very silent men. It's impossible to imagine what Wilton is thinking or feeling. He wears, no matter how hot the day, a buttoned-up waistcoat, and under the waistcoat a cotton shirt undone at the neck, and striped with the sort of thin stripes ruled in an exercise book. He doesn't ever wear a tie. His shirtsleeves are always rolled higher than his elbows. His arms are very brown indeed, much the same colour as the netting he lugs about; or as if they had been creosoted too, like the wooden pavilion. But once or twice I catch a glimpse of a part of his upper arms which is usually hidden, and the whiteness of that half-inch of skin revealed above where the sunburn stops astonishes and fascinates me.

His moustache also, in fact, is different from our father's. Wilton's moustache is black and thick and hangs down over his mouth, concealing it. He is respectful, or fairly respectful, to our father, calling him 'Sir', although not as frequently as our father considers he should. Wilton doesn't call all the members of the Tennis Club 'Sir': he chooses whom he will respect. There are those who say that the groundsman is Bolshie. He looks at them with contempt, in the same way as our father regards his bank manager, Mr Oxley, with contempt. Our father and Wilton were both in the Great War. They have this in common. Is it the Great War that Wilton is thinking about as he silently, broodingly mows the grass of the Tennis-Club courts? Is it

21

because our father was awarded a medal, the DSO, that Pam and I are allowed the out-of-season privilege of playing on the creosote-smelling step of the Tennis-Club pavilion?

*   *   *

One day in spring, a day of sunshine and blue skies—holiday weather—in a sudden fit of gaiety, our mother decides to abandon the usual household chores and take her brood of three solemn children for an outing instead: a morning ramble along beside the river. She is inventing a treat for us; or perhaps assuaging her own sad heart with memories of a country childhood, long ago, and happy.

We make our way down and down the further steep slope of Trenance Hill, passing, on our left, Wilton's cottage, which stands at right angles to and higher than the road; passing on the other side, also at right angles, a white-washed farmhouse where we occasionally buy eggs; and lower still, set into the stone hedge at a bend in the road, a small mysterious gate with nothing to see beyond it but a shadowy tunnel of dense foliage leading, apparently, nowhere. A few years later and the little gate will open often for my sister and me. But today this delightful familiarity is hidden from us in the future: as invisible today as is Mrs Miller's house, her garden, and the reclusive beautiful Mrs Miller herself.

In spite of the sunshine we are wearing gloves, and we have each of us been issued with a brown-paper bag. Our mother carries her shopping basket. A walk ought always, we know, to have a purpose, and this morning our purpose is to pluck the tender new shoots of nettles which, when cooked at home by Lucy, will be transformed from nasty weeds into nourishing green vegetables, and be good for us, and cost no money at all. Experience has taught us that whenever nettles happen to brush against our bare legs they sting most horribly, and the painful itchy white bumps have to be rubbed over and over again with scrunched-up dock leaves, and *still* the bumps hurt. Yet these horrible nettles, we are assured, once cooked will lose their evil sting and be perfectly safe to eat. Is this information reliable, though? Secretly, we have our doubts.

At the bottom of the hill we turn away from the famous railway viaduct that spans the valley, high—immeasureably high—in the air above our heads, and so at last arrive at our destination, the broad estuary of the River Gannel.

This morning the tide is out and we wander along a rough path, or track, of dry crumbly mud on almost the same level as the acres of corrugated sand it borders. Here and there, in imitation of our mother, we pause to pinch off, with due caution, the spiky tops of nettles and stuff them into our brown-paper bags until the bags are full to bursting. Then, having earned our reward, we can pull off the protective armour of gloves and let our fingers delve into the mossy, moist undergrowth, searching for stems of celandines and primroses. Finding and picking is the nice part; but I can't afterwards manage by myself the niggly task of tying these frail stalks together in bunches with bits of knitting wool. *It is too difficult*! Pam helps me. She winds a length of wool round and round my hotly clutched untidy fistful of pale yellow primroses, and fastens the ends in a bow. I admire and envy the dexterity of my older sister: she can do all sorts of things like this which I can't do. I wish I could.

Jim, however, won't be bothered with tying bows. He drops his flowers crossly, preferring to stand and stare instead at the fabulous piratical three-masted schooner, beached nowadays permanently, like a piece of exotic flotsam, on the foreshore of the Gannel.

Our mother spreads her coat and we sit in a row on the ground for a mid-morning picnic of biscuits, and a sultana bun each, and milk, which we share, poured into the metal cap of a Thermos flask. Behind us is a notice-board with DANGER painted on it in capital letters, warning people not to attempt at low tide to cross to the thickly wooded opposite bank of the estuary on foot, even though the river might appear to have shrunk to a little, easily fordable stream, running tamely down the middle. There are—we know—frightening rumours of quicksands which will suck you in and swallow you up, and you will never be seen again. They say that once upon a time a horse and cart and the man driving it—he intending, rashly, to take a short cut—all disappeared without a trace on the way over. And Lucy says there is a whole village hidden under the quicksands of the Gannel estuary. Can this be true? Today, as we sit and munch our ginger nuts, we eye the rippled empty stretches of sand in front of us and wonder what lies buried beneath them.

We eye as well, with an equal curiosity, the stranded black-hulled schooner looming above us,

24

tilted slightly, unmoving. She is the property of a said-to-be rich eccentric old man, who lives aboard his superannuated vessel. The masts and spars are stark, like trees in winter, without a shred of canvas: her sailing days are done. Beneath the bowsprit nestles a brightly painted figurehead: very strange! A gangplank leads up, tantalisingly, from shore to deck, but of the ship's owner, or of any other living soul, there is no sign.

And now, quick! We must go! We have dawdled too long! We must hurry! Our mother, in sudden alarm at the time, gathers up her coat, her basket, urges her children into a run. We hasten past the only house built on this side of the estuary—built so close to the edge of the Gannel that sometimes, at exceptionally high tides, the footpath is flooded, and water even laps up against the stones of the garden wall, making it impossible for any person to pass by dryshod. How wonderful to inhabit a house besieged by water!

But today, of course, the tide being low, we are in no danger of wetting our shoes: the danger is that we will be late arriving home. We have still to toil up the steep and narrow lane that brings us out at the far end of Mount Wise with the singing telegraph poles, have still, at a trot, to complete the big circle we set out upon earlier so as to be inside the Bungalow, hair brushed, hands and faces washed, before Daddy arrives back from work expecting to find his one o'clock lunch on the table, and his family assembled, ready and waiting. If this is not so, there will be trouble. He will be angry. And anger will spoil the treat we've had— our lovely morning treat of primrose-picking and biscuits and milk, and nettles and brown-paper

25

bags and sunshine, and nobody being scolded.

My legs ache. I want to stop. But Pam is pitiless: no stopping allowed. She lugs me along fiercely by the hand. 'Oh, come on, Ellie—come *on*—you're so slow!'

I stumble, whimpering, after her. For she's right, I know she is: we've got to hurry. Anger is what I daily dread, above all else, the nightmare threat that lurks round every corner. I have to be always on my guard; have to be clever; learn how to avoid it; invent places where I can hide.

*   *   *

In the spring-time we can pick wild flowers to arrange in bowls at home: primroses and campions, and then bluebells, and, later on, cowslips which grow in the field beyond the tennis courts where the club members park their cars. Wild flowers are free. But sometimes a gipsy-woman comes knocking at the back door with bunches of primroses for sale. Of course we don't buy them, because we can pick our own, thank you!

We refer to these gipsy people as *brusher-women*. For years and years I continue to believe that this is their real true name. Apart from the pretty little nosegays, their stock-in-trade consists of, chiefly, brooms and brushes, which is why, presumably, we have dubbed them brusher-women. They sell clothes pegs too, and shoelaces. We don't ever buy anything from any of them.

'Tell her there's nothing we want to buy from her, Lucy—nothing,' our mother calls out; or she may go to the back door to get rid of the undesirable person herself. We peep from the

26

window to watch the dark-skinned brusher-woman descending the steep flight of front steps with her baby. And because of her beads and her earrings and the colourful scarf around her head, she appears to us to be like an illustration from *The Arabian Nights*. But we catch a whiff of our mother's disapproval, and from Lucy a whiff of something besides disapproval. Why should Lucy be afraid of the brusher-woman? We don't know why, but we know she is, and we know she thinks we should be too.

It's different when a tramp knocks apologetically at the back door, as tramps quite often do. Instead of being shooed away with hard words, he will be given—not money, which is always in much too short supply for that—but a bowl of soup and slices of bread and butter and a cup of sugary tea in the kitchen, and a sandwich to take with him in his pocket when he shuffles off; sometimes even a pair of old socks or a scarf. Such ragged footsore men don't count as beggars, our mother tells us. Each one of them was a soldier, like Daddy was, in the Great War. But while our father works every day in the Bank, these tramps have no job, no home to go to.

'Poor man,' says our mother, shutting the door, and she is quiet for some time afterwards, and sorrowful, seeing things we can't see.

*   *   *

Shortness of money in our household is a constant anxiety. And of course our mother, not being a brusher-woman, can't earn us an extra silver sixpence or two by going from door to door,

27

offering for sale the primroses or the bluebells we've picked. Unthinkable—alas! Why then, with sixpences so sorely lacking and so hard to come by, does she sometimes allow herself to part with—to squander—carefully saved-up coins in exchange for a bunch of sweet-smelling velvety wallflowers from Mrs Wilton who has a garden? I wish we had a garden and could grow wallflowers in it, and be able to pick them as though they were wild, like cowslips or poppies. Mrs Wilton is the only person we ever do buy flowers from, and she doesn't charge much, says our mother, wanting to excuse the extravagance: not more than just a few pennies.

Mrs Wilton is tall and dark, like her husband, but a good deal thinner and without his habit of silence. She wears an apron and an unfashionably long skirt that blows round her ankles in the wind. Our mother and she stand on either side of the cottage gate and chat about the weather, and the new Wilton baby, which we admire, since, although dark enough to pass for a gipsy's child, it is not in fact so irredeemably tainted. People enjoy talking to our mother. She gets on well with everyone, but especially when our father isn't there. We call our mother *Mummy*. Mrs Wilton and Lucy call her *Mum*, which puzzles me. She's not their mother.

Names can be very puzzling. I shouldn't have said in the street one day—politely, as I thought: 'Good morning, Mrs Have-You-Heard'; or mentioned once in company, Pig-faced Ralph: a bad mistake, in each case. But how was I to know that these were not their proper names? My parents, in private conversation always call them that. And then there is Wilton, the Tennis-Club groundsman, who doesn't have a Mister tagged on to begin with, as most of the men I hear spoken of do. His wife, on the other hand, is known as Mrs Wilton, the same as are all married women. Or again, when our father speaks of his bank manager as Oxley, without a Mister in front, it's his way, I know, of expressing rudeness and contempt. But for Wilton to be deprived of a Mister is by no means intended to be insulting. It's merely to indicate the difference between club members who wear white flannel trousers—or white frocks—and play tennis, and the groundsman who doesn't play tennis, but puts up the nets for them and marks out the green grass he has mown with chalky white lines. That's how it is: I duly note and absorb these interesting distinctions.

*   *   *

We've been invited to stay with one of our father's relations, a rich old lady who lives a long way off, near London. For this visit Pam and I are to be fitted up with a whole range of new summer frocks: three frocks each. Samples of cotton material are sent for from a factory in the Midlands, and arrive by post. The prospect of so many new clothes, and in such a flurry of haste, is breathtaking.

Pam and I sit at the dining-room table with our mother while she hesitates over which of the samples to settle for. The small squares of cloth have ricky-racky edges, and are fastened in wads of identical patterns but a variety of colours. One of the samples is scattered over with tiny multi-coloured flowers. I am ravished by its prettiness. And yes—oh good!—she does eventually decide on it, selecting, in addition, a plain white cheesecloth and a checked gingham, all of which, it seems, are inexpensive and will wash and iron well.

The material chosen arrives, as did the samples, by post, and then our mother is terrifically busy for several days, measuring, cutting, pinning, and whirling the handle of her Singer sewing machine round and round with the energy of a demon. Lucy hovers admiringly in the background; and lo! we have our new dresses.

I love the flower-besprinkled one. It has little puffed sleeves and a gathered skirt. But I wish my gingham was a blue-and-white check, the same as Pam's is, instead of brown-and-white. I am dressed in brown often, because of having brown eyes: my father's eyes. It's a colour I hate. I would like never *ever* to have to wear brown. And I don't much care for the shades of green that are said to suit me. As for yellow and orange—colours that can be exhilarating—I don't want to have to wear them either. I long to have clothes of blue, or delicious pink; but in particular of blue. But blue is reserved for my sister Pam. She and her twin, Jim, have our mother's blue eyes, that's why. It *isn't fair*!

The plain cheesecloth dress would be dull had its dullness not been relieved by a scarlet tie and a narrow belt of scarlet. This colour, brilliant against the white, is very exciting. The tie, though, bothers me. We are girls, me and Pam. Ties are things that boys wear.

In what manner our brother Jim's wardrobe is refurbished in order to bring it up to scratch for the momentous visit to old Cousin Edith I do not know, not being interested in his clothes, which are as grey and as boring as all boys' clothing inevitably is.

In the middle of the lawn in front of the house of our father's elderly second-cousin-by-marriage, in the county of Surrey, there grows a gigantic copper beech. Coming, as we do, from a seaside town of hydrangea bushes and privet hedges, I am impressed by the grandeur of this immense tree, which is like a visible manifestation of the old lady's reputed wealth. Beneath its lofty spreading branches, in the sunshiney shade, we nibble at cucumber sandwiches and macaroons. Acutely conscious of the need for best behaviour, as well as of our new cheesecloth dresses, Pam and I don't say a word, except to answer 'Yes, please', and 'No, thank you'. Jim's habitual stammer makes even these utterances agonisingly difficult for him, and Cousin Edith is no help to us. Encased from head to toe in draperies of funereal black, she looks out on the world and her visitors with a fixed air of gloomy severity. It is our first meeting with this revered relation, and we three children are not attracted to her; nor she, plainly, to us.

Cousin Alec Martin, her lately departed stockbroker husband, had been Jim's godfather, and although the christening of our brother as James Martin might have appeared to be pushing the connection, yet the extra first name was not necessarily intended as a hopeful hint (and if so, a hope that was disappointed): Martins abound. Our father's mother, Granny Hallsmith, had been a Miss Mary Martin from Inverness, and his elder brother, killed in the last week of the Great War, was also baptised Martin.

31

Cousin Edith Martin has one older and one younger daughter, and a son, Cousin Reggie. The younger daughter, Mildred, lives at home, so as to be company for Cousin Edith. Although she is the younger, she's not really *young*, which is why we've been told always to call her *Cousin Mildred*. Only children, like us, or very young grown-ups, can be called by simply their first names without running the risk of impertinence.

The other daughter, Cousin Nancy, is married, and so is Cousin Reggie, and they both live out of sight, somewhere else. Cousin Mildred isn't married. She has two horses and a donkey instead. They wander about and chew grass in a paddock nearby. A paddock is the name for a field where you keep horses. We three stand, at a slightly apprehensive distance, and watch our Cousin Mildred while she grooms them and feeds them, and mucks out their stables; and when she invites each of us to offer up a lump of sugar we make very sure to flatten the palms of our hands, as instructed. If I haven't succeeded in squeezing my thumb down far enough, those huge horse's teeth, with the huge hairy tickly horse's lips, might accidentally bite it off, Cousin Mildred warns me. Horses can kick you, too, or trample on your feet, but if they did, it would be your own fault for standing in the wrong place.

Cousin Mildred also has charge of a troupe of Girl Guides, and one day we see her wearing a navy-blue uniform and a whistle, but even in this outfit she is not in the least alarming. Her friendly behaviour is so warm and so cheerful it quite outshines the chilliness of Cousin Edith, her mother, and the starched unsmiling disapproval of

32

Louise, their maidservant. We realise that neither Louise nor her mistress care for children. Cousin Mildred, however, luckily does.

For me the only real pleasure of this uncomfortable visit is due to Dandy, Cousin Mildred's little shaggy tail-wagging dog. To my lavish hugs and strokings he responds ecstatically. I so much want to have a pet of my own to love. Any pet would do.

Once I was given a white mouse in a cage by a customer of my father's Bank, a faintly remembered elegant lady called Mrs Pinwell who lived in a big house with a big garden somewhere outside Newquay. One afternoon I was taken, minus Pam—on my own—to have tea with her. Was it for me to make friends with a grand-daughter of the same age as myself? Possibly. I only know that when I left I brought away with me the snow-white mouse in its cage. It had pink eyes and a long pink tail. The love I felt for my white mouse, my fairy creature, my pet, was so intense it hurt. But it was a brief happiness: doomed. We aren't allowed to have pets. They smell and are dirty. I was obliged to return my gift the next day to its donor, kind Mrs Pinwell.

Once we had a goldfish in a bowl. That was nice. But we fed it with either too much food, or not enough, and whatever we may have done wrong, it died.

The ban on pets is extended to cover dolls, too. Dolls, our father declares, are nasty things: they have nasty cold faces. It seems a funny sort of a reason for dolls to be forbidden to us, but that's what Daddy says. Somebody's mother recently gave me a handed-down doll's pram, not knowing that we aren't allowed to have dolls. It was a wonderful present to be given. I enjoy pushing my doll's pram out for walks, even though it's empty. Sometimes I borrow Jim's toy terrier, Rough, and wrap him in a duster and pretend he's a dolly. But I don't really like Rough. Nor does Jim. He's been stuffed as hard as a rock, and he has no expression. I do wish I could have a dolly to put in my pram, even a small one.

You could say, I suppose, that Soccer Sid is a doll of sorts. Perhaps our father meant him to serve as a substitute for the dolls we don't have. He doesn't fill the void, of course—well, of course he doesn't. But one evening Daddy came back from the Bank in a good temper, whistling, with Soccer Sid under his arm, and proceeded to set him up, like a prize, on top of the chest of drawers in the bedroom that Pam and I share. Exactly how, or why, he acquired this grotesquely cheeky little dummy, I don't know. Soccer Sid is about eighteen inches tall, pedestal included, made of painted plaster, with a head that's too big for his body, and a cap that's too big for his head, and a grin on his face, and one foot propped on a football. He used to be displayed in the window of a shop selling garments for men: a gentlemen's outfitter. He's very heavy, so we mustn't lift him down, or touch him. I don't want to touch him. He both fascinates and repels me. I lie in bed and read, over and over, the writing on Soccer Sid's pedestal: *I'm Soccer Sid, the Liberty Kid, from Liberty Land, Market Harborough, England.* What can this curious message mean? Is it a poem?

*　　　*　　　*

34

How my sister Pam learned to read I'm not sure, but she decided to share her invaluable knowledge with me. I am more than willing to be her pupil. She teaches her pupil, not from books, which are practically non-existent in our family, but with the aid of a newspaper. One section in the newspaper is allotted to a junior readership. We lie on our stomachs on the floor, side by side, and I follow her pointing finger and listen to her translation of single letters which, when put together, turn into words. When the words are strung together, they make sentences; and from the sentences, little by little—speaking directly to us—comes the voice of Teddy Tail of the *Daily Mail*. This is how I learn to read.

*　　*　　*

We have been invited to a children's party given by a rich Newquay family whose name floats over my head, unheard. *Party* is all I hear, a word arousing instant excitement; also trepidation: a mixture. This will be the second Christmas season for the white organdie dresses that my sister and I wear to parties. Our mother, however, has hit upon the clever idea of transforming their appearance with a bottle of red ink. The contents of the bottle are emptied into a tub of cold water, and stirred, and our frocks, in due course, emerge from their soaking no longer white but instead a delightfully pale shade of rose: new dresses for old! A kind of magic, surely!

Being got ready for a party is a disturbing and not entirely enjoyable experience that has to be endured because of the reward which, we are promised, lies ahead. So we allow ourselves to be stripped of our warm serviceable winter clothes—jerseys, and thick socks and woolly combinations—and to stand in a state of shivering expectation, getting goose pimples, while we are washed: hands, faces, knees—especially knees. We have to start off clean for a party. But it does seem very strange indeed: we aren't usually *washed* in the afternoon. And then we are put into flimsy clothes, but with a cardigan on top to smother the goose pimples, and short cotton socks and, for me and Pam, not shoes but slippers. (Poor Jim—he still has to have clumpy lace-up shoes.)

Our exquisite party slippers, as delicate and thin, almost, as paper, only last out one winter of party jollification and are bound to be replaced each year, no matter what the cost. They are made of highly polished black, or alternatively, bronze kid leather, with fluffy pompoms on the toes and a narrow band of black elastic which must be stretched forward and twisted, so as to form a loop. When each foot is poked in turn through its loop the elastic will snap back and criss-cross neatly round your ankle, over your white sock, like a conjuring trick that never fails to hold your slipper securely in place. One party season my mother buys me silver slippers, because the shop has no more of black or of bronze kid in my size. Silver!— slippers fit for a princess!

But on the day of this party Pam isn't well. The glands in her neck are swollen and she's running a temperature and has to stay in bed with a copy of *Chicks Own* to compensate for the treat she's missing. Jim and I, without our leader to give us courage, climb up on to the bouncy back-step of the hired hansom cab—our mother's ingenious, and doubtless cheap, solution to the problem of transport on exceptional occasions—and from there into the cab's dark musty straw-and-leather smelling interior. I am wrapped in a fleecy shawl that covers my finery, and me, snugly, to the tip of my nose. Jim is buttoned into his ordinary coat. We settle ourselves on the sideways benches, opposite to one another, legs dangling, for the slow bumpy ride through the streets of Newquay: past the turning down to the harbour and on and up to the large red-brick house which is situated, with its imposing front steps and porch and the many sharply pointed gables crowned by red terracotta curlicues, close by the golf links. Beyond the links, over to the left, is Fistral Bay, a beach famous for its magnificently dangerous breakers, and its consequent reputation for drowning accidents: the reason why it has been deemed out of bounds for our family picnicking excursions.

Today Jim and I are obliged to make the journey from the Bungalow alone. Our mother can't come with us: she has to stay with Pam. It's Lucy's afternoon off. Clip-clop, go the old horse's hooves. Except when conveying us creakily to and from our Christmas party outings I never clap eyes on this romantically anachronistic horse-drawn carriage, which must have long since been retired to the shed of its equally retired and ancient cabby-owner, who is also its driver, and who, every so often, screws his neck round to squint at us through the little square window from his perch outside, and enquire if we are all right. We nod, and say yes, thank you, we are all right. Otherwise my brother and I remain quite dumb the whole way, sitting stock-still and apprehensive in the semi-darkness. We are neither of us brave, as our sister Pam is.

But the big house, when we get there, is ablaze with lights and overflowing with children and balloons and coloured streamers. A giant fir tree, topped by a star and festooned in tinsel, occupies a corner of the entrance hall: a sight to dazzle our eyes. We don't have a Christmas tree at the Bungalow. We don't believe in Father Christmas, either. Our own father doesn't approve of superstitious twaddle. We know who fills the stockings we hang at the end of our beds on Christmas Eve: Mummy and Daddy fill them.

Kindly voices greet us. Grown-up hands take hold of ours and conduct us to where the games are already in full swing: Oranges and Lemons, and Here We Go Gathering Nuts in May. And then there is a long table loaded with iced cakes, and jellies and chocolate biscuits, such as we never see at home; and I cause amusement by asking if I could please have some brown bread and butter.

38

This, actually, is what I prefer to eat above all else: brown bread and butter. But there isn't any here today, and so I have to accept the creamy cakes I'm offered that make me feel sick.

I don't want to pull any of the crackers, because I'm afraid of the bangs; they hurt my ears. And I dread the noise of balloons bursting. Some children burst them on purpose. After tea there is a treasure hunt, with a present for every child. You have to start by finding your string, with your name attached to it, and then the string will lead you to where your present is hidden in a room upstairs, in a cupboard or behind a cushion. It ought to be fun, but I don't properly understand what it is I'm meant to do, or how to unwind the string from round and round the bannister rail without it getting in a tangle. A nice older girl is kind and helps me. My present is a book. It's flat and wide, and mostly full of pictures. This is the very first book I've ever been given, exclusively for me to keep for myself. The nice older girl sits beside me at the top of the stairs and reads me the story, straight off. It's a bit upsetting, really, and so are the pictures, although they are beautiful and I love them too, in a painful sort of way. The book is called *Joanna and Her Dolls*. Joanna, unlike me, has lots of dolls, whole rows of them, all different.

Then, suddenly, there is our mother, standing tall in the doorway, come to fetch us home. And she bursts out laughing when she sees me, and says, very loudly: goodness, what a perfect little guy I look. I hadn't realised it, not till this moment, but I'm wearing Pam's pink organdie party dress by mistake, instead of my own, and it's much too big for me. Everyone turns then, and they stare up at me, and begin to laugh as well. They laugh and laugh. Because I must look silly—of course I must—in a dress that's too big for me: a perfect little Guy Fawkes person. I burn with the shame of it.

*   *   *

Children's Christmas holiday parties usually take place not in private houses but in hotels. The Victoria Hotel is the nearest; near enough for us to reach it on foot, walking soberly down Trenance Hill and on down Bury Road in our outdoor shoes, until we arrive at what might be considered a frontier, the majestic glass-and-mahogany swing doors dividing our everyday world from a world as rich and strange to us as would be the Xanadu of Kubla Khan. Armed with our legitimate passport of a party invitation card, we are emboldened to push open the swing doors and so to enter the grandly old-fashioned glamour of the Victoria Hotel's reception foyer. Coats and shawls are left in the cloakroom, shoes exchanged for slippers, and across the crimson Turkey carpeting we venture, breathless with anticipation, into the ballroom.

It is the ballrooms of these hotels that entrance us: the hugeness of them, the emptiness, the acres of slithery space that lies ready and waiting to be run at, skidded and slid over, fallen down on. If we have to join in Musical Chairs or Musical Bumps or Twos and Threes then, reluctantly, we will do as we are bidden: will line up, one behind another, hold on to the waist in front or grasp each other's hot hands, according to instructions. We will whisper *Oranges* into the ear of a smiling grown-up who bends down to catch the murmur of choice, (which is seldom for *Lemons*, a bitter fruit; Oranges, the popular team, always wins the tug-of-war). But all we really *want* is to be allowed the freedom to run and slide, and run and slide, again and again, across that enticing golden desert of a floor, and never have to stop till the party's over.

The Atlantic Hotel is a great square grey block of a building perched high up on the side of the headland that runs out beyond the harbour, and beyond the golf links, and even further, beyond the granite war memorial, windswept and stark. With its faintly forbidding air of a sentinel on perpetual guard duty, the Atlantic Hotel looks back towards the carefree Newquay beaches that spread below in curve after curve along the coastline.

The distance from here to there being considerable, an invitation to a children's party in the Atlantic Hotel means we have unavoidably to press into service the venerable hansom cab to trundle us to and fro. On this occasion Jim and I are spared the anxiety of travelling to an unknown destination by ourselves. This time Pam is with us, and also our mother; she too has been invited to the party and is in an unusually merry mood, as though intending to enjoy an afternoon off—such as Lucy is given every Thursday—from the daily demanding struggle of keeping up appearances on a next-to-nothing income.

Pam and I are each of us wearing a new party dress. Thanks to the unexpected bounty of a certain Mrs Wray, the red-ink dyed organdie frocks have been relegated to the ragbag, and here we are, setting forth in our new outfits, which are not,

41

for once, the result of our mother's industry and skill with the Singer sewing machine. But I can't rejoice at mine, or think it an improvement on inky-pinky organdie. Its dullness dismays me: brown velvet with a high neck and a cream lace collar. Hateful dress! I am said to look sweet in it. Pam's frock, in contrast, is a dream of desire. Made of a pale-green chiffon silk, it is called a handkerchief dress, because of the pieces of material shaped like hankies that hang down round the skirt and float out when she moves. Oh, lucky Pam!

Mrs Wray is a widow, elderly, childless, with a generous heart and appallingly bad breath. I hear, and learn, the interesting word *halitosis*. She insists on kissing us children every time we meet. She greatly admires our mother for her beauty, and pities her for her sadly reduced circumstances; and to demonstrate the sympathy she feels, has ordered a professional dressmaker to create these expensive garments so that poor brave charming Mrs Hallsmith's two little girls may be suitably clothed when they go a-partying. How kind of Mrs Wray! Say thank you, children! I am not thankful, but I say it. I always do say what I am told to say, and do as I am told to do. My obedience is a matter of policy, but my thoughts are rebellious.

*   *   *

The Twins have reached an age when they are required to attend an officially recognised real school. Jim is enrolled, therefore, at the County School for Boys, and Pam at the Girls' County School. They are duly kitted out with the uniforms compulsory at these establishments, and off they go every morning after breakfast to be educated.

I have to have it explained to me that a Council School is not the same—although the words are confusingly similar—as a County School. Not by any means the same! Boys who go to the Council School will shout rude things at you in the road, sometimes, and throw stones: that sort of behaviour. Why do they do that? Well, it's because they come from the lower classes and don't know any better, that's why. It's not their fault, says our mother. They're guttersnipes, our father says. *Guttersnipe* is a favourite epithet of his. And the difference is that boys who go to the County School, like Luke Gadstone, the doctor's son, or Peter Mitchell, the other doctor's son, can be invited to have tea at the Bungalow, and Council School boys can't. Is that clear?

Being three years younger than the Twins I find myself now, for the greater part of each day, in the position of an only child at home with my mother and Lucy. At first it's rather strange, but agreeable. The atmosphere is calm. Every morning, when the Twins have departed for school, I go shopping with Mummy. Every morning we call in at the Bank, and there is my father, seeming all at once like a stranger, who leaves whatever he was doing in the far recesses and comes forward to lean across the enormous high shiny counter and converse with Mummy in a low voice. What are they talking about? I can't hear. Except for the three of us, nobody else is visible in the Bank, but the Manager, so despised by my father, is lurking out of sight, I know, behind a door that remains permanently closed. The Manager is not a friend.

Does this mean he is an enemy?

The floor of the Bank is made of marble, black and white, and very hard and cold. There is a long shiny wooden bench I can sit on, if I want to, while I wait for my parents to finish talking; no other furniture. When I'm standing close to the counter I can scarcely see over the top of it. My father is wearing spectacles for work. He twitches his nose to keep the spectacles from slipping. He gives my mother money for her shopping. He never smiles. He looks at her, frowning, and tells her that the brim of her straw hat ought to be turned up at the back and down in front, instead of down at the back as well as the front. Why can't she realise, he says, that the way she has it is all wrong?—ugly! It's a question of line, he says—it's the line that matters. He sounds cross about it. He takes a slip of paper and sketches how the brim of her hat should be. I watch them; then I stand on tiptoe and see the drawing he's done of an S that's fallen over: a reclining S. My mother turns the brim of her hat up behind, and we go out together into the sunshine of the street.

I skip along beside her, skippety-skip, because it's such a relief to have escaped from the fearsome Bank. I take her hand while I confide to her my worry of not understanding what a bank is for or what you are supposed to do in it. My mother laughs and tells me I'm not to worry. It will be years and years before I have to use a bank myself, and by that time, she says, I *will* understand. This response of hers entirely reassures me: years and years is a very long time, as good as never. And so, as far as banks are concerned, I do stop worrying.

It sometimes happens that when you are gazing at a person's face, you don't hear what it is they're saying; or at least you are not quite sure afterwards what it was they said. You are so busy looking that you forget to listen.

Today is the day we are moving from one house to another, and to keep me out of the way until the worst of the upheaval is over I have been put into the charge of the two Misses Willisford, who live opposite the Bungalow. The two Misses Willisford are well-meaning but they have no experience of being in charge of children, only of Mrs Willisford, their mother; and besides, they have other things to see to on a Monday morning. So they leave me alone, with a ticking clock for company, in their claustrophobic airtight little sitting room, where the curtains are always drawn, to defeat the inquisitive eyes of passers-by.

How long am I expected to stay in this chair, waiting for Lucy to fetch me away? My thoughts are as muddled as the muddle today at home. But then all at once I remember Mummy saying something about the Great Western Beach, and saying—didn't she?—how I was to meet her there in our usual picnic place. Yes, that's what she said: I'm certain it is. And I'm beginning to get hungry, so it must be almost dinnertime. I shall have to hurry.

I wriggle off the chair and let myself quietly, quietly out of the front door. Then I run as fast as I can down the hill, and down Bury Road, and past the stone horse trough and the row of jingles and their patient ponies waiting for custom outside the

Great Western Railway Station. But by the time I come to where I have to cross the road I'm in a terrible fright. A voice has been growing inside me, louder and louder, telling me I've made a mistake—a dreadful mistake; I must have done.

I must have done, because never in my life have I run down Trenance Hill and down Bury Road and past the railway station on my own: I'm not allowed to go anywhere, not by myself. And why am I wearing my silver party slippers in the street? It is the slippers most of all that convince me of my horrendous error. They are shabby, it's true, post-party-season and in the process of being used up, but used up indoors, not *outside*. Whatever shall I do? I'm terrified at finding myself here, on the edge of the pavement, in my silver party slippers. It's like being in a nightmare. The beach, which I know so well, would be safer, but to cross the road on my own without holding the hand of a grown-up is absolutely forbidden.

I approach a very small, very bent old lady dressed in black, and ask her, timidly—please, would she see me across? And I put my hand in hers, and she leads me over. And then again I run—run—weeping with fear, through the shadow, deathly dark and cold and smelling of beer and urine, at the side of the Great Western Hotel, and out into the blaze of sunshine beyond; and down the steep road, with its hairpin bend halfway, to the bottom, where, on the heaps of dry soft sand that the high tides are seldom quite high enough to wash clean, I discover the blessed, familiar presence of little Sheila Hooper, playing contentedly with her nurse. And as I drop on my knees next to them, I know I am saved. The dreadful mistake I've made will eventually, I know now, have a happy ending. I shall be rescued. And so, indeed, I am; nor even punished, as I had thought I was sure to be, for my stupidity. The turmoil of moving house, the general worry surrounding it, somehow, mercifully, exonerates me from blame. Only Daddy must not be told: he would be furious with everyone.

*   *   *

The Great Western Hotel belongs to Sheila Hooper's father, who was given the nickname of Bo'sun as a small boy and has been known as Bo'sun ever since, in spite of having no connection with ships or the Navy. Sheila is younger than me, not much more than a baby. Her mother died when she was born, which is very sad for Sheila; and for her father, too, although he is a cheerful man, smallish, very suntanned and always good-tempered and smiling.

Bo'sun Hooper and Harry North, who is older, but also smallish, good-tempered and smiling, play tennis regularly with our father. To make up a foursome they have to get hold of another man, who might be Pig-faced Ralph, or possibly Douglas Adey. Neither of these two smiles. Douglas Adey is tall and melancholy; and Pig-faced Ralph has a rather gloomy character as well. But they like to join in and play tennis together. In summer, naturally, they play on one of the club's grass courts—the first one, nearest the pavilion, if they can get there early enough to bag it—but in spring, or even autumn when the weather's fine, they may decide to hire, for a couple of hours, a red-surfaced hard court in the vicinity of the railway viaduct. This just shows how much they enjoy playing tennis, because a red hard public court, which anybody can hire, is plainly inferior to the grass court of a private club for the benefit of members only.

*   *   *

Our change of address entails a move that could scarcely be easier. The house we are about to inhabit stands at the centre of a terrace, which is the name for a row of houses joined together, and the Bungalow is so close to it we are able to carry over many of our lesser belongings on foot, scooped up in our arms. John Julian's furniture van is employed to transport the larger items, and does so in a single speedy dash: we don't have a great deal of furniture.

Our father's desk is the biggest piece. Although a gigantic affair, it has a surprisingly flexible rolltop lid, a marvel of jointed slats, which performs the amazing trick of disappearing from sight with a rumble when pushed upwards. Daddy's huge desk was once the property of his father, our Scottish grandfather, a stern old man with a long white beard, who is dead. He died before I was born, but my sister Pam remembers being held on his knee. I know he had a stern appearance and a long white beard because our father painted a portrait of him looking like that.

It's on this desk that the cups our father won as a schoolboy for running and jumping and hurdling are always displayed, ranged in a line above the magical rolltop lid. Also displayed, in between the cups, is something else he won—but not for running or for hurdling, and certainly not when he was at school. It is the black and brass helmet of a German Army officer, with a chin-strap and a sinister spike sticking inches up from the middle. How he came by it our father will not say, but it is a souvenir of the Great War, about which he never speaks. Nobody speaks about the Great War, except, on occasion, our mother. She was a nurse, a VAD, in the war, and she learned to drive an ambulance: an unusual accomplishment in those days for a woman, requiring determination and courage. Our mother has both.

We know that a German can be called a Hun; or, alternatively, the Boche. And we know that our father was awarded a medal for an act of extreme bravery which made him a hero. And we know, furthermore, that he was taken prisoner by the Boche.

On the 11th of November every year, the day the Great War ended in 1918, he marches, with the other ex-servicemen (Mr Oxley, the Bank Manager, is not amongst them), through the narrow winding streets of Newquay, with his chin lifted, and his DSO medal pinned on his chest, and his eyes, his angry eyes, blindly staring ahead. We run and skip and hurry alongside him, up to the granite memorial cross on the headland above the sea, where the clergyman's words and the sad lament of the bugle are whirled out of hearing on the icy wind that always blows up there, perishingly cold, on November the 11th.

This is the reason why, whenever Daddy gets in a rage, we have to think of his medal and of him being a prisoner without enough to eat, and of the Boche and the Hun, and try not to mind. And we

50

do try not to mind. But it's hardest for Pam and Jim, because they are the ones he gets in a rage with most often, and his rages are frightening.

II
No. 9 Bay View Terrace

We have been given to understand that our new address is a step up, socially speaking, from our previous one, the commonplace gimcrack little hastily erected Bungalow. Bay View Terrace is more established, older, pre-dating the Great War, and, although situated, like the Bungalow, on the summit of Trenance Hill, was built as an arm branching off at right angles, and has thus the benefit of a greatly superior aspect. The panoramic vista that its name implies may be a slight exaggeration, but we are fortunate in having, immediately opposite our new address, an area neatly parcelled out into agricultural allotments which, by sloping away steeply downhill, enables us to overlook the lower level of chimneys and roofs, and the town's gasometer, and to glimpse the ocean's far horizon. Up here we are kings of the castle!

Our house, No. 9 Bay View Terrace, is approached by what more resembles a country track than an urban road. It is *unadopted*, which means that it's not the responsibility of the Council, and so, instead of being covered in tarmac, it remains as rough as the track alongside the River Gannel or the lane behind the Tennis Club. We rather like this. It makes us seem different. We like to seem different: to be different is to be special.

Our bumpy road goes nowhere. It is a cul-de-sac, the end of it blocked by a substantial white-painted gate, forever closed, the entrance to somebody else's grander shrubbery-screened residence. The pocket-handkerchief-sized front garden of our new house is filled only and completely with rampant hydrangea bushes. At the back of the house is a yard, the same width as the house—which is to say, not very wide—but longish, with a chipped grey concrete path leading from the kitchen door to another wooden door, set in a high brick wall. This door-in-the-wall, when unbolted, opens into a road that presumably—being macadamised and in a decently maintained condition—*is* adopted by the Council.

A few yards down to the right is a small crowded general dry-goods grocery shop, (very convenient in a cooking emergency when there may be a sudden shortage of sultanas or demerara sugar). We can also visit Mrs Clements' handy stores by means of a squeezed-in passageway that cuts through between the front garden and backyard of No. 1 Bay View Terrace and the back gardens of the Willisfords and their neighbours. This alternative access has the mildly adventurous allure of a footpath known to few people and seldom used, except by us. We prefer it to wrestling with the stiff rusty bolts of our door-in-the-wall.

To the left of our back entrance, but rather further off along the road than the grocery store to its right, is the combined home and business premises of the Stafferi family, Italian-born makers and purveyors of ice-creams. The Stafferi tribe is frowned upon by our parents to such an extent, its numerous noisy progeny and their lively street behaviour *so* disapproved of, that, inevitably, these low-class neighbours become a magnet of secret fascination for we three children. Our father declares catagorically that the Stafferis— foreigners!—have the revolting habit of storing the

56

ice-cream they manufacture by day underneath their beds at night. Well, we all know what most people keep under their beds at night: potties! If true, then it's understandable that no Hallsmith should be permitted ever to sample a disgusting unhygienic Stafferi ice-cream. But deep down in our doubting hearts we wonder—as we so often wonder—*is* it true?

We have moved house, but we still don't have the sort of real garden with real flowers in it that I yearn for. The backyard—referred to, inaccurately, as a back garden—is weedy, unkempt and sunless; and as for the prolific eye-catching hydrangea bushes in front (*our* hydrangea bushes now, a Terrace feature unparalleled), I am not able to take the same proprietary pride in them as my parents at once do, quite as much as though they had planted and nurtured the bushes themselves.

What happiness it would be to have a garden crammed with pansies and delphiniums and carnations and lupins and sweet peas; a garden, however small, of colours and scents, with butterflies flitting, and bees droning. I know there can be a garden like this because Granny Laurie, who lives at 59 Victoria Road, Summertown, Oxford, has just such a one. I've seen it.

Granny Laurie is our mother's mother and she is looked after, being elderly, by Aunt Margaret and Aunt Molly. She is a widow. Our mother's father was agent to the Fawley Estate and he was drowned when Mummy was a little girl, twelve years old. He was sailing with Andrew, her brother, in Southampton Sound when the wash from the passing ferry tipped over their boat, and that was the end of him: he wasn't a swimmer. Although, indisputably, a very sad accident, I can't help thinking her father, James Laurie, must have been asking for trouble to go sailing in choppy water when he couldn't swim. He should have learnt how to swim. Andrew, our uncle, who was fifteen then, could swim, and he swam ashore and is alive to this day. Mummy says she won't allow any of her children to risk their lives in a boat. I think this is a pity, considering that we live beside the sea. I should like very much to go sailing. I mean to learn to swim as soon as possible.

*   *   *

When our mother's father, James Laurie, was drowned, his widow, who later became our granny, was obliged to leave The Home Farm where they had lived until then, and move into a poky little semi-detached house in Oxford with her six children: five daughters and one son, Andrew. She had fallen on hard times. We were taken twice to visit her. Almost my only remembrance of the first occasion is of a picnic by a river, where all the world was green and moist and sun-speckled; and a frog jumped out from beneath the rug I sat on, and hopped away into the river. I had never seen a frog before. I was very young indeed, and frogs are not to be found on the top of Trenance Hill, Newquay. And another afternoon our Aunt Molly came towards us, tall and laughing, across a great stretch of grass, with a long skirt and a white head-dress billowing in the breeze. She was the matron of a boys school, St Edward's, we were told.

It was several years later that we visited our poor mournful old Granny Laurie for a second time, which was when I was unforgettably impressed by the sight of a small garden packed with flowers in full bloom.

Gardens: they intoxicate me. The attraction I feel for them is so overwhelming and so inexplicable it renders me dumb. Lucy's family have a garden. The cottage where they live is in the country outside Newquay, surrounded by deep lanes and high overgrown hedges. She took me there once on her half-day off and I found and picked some primroses which, instead of being yellow, were the palest pink. How wonderful! I had believed that primroses were always yellow! You have to be lucky to find pink primroses—they are as rare as buried treasure.

Lucy's mother and father are very little people, the size, almost, of dwarfs and very friendly, but with ugly knobbly hands. All her family are very friendly to me. Her two brothers, Frank and Dick, work on a farm and are as big and clumsy as giants, quite the opposite of Mr and Mrs Coles, their parents. They are fair-haired, the same as Lucy and the same as Lily, their other sister; but Dick is married to Ada, who is dark, and has no front teeth.

Funnily enough, except for being fair-haired, Lucy doesn't seem to resemble any of them much, not really. She seems to belong more to us Hallsmiths than to her own family, and I'm glad of that. But I notice how, when she's with them, her voice changes. That's because, at home, she tries to imitate our mother in everything—the way Mummy talks and the way Mummy laughs: everything.

I enjoyed my visit to Lucy's cottage very much,

all of it, because the Coles were so welcoming and made such a fuss of me. But what I most enjoyed, apart from finding the pink primroses, was being conducted round their garden. It was extremely well-tended and flourishing, a mixture of flowers growing in unregulated abundance and vegetables planted in straight precise rows, and with not an inch of earthy space wasted.

I was allowed to go by bus with Lucy on this visit to her family because that day our mother wasn't well. She was lying down with a bad headache. Mummy often does have headaches. And sometimes she has dizzy spells, and feels faint, and has to sniff at a tiny green bottle of smelling salts to recover. When I sniff the smelling salts, to investigate what they're like, my eyes water and sting.

*   *   *

A telegraph boy pedalling up to the front door on his pushbike, and extracting an orange envelope from his leather wallet and ringing the bell, almost certainly means the bringing of bad news. My mother goes white in the face when Lucy hands her the orange envelope, and has to sit down before she tears it open. Not so long ago a telegram was what everyone dreaded most of all to receive. Lucy fetches the green bottle of smelling salts and takes me away with her into the kitchen.

When Daddy gets back from the Bank for his midday meal I learn that our mother's beloved Aunt Jessie, who lives in Anglesey, Wales, with Mummy's Uncle Stuart and her other aunt, is very ill: so ill, in fact, that Mummy has to rush upstairs

60

and pack a bag and be away down to the Great Western Railway Station in such a tremendous hurry to catch a train that when Pam and Jim return from school she's already gone. Despite her haste our mother has nevertheless found enough time to arrange for Mrs Dutton, a pale nervous little Scottish widow with one child, to take over the running of our Bay View Terrace household in her absence. How many days her absence may last we don't yet know.

Our father says there's no need at all for the Dutton woman: he can't stand having her about the place, and her boy is a snivelling halfwit. He doesn't see why he should have to pay good money for Mrs Dutton to be making a nuisance of herself. And Lucy supports this opinion, declaring huffily that she knows how Mrs Hallsmith likes things done. Didn't she manage perfectly well alone during that emergency when Jim was whisked off to Truro Hospital at a moment's notice to be examined by doctors on account of his double hernia? If she could manage those two nights when Mrs Hallsmith stopped on in Truro, says Lucy, she can manage quite as well again for just as long as is necessary, and will be glad to take her orders from Mr Hallsmith, but not from someone who doesn't understand our ways. And so meek obliging Mrs Dutton and her son (both of them rather nice, I privately think) are dispatched forthwith, having lasted the course for no more than twenty-four hours.

As soon as they have been got rid of, an unexpected holiday atmosphere sets in, generated by our intimidating father assuming the unfamiliar guise of children's friend and benefactor: a remarkable transformation. Indeed, a veritable change of personality! We have sometimes in the past encountered this other Daddy, but the light-hearted mood, like a burst of wintry sunshine, is always brief and quickly over. And so, while we are thankful for a blue-sky interlude, we are wary, sensing the situation to be precarious and not under guarantee.

Besides, is it right that we should be playing endless games of Ludo and Snakes and Ladders, and having extra ju-jube sweeties, and staying up late, when a letter from Mummy in the morning's post informs us that her dearly loved Aunt Jessie has died? Ought we not to be sad also, instead of romping off excitedly to the cinema to see an actor called Will Hay in a full-length farcical grown-up film?

Our only previous experience of moving pictures—films—was in a darkened makeshift hall behind a newspaper shop when Daddy took us to see a programme of Jackie Coogan in *The Kid,* and Charlie Chaplin and a cartoon of Felix the Cat. But this time we have tickets for the Victoria Cinema, a palace of entertainment recently refurbished with splendid velvet curtains, and a rise-and-fall organ belting out popular music, and plush tip-up seats. The story is mostly incomprehensible, but we can, and do, laugh loudly at the funny bits. Even our father, who never laughs, is laughing, leaning forward eagerly in his seat—having a good time; and with us! Amazing!

Going to the cinema continues, throughout the Newquay years, to be an occasional treat doled out to us children exclusively by our father, who is a film buff. When we go to the pictures we go without our mother. She doesn't care for the flickering silver screen: it gives her a headache.

The present good time doesn't last. We knew that it wouldn't—couldn't. But before the storm clouds gather again—before Mummy returns from the funeral of her Aunt Jessie in Beaumaris, Anglesey—Newquay has its summer Carnival, and our father, at the eleventh hour, decides that we too will take part in the parade. The Hallsmith contingent, moreover, by some means or other, will be outstanding. This is how we contrive to do it.

Ever since our ABC burnt out on Mevagissey hill we have had no car; not until, that's to say, a certain Mr Cooper, who lives at the far end of Mount Wise and is one of the Bank's customers, offered to share his Ford and its expenses with us. His offer was accepted, and nowadays our father and Mr Cooper take it in turns to get behind the steering wheel of the Ford on alternate weekends. It happens, by a lucky chance, to be our turn this weekend, the date of the annual Carnival.

Our father's brainwave is for us, having folded flat the canvas hood of the Ford, a smallish grey tourer, to cover the car, every inch of it, with the round pink rosettes of the hydrangeas growing in our front garden, thereby converting it into what will amount to a mobile hydrangea bush. The only cash outlay required is on the purchase of a great many balls of string. As commanding officer of a tricky camouflage operation, our father is in his element, deploying a volunteer squad of three enthusiastic foot soldiers, who scamper tirelessly to and fro at his behest. Lucy, though, is dubious. From the doorway she watches us, but won't help,

63

except to fetch the scissors.

With not a minute to spare, the final knot is tied. We climb aboard our flower-encrusted conveyance, a jubilant crew, and set off, just in time to tag on to the tail of a slow-moving cavalcade of decorated floats and wagons and tradesmen's vans and pony-drawn jingles wending their way through the streets of Newquay. Cheered by the crowds as we go past, our father honks the squeeze-hooter in boastful acknowledgement. Spectators throw paper streamers at us, jump on the running board, hand us flags to wave; and the judges award our garden-on-wheels fourth prize for originality. We think we deserve to have won first prize, or second at least. But never mind—we have scored a triumph!

This year's carnival junketing is the high-watermark of our relationship with Daddy, a moment of comradeship never quite, alas, to be equalled.

On Monday morning Mummy returns. Waiting for her, we have been divided between excitement and anxiety. In her Saturday letter she wrote that she would be bringing back books for us— recovered from our Granny Laurie's house in Oxford, where she will spend a night on the way home—a fund of wonderful stories that Mummy can remember reading herself when she was a child. We are book-deprived, my sister Pam and I: book-hungry. We long for books. Our anticipation of what, according to this promise, we are about to receive is fever-high; and our disappointment at what we do receive when our mother unpacks her bag, correspondingly profound. The books with which we are presented are considered by us to be dismal in the extreme. One of them relates the tale of the little drummer-boy who dies, drumming to the end, on the battlefield—how dreadful! Then there is the story of the naughty eldest girl in *Ten Little Australians* who makes amends for her naughtiness by being killed heroically saving the life of her baby brother from a falling tree—how horrible! How could Mummy have possibly thought that we would enjoy reading about such depressing happenings? How could *she* have thought them fun when she was a child?

Our mother's reaction, on being confronted by the desecration of No. 9 Bay View Terrace's garden, was as predicted by Lucy: incredulous and shocked. She cannot believe her eyes. Not a single bloom did we leave in it—not one; only barren sticks remain. This, on returning from the unhappiness of her much-loved Aunt Jessie's death and funeral, is what greets her. Sounds of weeping, and of shouting, filter out from our parents' bedroom, and gloom descends once more on the Hallsmith household.

*   *   *

At this stage in our lives our father still sometimes receives mail addressed to Captain G. Hallsmith, DSO: a gratifying confirmation of the position he once held in a society to which he feels he rightfully belongs, but whose qualifications for membership he is painfully aware of having forfeited on becoming, not just the employee of a Bank—a dreary enough occupation when you had set your heart on being a world-famous painter— but an example of the lowest form of that species:

a mere miserable clerk. Oh, how the bitterness of it rankles and eats like acid into his soul!

Many years ago our father's father, the dour old Scotsman with the long white beard—thirteenth child of a Presbyterian minister—had also, it seems, been employed in the service of a Bank; but on a far more elevated plane and in financial circumstances that were modestly affluent, even prosperous. Migrating south from Aberdeen, he had crossed the border to take up his post as manager of the Bank of New Zealand's prestigious London Head Office. Tragically, however, the wife he brought with him from Scotland, and three of their five children, died almost immediately on arrival in Hampstead, London, from the fatal consequences of insanitary drains.

As a widower in his forties, Harvey Hallsmith married a second wife, young—very young—Mary Martin from Inverness, daughter of a tea-planter in Assam, whose dowry, in lieu of money, was a beautiful face and a beautiful sunny laughing disposition. Five more children were born, our father Guthrie being the second of this replacement brood, and our grandmother Mary, née Martin, proceeded to bring up all five of them, as well as the two surviving step-sons who were not much younger than herself.

Then, one fateful day, she too suffered a similar catastrophe to that which had overtaken our maternal Granny, and fell, with the same shocking suddenness, on hard times. But in her case it was not the result of an accidental drowning, nor did it reduce her to widowhood.

Her elderly husband, the bank manager, had been foolish enough to take the advice of Alec

Martin, Mary's rich stockbroker cousin, (our old Cousin Edith's now-deceased husband) and invested every penny of his accumulated capital in a tin mine in the Argentine; or perhaps it was a copper mine in Chile, or a gold mine in Brazil: who now knows? The South American mine, whatever and wherever it was—if, indeed, it had ever existed—went bust, and Grandfather Hallsmith, and his whole family along with him, was ruined overnight. I cannot think the Bank of New Zealand had shown much acumen in appointing Grandfather Hallsmith as the caretaker of their customers' money when he turned out to be so incredibly reckless with his own. How could he have demonstrated such an inexcusable lack of professional common sense? And why should his wife's Cousin Alec, the well-to-do stockbroker, have proffered such disastrous advice but refrained from following that advice himself?

The crash came just prior to the start of the Great War. Our father Guthrie, aged eighteen, was given the task of fetching home his sister, Dorothy, from her finishing school in Switzerland, while he, instead of being enrolled in a college of art as he had hoped, was placed by his bankrupt old father in a bank, on the lowest rung, and told he must immediately set about earning his living. It was only the outbreak of hostilities in August, 1914, that presented him, ironically, with his chance to escape.

And yet now, with the Great War concluded and a receding horror, here he is today, chained once again to a job he hates, married to a woman eight years his senior, father of three, with a wretched income and no prospects. How has it—how *can* it—have happened?

He lives in a state of perpetual mortification, repeatedly, through gritted teeth, impressing on his bewildered children what we are never to forget—always to remember—that although the necessity of providing for us, his family, forces him to work as an ignominious bank clerk, our father is, nonetheless, *a gentleman*!

What exactly does it mean, to be a gentleman? We don't know; and nor, perhaps, does he. But thus are his three children taught, by this anguished angry refrain, to feel obscurely ashamed of Daddy for his despicable status. An innate superiority, duly acknowledged and unquestionable, is the birthright, we dimly gather, of every gentleman. But a bank clerk is not viewed by the world as a superior being; quite the opposite. Nor does the world pay tribute to an artist, no matter how much he deserves it, who appears in the guise of a bank clerk. Contradictory emotions of pride and shame forever churn away inside our father, tormenting him.

*   *   *

We find ourselves, after the Carnival, once more car-less. Mr Cooper is outraged by our use, or misuse, of his precious Ford, the car that he was good enough to share with us and wishes to share no longer. The photograph in our local paper showing a proudly flower-bedecked winner of the parade's fourth prize only increases his wrath. We had not asked for his permission!—and look at the damage done!—the scratches! There is a heated scene. Increasingly affronted, Mr Cooper withdraws our car-sharing benefit. That he also withdraws his account from Midland Bank and transfers it to a rival establishment neither we children nor our father care in the least. Daddy, indeed, is rather pleased by what he takes to be proof of having won a ding-dong battle with a customer beneath contempt. But we do care, and care very much, at being deprived of the means whereby the Hallsmiths can drive out of Newquay every other weekend for those beach-picnics we depend upon—winter months excluded, naturally—throughout the year.

Picnics-on-the-beach is the one area of an otherwise discordant marriage where our parents are in harmonious, if tacit, agreement. To be out of the house, out-of-doors, to be sitting on the sand, or on smooth rocks, with the sounds of the sea making unnecessary any attempt at conversation: this has for them, it would seem, a significance of almost religious intensity, notwithstanding the acrimonious preparations always attendant on these regular family outings. The truth of the matter is, our beach-picnics have a far greater importance for us than simply the eating of meals outside: they are a form of salvation for our mother and father, and so, by association, for their children.

When the chosen picnic place is finally reached, and the rug unfolded on the ground, establishing our ownership of a certain footage of sand for the morning and afternoon ahead, we become aware of a letting-go at last, a blessed loosening of tension traceable to our parents' release, like a sigh exhaled, from the daily bondage of a pain that is well-nigh unendurable and yet has somehow to be endured. The neutral splash of waves breaking, retreating, breaking again, endlessly; the tides that ebb and flow, ebb and flow; the sting of salty spray blowing on the wind; the wide sky above, whether blue or cloudy—all this has the effect of ministering to a need of theirs, unspoken, but so profound we children (and possibly they too) can only guess at it: a cleansing of invisible wounds, a rinsing of stains, a purifying of memories that have to be washed over and over, and still can never quite be washed away.

*   *   *

Our father isn't going to have somebody like Mr Cooper, whom he describes as 'that little pipsqueak', interfering with his arrangements. He makes a few discreet enquiries amongst his other customers and comes home one evening, cock-a-hoop, driving a motor car he has just bought from the owner of the garage where we used to fill up with petrol. We shan't have to share the rather battered old second-hand Fiat (a tourer, of course, to satisfy our parents' passion for fresh air) with anyone. It belongs entirely to us; or at least it will belong to us entirely as soon as a sufficient number of monthly payments have been made.

'Oh, Guth!' says our mother, doubting the wisdom of such an impulsive action. She has never herself bought anything by instalments, and in her housekeeping economy every single penny counts, and is accounted for.

Daddy, who was expecting to be congratulated, gets cross. The garage-owner let him have the Fiat on extremely easy terms, he says; which means that the monthly payments are small—very small. How small? Daddy refuses to say. Who, he demands— getting crosser—who brings in the money to ensure this family is clothed and fed? He does! He earns it by the slavery of working for a mere pittance behind the counter of a beastly bank. Well, then! It's for him, and for no one else, to decide on how the money should be spent.

We look from parent to parent, hardly daring to breathe. Do we or don't we have a motor car? Can we rejoice? Does Daddy know best? He says that he does.

We keep the Fiat, and from the beginning consider it to be, not a gradually acquired possession, but entirely ours. Now every weekend—instead of, as previously, every alternate weekend—we drive out with our picnic baskets, our rug for sitting on, our bathing togs, to beaches judged to be remote enough to avoid the danger of

71

bumping into Newquay residents.

It is our father who looks upon such possible encounters as a danger. Our mother would welcome them. She has a sociable nature and enjoys meeting and exchanging chit-chat with acquaintances, or even with total strangers. Our father, on the contrary, views almost all people, and always when first introduced, with suspicion. On seeing a face approaching in the distance that might at closer quarters turn out to be familiar, he will stop short, utter an imprecation under his breath—'*Hell's Teeth*'—and then, with perhaps a child, who would give the game away, in tow, will bolt off, shoulders hunched protectively, in an opposite direction, taking cover until the person, known or unknown, has gone by and he and his hostage can safely emerge from hiding.

In our new-old motor car, Daddy at the wheel, we explore the northern coastline on both sides of Newquay, and occasionally, but less frequently, cross over the Cornish hinterland by way of Quintrel Downs and Indian Queens to investigate the milder bays and inlets and villages bordering the English Channel: Kynance Cove, Marazian, Lamorna Cove. We try them all, usually once only, as if we are searching for something which we never find, because we have forgotten what it is. Next week we will pick a different name on the map, and if that proves to be unrewarding too, the following week we can pick another. We have a car of our own! We can escape to somewhere every Sunday, rain or shine! And this is what we do.

But the south coast of Cornwall has less appeal for our parents, and for us children as well, than the taller cliffs and stronger winds and long, crested breakers of the Atlantic shoreline. Eventually, after many trial outings to different locations weekend after weekend, two of them become our accredited favourites. We develop a personal and possessive relationship with Porth, to one side of Newquay, and Holywell Bay to the other, in time regarding these most often visited picnic places as indisputably ours: weekend extensions of the Hallsmiths' restricted urban domain.

Holywell Bay has a beach that stretches on and on, backed by soft piled-up slippery silvery sliding sand-dunes, over which grows a profusion of coarse grass, the points of its tall stalks as sharp as spears to prick the flesh of bare legs passing through them. Picnics in Holywell Bay are exhausting affairs. We are obliged to park the car a quite considerable way from the sea. But this is only the start of it. Having traipsed across the dry desert-like approach to the beach, laden down in the manner of pack animals with picnic paraphernalia, and having reached firm sand, we must then trudge along the foreshore for what seems to us children like much more than a mile—*miles*!—to reach the rocks and caves and cliffs and pools at its furthest end.

This is where our picnic has to be. Dunes are not thought acceptable for a day's camping site, though exactly why not is unclear. Are they too featureless, lacking a definite character that would have some sort of an affinity with the Hallsmith character? Is it because the sand of the dunes is so fine and soft its particles are more liable to blow into our food than the sea-washed harder damper sand of the cove upon which our sights are set? Or is it because—which is true—hardly anybody else except us would bother to undertake such a toilsome journey, and the danger, therefore, of bumping into another human being will be minimal? A more sensible reason (and perhaps, after all, the main one) is that the deep still pools left behind by outgoing tides amongst the rocks at the far end offer safer bathing for children than the enticing waves of an untrustworthy sea.

Here, at any rate—here and nowhere else, immutable as a law—we will plant ourselves for the rest of the day to have our picnic. The rug, laid carefully out on the ground, its corners weighted with pebbles—we are not allowed to sit on the wet sand—is really an old grey Army hospital blanket. Acting as subsidiary rug, or blanket, is a faded khaki-coloured garment of a curiously silky texture

74

known as Daddy's trench coat. We have wondered whether the splodges of scarlet on it might be blood-of-the-Boche, but there are smears of yellow too, and we learn—disappointed—that the trench coat we now sit on has also done service as a painting smock.

Our first assignment on arrival is to find, each of us, a shell, the sort that looks like an upturned open hand. Ribbed and brown on the outside, smooth on the inside, washed clean by the sea, these cockle shells, of which there are many scattered about, provide us with individual salt cellars wherein we dip our hard-boiled eggs and new potatoes. Picnic fare on these outings never varies: everyone has an egg, a tomato, several small waxy boiled potatoes, a home-made pasty, some lettuce leaves (representing what our father describes generically as *green stuff*—essential, he informs us, to ward off the scurvy), and always, to finish with, a Fyffes banana, big and curved like a scimitar. We drink either a limited ration of lemon squash, so frugally diluted as to be insipid, or, if we are still thirsty when that's gone, plain water. Nothing the matter, says Daddy, with plain water: we can count ourselves lucky to have it. In a war, remember, we'd thank our stars for having muddy water out of ditches to drink. We do thank our stars, indeed we do, to be drinking water which isn't muddy and has come, we know, from our scullery tap and not out of a ditch.

Before eating lunch we bathe once, to sharpen our appetites, and earn us our meal. After lunch an obligatory three-quarters-of-an-hour has to elapse before we bathe again. Should this last rule be disobeyed, or skimped, our digestions, disrupted

75

while working away busily inside us, will repay such disobedience by causing an attack of the cramps, or heart failure, followed, most probably, by death—and serve us jolly well right! We, who doubt so much, believe this absolutely, and when foolhardy visiting friends rush into the water within half-an-hour, or less, of eating, we expect to see them throw up their arms and die in front of our eyes; and we are surprised and inclined to be put out when they inexplicably don't suffer the fate they deserve.

Our parents consider that simply by transporting us here and setting us free to do as we please, we children will have been supplied with sufficient amusement for the whole of the day ahead. And yes, it is entirely sufficient. We ask for no more. Our mother can knit. Our father can doze, or go off on his own with his painting gear. We will draw pictures in the sand, practise catching and throwing with an old tennis ball, hunt for shells, paddle in the fringes of the perilous waves, splash about in one of the pools, run races, play French cricket with a piece of driftwood for a bat, explore the seaweedy rocks, amongst the cracks and crevices of which are the crystals that my sister Pam and I (Jim isn't interested) patiently prise out one by one as if extricating individual yellowish pointed teeth. Diamonds!—ours for the taking!

And so the peaceful hours drift by until we hear our mother call to us. Time for strawberry jam sandwiches and sultana scones, and a mug of weak tea, tepid and milky, poured from the two aluminium-capped Thermos flasks. Then the blanket and the trench coat are picked up and shaken and folded, the baskets re-packed, and the wet cotton bathing costumes rolled up in our striped and scrubby towels. Each of us has his or her own stripey towel, and is responsible for bringing or taking away a tightly rolled sausage of *bathing togs*: our father's term. If any part of this bathing-togs equipment can't be found at the moment of setting forth for the picnic in the morning, or gets left behind when the picnic's over, or dropped on the way home, as has happened more than once, there is bound to be an almighty row. So, ever-anxious, I make very sure my unfortunate brother Jim does have his sausage tucked securely under his arm, both coming and going. Rows, at all costs, are to be avoided. Above the dunes, as we trudge homewards, the larks, in the clear blue summer sky, sing and sing and sing, on and on, up and up, as though they would never stop. Life can be happy. If only it could always be like this.

But one Sunday, as we make our tired way back along the beach, our father sees, lying on the sand and surrounded by pebbles, a brooch. It must have fallen quite recently, from the dress of some person, a woman, as she was stooping, perhaps, to pick up a shell. There is not a soul in sight. The large opal, set in gold, is at the centre of a looped and twisted triangular design, vaguely heart-shaped: a beautiful brooch; a valuable one. Our father gives it to our mother.

We must take it, she says, at once, Guth—as soon as we reach Newquay—to the police station. Whoever has lost it is certain, she says, to be feeling dreadfully upset, and will be so pleased, so thankful to have it returned.

We shall do no such thing, says our father. What

77

a ridiculous idea! He found the brooch, carelessly dropped on the ground—left there, forgotten; so now it's his. He estimates that he could, if he wanted to, sell it for a considerable sum of money. Instead he chooses to give it to his wife. She ought to be glad, he says, be proud to have a husband who would rather present her with the treasure trove he has happened upon by chance, than keep it for himself; as he has every right to do. Not all husbands would be so generous!

The high unending song of the larks is too far-off to sweeten the bitterness of this earthbound quarrel; nor can the regular splash of waves on the seashore drown the pleading and angry exchange of words. We three children stand by in silence on the deserted beach, listening, judging. Daddy is wrong, we know it: shockingly wrong. Crowning the ruination of our picnic Sunday, the beautiful brooch has been turned now into what is worse than base metal: it has become stolen goods. Our mother, who possesses no jewellery, keeps the exquisite opal-and-gold ornament, somebody else's treasure, on her dressing table for years, unworn.

*　　　*　　　*

Our other favourite picnic place, Porth, is in complete contrast to Holywell Bay. It has no dunes, no empty stretch of beach, no long fatiguing walk to arrive at the site for our picnic. Porth is a deep inlet where once, instead of the present little meandering streams, a sizeable river must have carved its way out across low-lying land to reach the sea. The estuary has silted up. On either side today there are banks rather than cliffs, where springy turf and bushes of pungent-smelling tamarisk, and the flowers of thrift and bladderwort spill down over the rocks to the level almost of the sandy coves below. It's easy enough to scramble the few necessary steps down by a well-worn path into any one of these little coves, and to scramble back up again to the safety of the grass above when the ebbing tide ceases to ebb, and turns, and comes flooding in.

The Newquay side of the estuary is somewhat higher, rockier, less friendly and sunlit than what we think of as *our* side, and the whole of that headland is private property, owned by the Tangye family, with here and there a notice-board warning that Trespassers Will Be Prosecuted. The opposite headland—*our side*—is common land, where anyone may wander at will: so that's all right. This headland, as it approaches the sea, begins to tilt upwards more and more, to bring it into conformity with the towering cliff-height of the rest of the north Cornish coastline; and the point itself, a quite extensive grassy area inhabited by scores of rabbit colonies, has actually at some time in the past become separated from the mainland. The narrow ravine that cuts it off, effectively creating an island at the end of the estuary's enclosing northern arm, is deep and dark, a sheer drop. Spanning the draughty gap is a wooden bridge, barely a yard in width and pleasurably unsteady: a bridge that bounces as you run across it.

Full tide in Porth estuary is, generally speaking, a mild affair, the water spreading gently between its confining boundaries like a lagoon; but it can, on occasion—especially in autumn and winter—be stormy. And even when it isn't rough out at sea, the meeting of those waves which come swirling uncontrollably in beneath the footbridge from either side of the island is always a violent spectacle, breathtaking to watch from above, the battling churning white commotion of opposing forces flinging up high fountains of spray to soak us children as we hang, enthralled, over the railing.

The road from Newquay skirts, at a safe height, the wide head of Porth estuary. But it has already been obliged to descend from its lofty eminence in order to cross over the first of the two streams flowing out on to the sand at either corner, and it has to descend again to cross the second stream. This done, it turns away to the right and mounting steeply up continues its windy cliff-top progress, following the coastline north-eastwards in the direction of Padstow.

Immediately before the road swerves off and vanishes uphill there stands a rather ramshackle weather-boarded and weather-beaten single-storey building. Once upon a time, when pilchard fishing was a thriving Cornish industry, the building had been a boatshed belonging to local Porth fishermen. Sunk a little below the level of the road, which runs close behind it, only a few feet of roughly concrete-covered rock separates this long low-lying shed from the foreshore. We can tell by two remaining bollards and the great iron rings let into the concrete how fishing smacks used to be steered in and made fast against what in those days counted as a quay. Boats would have been hauled up the slipway during the winter months for painting and necessary repairs, or to save them perhaps from the buffeting of exceptionally stormy seas.

Today the boatshed is a tearoom: the Rose Café. We know it well. Two elderly sisters, the Misses Clark-Ourry, who happen to live quite close to us on Mount Wise, open it every summer season to visitors, dispensing delicious cream teas at very moderate prices. Considering how extremely moderate their prices are, and how lavish the cream dispensed, it is a wonder the two old ladies manage by this means to scrape a living; but somehow they do.

The Clark-Ourry sisters, although devoted to one another, could hardly be more different. Veah is plump and blonde and blue-eyed, with a wheezy voice and an array of bangles chinking on her soft fat arms, and her feet squeezed into and bulging out of shoes a size too small. Isobel isn't able to indulge herself in pretty shoes with heels and pointed toes and sparkly buckles. One of her legs is shorter by inches than the other and she hobbles about in a clumsy black built-up boot. She is as dark as Veah—whose youthful frizzy curls are suspiciously golden—is fair, and as thin and angular as her sister is rounded and podgy. We children, indeed, are slightly afraid of Isobel's appearance: her very sharp features, the jutting chin, the bright observant black eyes—is this not how witches are supposed to look? But the overflowing generosity and kindness of both the Misses Clark-Ourry are beyond any doubt. And their cakes—ah, their cakes!—in particular, the sponges, lemon-iced and as light as air: their cakes are heavenly!

Only once during the summer will they abandon the Rose Café in Porth and return briefly to

Newquay. This is on the occasion of our Tennis Club's annual tournament when Miss Veah and Miss Isobel are invariably requested to provide the so-called refreshments—in actual fact, a sumptuous feast—for competitors and spectators. By a happy chance their back garden runs up to the lane that borders the Club's grounds, and on tournament day the two ladies manage to creep through a specially maintained hole in the hedge bearing trayload after trayload of cakes and buns and sandwiches and shortbreads and jellies and extravagant trifles, all to be laid out on the trestle tables which their accomplice Wilton has set up ready for them in the hut where in winter-time he stores the bulky nets and other out-of-season equipment. He also sees to it that the convenient hole is blocked again afterwards, and will remain so until next year's tournament.

The Clark-Ourrys' house on Mount Wise is crammed to capacity with furniture: with sofas and small mother o'pearl-encrusted tables, and footstools and Oriental screens; with fans and shawls and yellow silk lampshades, and tassels and artificial flowers and cabinets full of sentimental knickknacks. There is a dingly-dangly curtain of glass beads, like a shower of sweeties, at the entrance to the porch, and inside, everywhere, piles of cushions, plump and soft and be-frilled like Miss Veah herself. Being artistic, and industrious, and with a passion for decoration, they have painted the fans, and embroidered the cushions, and embellished whatever they find to be capable of added adornment: pencils are tipped with blobs of sealing wax, glass bonbon dishes and ashtrays are backed with the multi-coloured silver-paper wrappings from chocolates. Nothing pretty is wasted or thrown away.

Their superstitions, which are many, cause them great anxiety. Hawthorn blossom, for instance, must on no account be brought indoors: to do so would be disastrous. But when fortunes are told from the tarot cards, or the leaves at the bottom of a teacup, or the palms of hands, their predictions are always optimistic, never upsetting. The Clark-Ourrys own a fluffy cat, a pampered and much-loved animal, but the cause also of anguish, since, like all cats, it has the distressing habit of killing birds and little defenceless mice. Less harrowing to their tender emotions is the companionship of a green parrot on a perch and a couple of lumbering winter-hibernating tortoises. These exotic and interesting pets, encountered by us for the first time, we study closely with amazement and awe.

No footsore tramp, passing through Newquay, ever fails to trudge up the steep gravel drive of their Mount Wise residence, or ever returns down it empty-handed. The Clark-Ourry sisters would, if they could, feed and clothe and care for the hungry and wretched—whether human or otherwise—of the whole world, but their financial circumstances are in reality so limited they have a struggle to keep themselves afloat.

Our father is inclined to look askance at this friendship which our mother, who makes friends easily with everyone, has struck up with these innocently unorthodox neighbours of ours, the Misses Clark-Ourry, and to distance himself from it. But the unorthodox element is just exactly what we children find irresistibly fascinating.

Every year, as soon as Easter has come and gone, the sisters resolutely shut up their house on Mount Wise and migrate to Porth. This is how they solve the problem of being two unmarried untrained elderly ladies who have somehow to earn a living.

People driving out from Newquay are greeted, the moment the road dips down clear of its over-arching trees, by the sight of the Rose Café facing them across the breadth of the estuary. There it sits, the long low white building on its rocky promontory at the very edge of the sand or the water—according to whether the tide is in or out—its huge pink letters painted on the shabby weatherboard exterior proclaiming, like a welcome, what it is and what it has to offer: THE ROSE CAFÉ: TEAS. Who could resist the invitation?

As well as the old boatshed they rent the triangular flat field on the other side of the road, an area flooded in winter by a combination of high tides and the swollen stream, but judged in summertime to be dry enough and firm enough for their customers to use it as a carpark. At the gateway to the field is another smaller shed and here Miss Isobel Clark-Ourry, handicapped by her lame leg and ungainly boot, spends the day, seated at a table, issuing tickets to the motorists, and selling them confectionery and Capstan cigarettes and ice-creams. She also has charge of the lending library. Behind her chair there is space enough in the shed for several rows of faded red cloth-bound Edwardian and Victorian novels. Any one of these out-of-date romances may be borrowed, the notice advises, for tuppence per volume. But people don't

84

as a rule come to Porth to read; and so the lending library's books continue to moulder away on their shelves, undisturbed.

Inside the Rose Café, pink is the colour that predominates: curtains and china, even the paper napkins, all favour shades of pink, and a boldly executed design of stencilled roses, with pink petals and green leaves, decorates the walls of the tea room, which is entered by three shallow steps leading down into it from the bumpy concrete-covered quay. At the furthermost end of the tea room, past a proliferation of rickety tables and chairs, is the miniscule kitchen, and on beyond it a door, firmly closed, marked: PRIVATE. This door guards a haven: the tiny sitting-room, filled almost entirely by a baggy sofa, where Veah and her team of waitresses can rest and put their feet up whenever business is slack enough to allow them a few minutes respite. Outside, in a lean-to, the clean—if primitive—El-San lavatory is for the convenience of staff and proprietors only, not for customers. We, however, as privileged friends of the management, are allowed in dire emergencies to use it.

Although the waitresses (who wear pink cotton frocks when working) travel daily to and fro on the Newquay bus, the Clark-Ourry sisters have succeeded in obtaining for themselves accommodation locally of a sort that enables them to stay on in the evenings after closing time, and be near, still, to their Rose Café.

At the back of the field opposite, right under the hill, is a discarded Great Western Railway carriage. It stands on stilts to keep it clear of winter flooding. A short flight of wooden steps gives access to one of its doors. The other doors have been blocked, and the box-like compartments been subjected to a certain amount of modification, resulting in bedrooms—not spacious, to be sure, but adequate in size—for the two old ladies to occupy during their summer residence in Porth.

This form of temporary shelter has been adopted by the Misses Clark-Ourry as a sensible measure, and for purely pragmatic reasons: it was there, it was cheap, it was possible. Custom has rendered commonplace what might once have seemed a quaint idea, and their seasonal lodging, surprising to some, they now take simply as a matter of course. But we children view such behaviour differently. To cross a field at night under the stars, to mount a ladder stairway, and undress and lay your head down on a pillow in a bed in a *railway carriage*, within sound of the sea— this to us is the very essence of true romance! Oh, how lucky they are, we think—these old ladies! How thrilling to be the Misses Clark-Ourry and live in a converted boatshed and a railway carriage!

*   *   *

Mummy and Pam are back home again in Bay View Terrace after being away together. It wasn't a holiday for them. The glands which had made Pam ill before, kept on getting worse and swelling up and hurting her, and eventually this meant that the bad bits were going to have to be cut out. That's why they went off to stay with our father's rich, old Cousin Edith in her big house with the enormous copper beech tree on the lawn. At least, our mother stayed there, and Pam did for a while, when she wasn't being operated on in a hospital.

Since her operation my sister seems to be different, somehow. She has a scar now on the right side of her neck; but that isn't the difference. Although they weren't away for very long, it seems to me she's changed, as if she's become suddenly more grown-up.

During our mother's absence with Pam the rest of the Hallsmith family, and Lucy, had to manage as best we could. Aunt Margaret came to stay. Aunt Margaret is our mother's oldest sister, older than Aunt Molly, or Aunt Nancy, or Aunt Christine. We love our Aunt Molly, who laughs and is fun, but we don't love Aunt Margaret. She's rather stout, and she walks and talks very slowly, and she has a bristly chin, and wears pince-nez. And she insisted on me and Jim saying our prayers in the morning as well as in the evening, which we never usually do. She's not unkind, but she is dreadfully dull, like the stories she told us at bedtime that went on and on and *on* about children being good. As soon as Mummy and Pam arrived home Aunt Margaret said goodbye, and for Jim and me—and for our father *and* for Lucy—it was a relief when she left.

Things are different, though, since my sister's operation, and it isn't just the new scar. Nor is it Pam's new tortoiseshell hairslide—the first time she's had a round one—which I regard with hopeless yearning envy: my hair, unlike hers, is floppy and dead straight with a fringe, a dark slippery red that doesn't require, to my disappointment, any slides of any sort at all. Pam's round hairslide is the same shape and about the same size as her scar. How curious! Both are new, but whereas one of them is pretty, the other is decidedly ugly.

But the real difference is this: my sister Pam won't, in future, be going to school. The glands that the surgeon chopped out of her neck were infected by tuberculosis, otherwise known as TB, a shocking disease, and therefore, instead of being cooped up at a school desk, she is to spend as much time as possible out-of-doors in the fresh air. For Pam, who passionately hated having to attend the Girls' County School, this is wonderful news indeed. We hear that, instead, she is to be given half-day lessons by somebody called Mrs Oliver, an ex-governess, and that *I* am to join in the scheme. The two of us, Pam and Elspeth, are to share these lessons. How much more important is this than tortoiseshell hairslides! A whole new era of education has dawned! Or so we joyfully imagine.

*   *   *

Mrs Oliver, our teacher, doesn't come up to us on the heights of Bay View Terrace; Pam and I, holding hands, descend to her, picking a path down through the allotments, a direct if muddy route that bypasses Trenance Hill and Bury Road, thus being safer as well as quicker. She lives by herself in a small house in a quiet side street, a short way on beyond the Great Western Railway Station. It is a genteel area, tucked in behind the terraced row of stucco-fronted hotels overlooking Tolcarne Beach.

Some years ago our governess, Mrs Oliver, retired from her former employment with a prosperous—or even, perhaps, it is delicately

88

hinted, aristocratic—family. She is a tall thin gaunt elderly childless widow, and she wears loose grey garments, V-necked blouses and cardigans, and a collection of long dangling chains with medallions attached. Her grey hair, fastened insecurely in a knob at the back of her neck, straggles wispily out of its confining net, and when hairpins patter down on to our exercise books or drawing paper she retrieves them absent-mindedly and pushes them back into her head without apology. We sit, passively waiting, and Mrs Oliver wanders about her parlour, munching away hungrily at a currant bun. She is forever munching a bun, and the currants and crumbs fly out of her mouth and drop, like her hairpins, on to the written or printed pages open on the table. When she stoops over us, as she constantly does, we cannot avoid glimpsing, with horror, the dreadful shrivelled breasts and bony sternum that her loose-fitting blouses fail to conceal.

What does she teach us, her pupils, eager as we are to learn? Not much! Mrs Oliver depends for our education on the support of a few, a very few, books. Her illustrated anthology of tales founded on the myths of Ancient Greece is, it's true, a source of delight. We pore over pictures of Pegasus, the flying horse; the sowing of dragon's teeth; the king on a cliff-top, watching out for the sails of his returning son. We read about Jason and the Golden Fleece, the Minotaur, the saving thread of Ariadne: gripping stuff, all of it, even when perused, for lack of anything else, over and over again.

Another volume, a good deal weightier, entitled *Letters to Hilary*, has for the frontispiece a photographed profile of its author, Lieutenant-Commander Stephen King-Hall, at which portrait Mrs Oliver gazes frequently with reverend adoration. Plainly she dotes on the handsome Commander, and his writing. We, on the contrary, find the daily readings from his *Letters* so excessively boring that our ears rebel and refuse to listen.

For some part of the hours we spend each morning in Mrs Oliver's dim little front room, cluttered with souvenir mementos of Florence, Italy, and sepia prints of the Roman Colosseum framed in black passe-partout, we are given sheets of paper, a ruler and compass, and a paintbox, and bidden to occupy ourselves, either by making geometric patterns or by drawing freehand whatever takes our fancy. Drawing and painting is what we do at home. We had been hoping for more from Mrs Oliver: for instruction.

On her upright piano we master with one finger the air of '*Au Claire de la Lune*', and learn to sing, fairly accurately, the words that go with it. This represents the sum total of our French tuition— and it is *not* enough: we want *more than this*.

Other subjects our governess deals with in a manner equally vague and haphazard. History lessons are extracted by her from a certain textbook bound limply in linen, thanks to the contents of which manual we acquire a magpie fund of singular, unforgettable information: for instance, that King Alfred, through culpable inattention, burnt the cakes; that poor King Harold had his eye shot out at the Battle of Hastings; that Queen Boadicea mowed down the Roman enemy by driving pell-mell in a chariot with swords sticking out of its wheels; that St. Augustine came to Britain from somewhere-or-other, laid his hands on the flaxen heads of little children and remarked, 'Not Angles but Angels', causing them all immediately to become Christians; that a talking spider said to Robert the Bruce, 'Try, try, try again,' and when he did, he won; that King Henry lost his clothes in the Wash, which was a kind of joke, and afterwards he turned his face to the wall and never uttered another word.

These, and similar fragments, reach us sporadically in a shower of crumbs and currants, and, although graphic, are so disconnected that the significance of them, their why and wherefore, remains obscure. We would like explanation. What we want, in fact, is to be taught. We know in our hearts, my sister and I, that we are wasting our precious time here with Mrs Oliver; that there is something basically wrong in accepting, week after week, such boredom. How can it have happened?

Did our parents not take the trouble to enquire into this old retired governess's competence in the educational field? Did they not try to find out what are her qualifications to teach two little girls (with a three-year gap in their ages) the rudiments of a school syllabus? Surely they cannot have done! Who was the false adviser who recommended Mrs Oliver to them? Or is it, perhaps, considered by our mother and father to be unimportant whether or not our minds, in addition to our bodies, receive nourishment at this early stage in life? Is nothing further expected of us than that we should, as daughters, (for sons, of course, are a different kettle of fish) grow up with only as much in the field of accomplishments as will ensure us each pulling off a marriage of social acceptibility?

Well, this is not all *we* expect for ourselves. The sort of nourishing we feel in need of can't be satisfied by a diet of healthy greens to ward off the scurvy. We are hungry, my sister and I, for something more.

We are hungry for more, but we don't know how to ask for it. Decisions are not discussed in our family. Opinions are not canvassed, and questions are discouraged. Compliance is the rule, and *please don't argue*! Argument is dangerous. It brings trouble; as also does complaint. Children take what they are lucky enough to have handed out to them—be it clothes, education, boiled cabbage, cod-liver oil, treats or punishments—without murmuring; and must always be grateful. Our discontent, therefore, at the limited nature of our tutoring goes unreported. We realise, my sister Pam and I, that it's up to us. We shall have, somehow, to supply our own intellectual sustenance, to plug the gaps, from whatever material may, by chance, be lying about.

Mrs Oliver isn't interested in arithmetic. She does occasionally set us sums of addition or subtraction, and corrects them offhandedly, without enthusiasm. But printed on the back of each of our exercise books, crowded together in a disorderly patchwork on the brown paper cover, are lists of weights and measures (outlandish, some of them: rods, poles and perches—what are *they*?) and at the bottom of the page, in a regular row like a border of neat cross-stitch embroidery, the multiplication tables up to and including twelve.

We don't attempt to master fathoms and furlongs, our daily measuring requirements being adequately served by a wooden ruler marked in inches. But the multiplication tables present a worthwhile challenge. My sister tackles it first, unaided, and only when she can chant the rows of figures triumphantly, right the way through to twelvetimestwelveareahundredandfortyfour without once tripping over her tongue, then and only then does she turn her attention, with patience and perseverence, to teaching me this arithmetical discipline.

I am a willing pupil. I love to memorise the easy tables—the twos and the fives, the tens and elevens; although the eights table remains an awkward sticking point. However, we conquer the difficulties, both of us, in the end; and the pride we take in this achievement is because it has had nothing to do with our governess, Mrs Oliver.

We've scaled the heights, and reached the top of the mountain range, and managed it quite by ourselves! Well, then! If we can learn the multiplication tables on our own, it stands to reason there must be, surely, other things we are capable of learning on our own. What other things? Appetite sharpened and confidence bolstered, we search around and hit on poetry. Although books are scarce in No. 9 Bay View Terrace, some have drifted in from unspecified sources. A copy of *Alice Through the Looking-Glass* gives us 'The Walrus and the Carpenter', and after we have succeeded in reciting aloud at each other the eighteen stanzas, word perfect, we come upon John Gilpin's comic misadventure, described in rollicking verses that we gobble up with the greatest facility. 'A train-band captain eke was he'—what on earth was a train-band captain?

What does *eke* mean? We neither know nor care. To commit to memory the farcical story in its galloping rythm is all that concerns us. This learning of poetry—doggerel, chiefly—becomes our secret pleasure, from which we derive a sense of secret power; and it has the magical property of banishing boredom.

The last of the poetic sagas we discover—the hardest for us to learn by heart, but the most exciting—is *The Pied Piper of Hamelin*. We are enraptured by this richly moral folk tale: '*Come in, said the Mayor, looking bigger/And in did come the strangest figure . . .*' Oh, the huge drama of it! '*Rats!/They fought the dogs and killed the cats . . .*' We shout the lines at each other on our way home from lessons, in our bedroom, outside on the beach, on the windy cliffs: never in Mrs Oliver's hearing. This is how we save ourselves from the stultifying dreariness of her inept ministrations.

Our other saving grace—the presence that underpins, overarches, encircles our lives, ever-present and omnipotent as God, but, unlike that inexplicable Being, a visible, audible companion—is the sea: the sea, both feared and loved, as God is supposed to be feared and loved; endlessly interesting in its unchanging changeability; always, inevitably, there.

One of the main benefits of our lack of conventional schooling is that each morning, throughout the greater part of the year, we escape from Mrs Oliver's dull little front room at 12.30 on the dot, career up her garden path, pausing only—in season—to pluck the green elves' caps from the budding eschscholtzia clumps at her gate, and race on: across *this* road, across *that* road, and so down

94

to the Great Western Beach, our playground.

Once arrived here it is our immediate duty to bag a certain corner formed by the wall and a concrete buttress that we consider belongs to the Hallsmith family. This is *our* exclusive patch of sand, as much ours by right of continuous occupation, we think, as the superannuated beach hut which our parents rent and use as a somewhat flimsy but permanent seaside home-from-home.

Lapping at our bare feet, the cool ocean invites us to wade in further, deeper, to submerge ourselves entirely in its delicious embrace. We resist the temptation. We have to: we are not allowed to bathe until the arrival of our mother. This is a rule we dare not break. So we stand, impatient, with our backs to the sea, gazing up at the cliff-top for a first glimpse of the familiar straw hat appearing over the wall, just where the road, far above, begins its downward spiral. Why doesn't she come? We are dying to bathe! We shut our eyes and count to ten, to fifty, to one hundred, peeking through our fingers. And suddenly we see the hat—her hat. She's here! We wave and wave: *Look at us, Mummy—look*! She waves in reply, and vanishes, coming into sight again a minute later round the bend in the hill, laden with baskets of food. We run to meet and escort her to our specially prepared corner, thankful that now, at last, with our mother's watchful eye upon us, we can bathe.

But not for long: a quick splash and we have to be out of the water. It's time to eat, and there can be no dawdling, on account of our brother Jim, who is hurrying to join us from his County School—the school to which, poor boy, he must return, wretchedly, as soon as he has swallowed his lunchtime picnic. When his head, high up, bobs over the wall we wave a welcome greeting; whereupon the head disappears. We meet him in silence at the slipway: silenced by pity. Wearing his clumsy lace-up black shoes and scratchy knee-length grey wool socks, he trails across to our corner and sits on the sand in his ill-fitting grey flannel shorts and school tie, with his cap beside him. He doesn't speak. He concentrates on eating. What is he thinking about? Does he wish he was in a bathing costume (which we call, whatever the gender of its wearer, a bathing *dress*), all but naked under the hot summer sun, and dripping wet, as we are? Possibly not. Jim doesn't share his sisters' passionate engagement with the sea. It is too cold for him. It makes him shiver, and turns him blue. The sea isn't his friend, as it is ours. He regards it apprehensively, afraid of what it may do to him: cause his teeth to chatter; drown him, perhaps, as it once drowned a grandfather.

Now and then, if the sea happens to be sufficiently far out in the middle of the day, we are joined for the picnic lunch by our father, too. The Midland Bank being at the harbour end of Newquay he is able on such occasions to take a short cut from the Towan Beach to the Great Western Beach along the sands.

At low tide these two beaches are, for a few hours, united, like two separate continents in pre-history, to become a single vast area, flat and newly washed, a space dotted over with deckchairs and speedily colonised by family parties playing cricket and rounders.

We see him, our father, small in the distance, a

solitary unmistakeable figure, walking briskly towards us. If he's swinging his stick it's the sign that he's in a good mood: we can relax. It means that this morning's customers have appreciated they were being dealt with by no ordinary common-or-garden clerk, but a gentleman in disguise, who is also an artist and a war-hero. Not all of the bank's clientele do appreciate this, but when they do, he swings his stick.

Swinging his stick, he walks across the shining acres of sand. Is this what he once dreamed of doing, not so many years ago, on the muddy bloody nightmare fields of France?—the celestial vision he had inside his head of peace and blue summer skies and the lulling sound of a far-off sea? Is this the dream come true? We shall never know. He doesn't say. He eats, like Jim, in silence; lies back for a minute or so, eyes closed, a figure no longer frightening but incongruous here on the beach in his behind-the-counter suit of clothes, his polished

leather shoes, his socks held up by garters.

It's time to leave or he will have over-stayed the allotted hour, thus giving Mr Oxley the advantage—he is convinced—of scoring a spiteful point. He stands up, faces about and sets off on the return journey, not now swinging his stick but grasping it like a weapon. For some part of the way I accompany him, running and skipping to keep abreast, and taking his hand to show I'm very sorry he's going to have to spend a horrid afternoon, a prisoner, shut up in a bank, instead of being free outside, like me.

*   *   *

The inexorable movement of the tides, alternately outgoing and incoming, dictates the daily summer routine of Jack the Beachman, who is tall and straight and young and sunburnt, and his team-mate, Stevens, equally sunburnt, but quite old, it seems to me, a small elderly man, bent over, wizened, and always in a hurry, hastening from one task to another. Stevens wears trousers rolled up to his knees, and smokes a pipe. Jack the Beachman doesn't smoke, never hurries, and his khaki shorts with a ragged hem reach *down* to his knees. They both go barefoot, and are both, like their horses, reliably good-humoured, appearing not to mind in the least how much we children, me and Pam, hang around or tag along after them, staring at everything they do.

We are careful never to be a nuisance, or to get too close to the horses. These patient docile animals are blinkered, to prevent them from being startled by anything unusual or sudden. Blinkers are squares of brass-studded leather that stick out like little shields at a forward angle on either side of the horse's nose. Their necks are encircled by massively heavy blackish leather collars, with brass rings attached. Working beach-horses don't have saddles or stirrups because—unlike Cousin Mildred's horse—they aren't supposed to be ridden: they're meant for the business of pulling. Queenie is Jack the Beachman's horse, and very big and strong, the same as him. The second horse, which belongs to Stevens, is smaller—so the two men and their two animals match each other, in pairs. When I'm tossed up on to Queenie's broad glossy brown back, except for slightly shuffling her hooves and whisking her tail, she remains passive. The ground, from this height, looks a long way below; but of course it's only sand, and soft, so I feel safe. I enjoy being flung aloft by a laughing Jack the Beachman, and then, after sitting perched up there for three or four minutes, being lifted down again: it's a treat.

Great Western Beach visitors are funny people. They have peculiar whims and inhibitions. To be spared the embarrassment of crossing a wide expanse of sand in a state of semi-nakedness, they will pay money to Jack the Beachman to be able to undress and dress themselves privately in a wooden box on wheels, drawn, for their convenience, to within a few yards of the frothy water's edge. Queenie's job is to drag the bathing huts from place to place in pursuit of the outgoing sea, chasing it to its furthest limit, like a line of soldiers obeying the orders of King Canute.

But as soon as the tide turns the situation is reversed and the flimsy matchbox army forced then to take flight, retreating little by little, each of the staging-posts on the way back being held for a short while and abandoned only at the very last moment, always just in the nick of time as another fierce counter-attack of swiftly advancing waves threatens to surround and swamp these puny man-made shelters that have dared to challenge the mighty power of the Atlantic Ocean.

In this game of catch-as-catch-can—a game played by Jack the Beachman and his horse, Queenie, repeatedly, tirelessly, against an unconquerable opponent—success or failure depends on him judging correctly where to position and when to retrieve the half-dozen or so huts for which he is responsible. Calculations are tricky. Winds have to be reckoned with: on- or off-shore. Tides vary with the calendar months: Spring or Neap. Jack the Beachman has never lost a bathing hut yet, but it can sometimes be a near thing, and give rise to much pleasureable drama for the lucky spectators. More than once my sister

Pam and I, as members of an enthralled audience, have heard cries of alarm issuing from a bathing hut in bumpy motion but still occupied, with Queenie straining and struggling to pull it safely clear of the ravenous waves and Jack the Beachman splashing alongside, encouraging simultaneously his faithful Queenie and his anxious invisible tenant.

Stevens is in charge of the deckchairs. Throughout the season these are stacked at the bottom of the hill where the sea wall, by completing its descent in a right angle just above the slipway, provides a protective corner for the chairs to be banked overnight beneath a securely lashed immense green tarpaulin. Mornings are always begun by Stevens and his horse, Bonny, setting forth at a clattering trot to distribute their wagon-load of deckchairs over an empty beach—a huge area if the tide happens to be out.

At every halt they make Stevens, as agile as a monkey, leap to the ground, and having snatched an armful of chairs from the pile aboard, unfolds these flattened constructions of wood and canvas and proceeds to arrange them, either two by two, or else in sociable clusters of three or four together. Then, the scene being laid for whoever may wish to take advantage of it, he springs up behind Bonny's tail, clicks his tongue, without dislodging the pipe between his teeth, and away they speed, to repeat the performance some few yards further on.

The deckchairs they leave scattered about so invitingly in their wake are seldom unclaimed for long. Visitors arriving on the beach, at first in a hesitant trickle, later in a steady stream, from

Newquay's many hotels and bed-and-breakfast establishments, are thankful to find such a choice of seating put out ready and waiting, and will gladly pay the price of tuppence a chair for a morning's occupation, and a further tuppence again if they should decide to renew the lease that afternoon.

Stevens and his horse-and-cart are continually on the go, for his life too is ruled by the tides and their unceasing fluctuations. After the chairs have been strategically planted, far and wide, he has immediately to start off on his rounds again: tickets must be dispensed and the money for them taken. When somebody offers him half-a-crown instead of the couple of pennies per chair required, he's obliged to rummage for change in the depths of a big shiny battered leather wallet that dangles at his hip. The shoulder strap from which this wallet hangs is criss-crossed on his chest with another strap, a thinner one, threaded through the pink paper roll of tickets.

And then, of course, finally, the chairs have to be chased after, collected and brought in like straying cattle at the end of the day—or, indeed, it may be well before the day ends if an incoming sea causes the visitors to pack up their traps in sudden alarm and hurry to gain the safety of dry sand above the high-tide-mark. There are times when Stevens has almost had to order people to relinquish their seats before it becomes too late for him to be able to salvage his deckchairs; (which are not really his chairs at all, but the property of Mr Poole, the absentee employer of Stevens and Jack the Beachman).

Sitting up on the front of the cart beside Stevens

when he does his deckchair rounds, as I am occasionally allowed to do, staring at the visitors, unrebuked, as we trit-trot hither and thither, from group to group, is a better treat even, I consider, than being tossed high on to Queenie's back by Jack the Beachman. Of all the various treats and entertainments to be enjoyed on the Great Western Beach, it is, in fact, my favourite.

If the sea touches its high-water-mark at a comparatively early hour in the afternoon, Stevens and Jack the Beachman can benefit by a shortened working day. The deckchairs having been all fetched in, stacked against the wall and sheeted over, and the bathing huts drawn close up under the cliffs, out of reach of the waves, they are at liberty to depart.

Barefooted, I stand in the road alone to watch Stevens and Jack the Beachman, my friends, going home. Stevens walks quickly, bent and bandy-legged, at Bonny's head, smoking his pipe, and with one hand holding the reins near to her velvety mouth, although she doesn't need to be guided. Jack the Beachman rides up the hill, sitting negligently sideways on good old Queenie's broad back. Men and horses: their working day is done. But where are they going, I wonder, now? Their home—where is it? And what will they do when they get there? I have no idea. They are simply disappearing out of my sight until tomorrow: gone! I feel a vague but painful sense of loss, as inexplicably sad as though they were carrying off a necessary piece of my happiness up the hill with them, and had left me here in the road, watching them go, bereft.

We take it for granted that Newquay residents are, *almost* without exception, a superior breed to Newquay visitors. The Hallsmiths can thus, being residents, regard the seasonal influx of holiday-makers on their beach—*our* beach—with aloof condescension and a certain degree of pity. They are truly pitiable, these poor transients, who hardly ever stay for more than a fortnight. Their ignorance is pathetic. They can't wait to tear off their clothes and lie in the full glare of the sun; whereupon their skin goes a bright pink, their noses peel and they suffer from blisters. They haven't the faintest notion of how to deal with a surfboard. We observe them trying and trying to grab a lift with every wave that passes: trying and failing, over and over. Their efforts are ludicrous. But it isn't their fault. You have to have an instinct that will tell you precisely when to launch yourself unhesitatingly forwards in order to be picked up and carried on by the smothering rush of water. A second too soon, or a second too late, and the wave will be lost to you. Pam has this instinct, and so do I; but we are residents.

Mr Poole's grown-up daughter, Jenny, is our local champion surfer. Any day, if the tide happens to be high and rough—even, it may be, terrifyingly rough—she will arrive on foot, always unaccompanied, a small young woman wearing her beach-robe, her board tucked under her arm. She speaks to no one, takes no notice of the onlookers who gather expectantly, but plunges directly in amongst the breakers, and swims out and out, pushing the board ahead of her, before facing shorewards and waiting for the roller she has chosen to bring her shooting back to land. No wonder she draws a crowd: her performance is spectacular. And although my sister and I have never exchanged a word of conversation with Jenny Poole, we revere her as a surfing star who sheds a glory, we proudly feel, on all of us Great Western Beach regulars. When she has surfed enough to please herself, she departs, as unobtrusively as she came.

Residents do not make a commotion. When bathing, we do not shriek and scream. According to our unstated code of honour, however icy the water or crashingly sudden a wave, we, the inhabitants of a seaside town, remain stoically mute. In this, as in other ways, we are conscious of being different from holiday-makers, who are not so restrained. Indeed, no! They shriek and scream unceasingly, piercingly, as though their lives depended on it—which sometimes, in fact, is the case: for their ignorance extends to tides and currents, and cliffs they ought to have the sense to realise are beyond their capability to scale. Every summer we are sure to witness the dramatic rescue of some idiotically reckless visitor, either stuck halfway up a precipice or else being swept, panic-striken, out to sea. And who rescues them? Again and again it is one or other of the Stafferi brothers, members of that swarming foreign family tribe, our unacknowledged Bay View Terrace back door neighbours.

We children are of the private opinion that young men who canter gaily about the beach, standing upright, as if they were Roman charioteers, beneath the jingling bells and pretty painted canopy of a trim little two-wheeler cart pulled by a pony smaller than Bonny but twice as sprightly—these handsome young men, who can climb and swim with the natural ease of born athletes and who make nothing at all of sprinting into the sea, fully-clothed, to save the life of a silly stranger—*we* think, in our secret admiration of them, it is most improbable such heroes would conceal their ice-cream merchandise under their beds at night. But this plainly subversive opinion we are careful to keep to ourselves, our parents having decreed that anything edible from a Stafferi source, whether in the form of wafer or cone, would be bound to have a contaminating effect upon our stomachs. It is forbidden for Hallsmith children to consume Stafferi ice-cream: no argument, please!

*   *   *

When Pam came home after the operation on her neck for TB glands, she was given a present by Lewarne Hosking: her own special surfboard. What made it special was the size. It's as wide as a normal surfboard, but shorter by several inches, and consequently that much lighter and easier to handle. Usually you can't tell surfboards apart—they are all exactly the same: two lengths of plank, squared off at the bottom and rounded at the top, put side by side and clamped together by two pieces of wood nailed across on the back. That's how a surfboard is constructed. And the proper way to surf is to lie on it as flat as you can, with your arms stretched out in front of you and your head on your arms. Visitors who haven't been

106

taught how to surf look ridiculous because they don't lie flat and don't stretch out their arms, and don't keep their heads down.

My sister painted her new surfboard yellow, the colour of a canary; and then she painted a lattice pattern of grass-green lines on the front, and on the back her name—PAM—in big green letters. She was allowed to buy the pots of shiny enamel paint with her own saved-up pocket money from Timothy White's, the ironmongery shop that's next to Daddy's Midland Bank, and to choose the colours herself. Nobody else in the world has a surfboard the same as hers: a *painted* surfboard, grass-green and canary yellow. She lets me borrow it sometimes, but not often. Generally I have to use one of our ordinary full-sized boards, which is rather heavy for me to carry—until I'm in the sea, when, of course, it floats.

We keep our surfboards, and the deckchairs that belong to us, as well as bathing towels and picnic mugs and plates and so on, stored inside the beach hut that we rent by the year from Mr Poole, Jenny Poole's father. To our eyes it represents more of a beach house than a beach hut, being quite unlike the uninteresting modern matchbox contraptions that Queenie and Jack the Beachman trundle to and fro, and rent out by the hour as a convenience for bathers. *Our* hut, and its few flanking companions, will never move again. These antiquated vehicles, now immobilised, are drawn up at the base of the Great Western Hill, close to the sea-wall, a permanent reminder of once fashionable seaside outings in days long ago vanished. Raised high off the ground by their iron-bound, immensely tall carriage wheels, and with flights of wooden steps and hand-rails leading up to their doors, they still retain, despite age and dilapidation, a ghostly air of elegance. And we Hallsmiths, who are lease-holders, feel that something of their distinctive—distinguishing— old-world dignity must rub off on us, thereby enhancing and giving credence to our status as residents. For we like it to be known that we are not merely birds of passage. We live here: the Great Western Beach is *our* beach.

It lies in the middle of three local beaches, a group enclosed by headlands jutting out to north and south, beyond which Porth, along the coast on one side, and Fistral Bay on the other, although not far off, are less immediately accessible.

I remember a time of innocence before we had learnt the nuances of what was what, and who went where, when our mother would take us, her children, down on to the Towan Beach, after first calling in for a brief mid-morning conversation with our father over his high shiny counter. The Towan Beach is at the commercial end of Newquay where the banks, and the shops, and the Victoria Cinema all congregate, and where the road, having wound its narrow way between a clutter of butchers and fishmongers, grocers and newsagents, and shoe shops and drapers, eventually veers to the right and divides, a branch of it dropping down, steep and cobbled and uneven, to the sands, while the main street, widening, pursues an upwards direction behind the harbour, towards the bleakly exposed war memorial and the grey Atlantic Hotel in the distance.

Why the Towan Beach should have had an apparent misspelling foisted on it, instead of being

given its correctly descriptive title of *Town* Beach, remains an unsolved puzzle. For this is what, by virtue of its location, it demonstrably is: a beach for the townspeople to spill out upon during their hours of leisure. Unaware, in those early Bungalow days, of any such prerogative operating to the advantage of Newquay's lower classes—an uneducated and, on the whole, roughish lot—we would come running down on to the Towan Beach, happily armed with buckets and spades, to dig sandcastles and splash about in the shallow paddling pool that is twice daily replenished by incoming tides.

Then, at some point, it must have dawned on our parents (who, in 1921, had newly arrived in Cornwall) that the Towan Beach was not territory suitable for Hallsmiths to frequent; an initial mistake repaired, once recognised, by a hasty withdrawal, and allegiance transferred to the adjoining Great Western Beach. Here they found an environment much more congenial and to their liking. The Great Western Beach, being so placed as to serve the residential quarter of Newquay, has an orientation, social as well as geographic, reassuringly in the middle.

But our removal from the awkward possibility of having to rub shoulders with Newquay's *hoi polloi* (and one must, it seems, admit that even the *nicest* tradespeople cannot be entirely disassociated from *hoi polloi* elements), has also meant our removal from the vicinity of the single outstandingly romantic feature of an otherwise vulgar Towan Beach. At some unrecorded time in history the projecting cliff on the opposite side of the beach to the harbour has had its tip cut off from the mainland by the sea's endlessly restless action. So there it stands today, a tall rock, the summit of which, covered in rampantly flourishing vegetation, is large enough, but only just, to accommodate the dwelling that crowns it. Everything about this miniscule island, and the house that has been built upon it, is fabulous, including its owner, Sir Oliver Lodge, an old gentleman with a long white beard, celebrated for his scientific investigations of the paranormal. Once a year, Sir Oliver descends on Newquay and shuts himself up in his uniquely secluded retreat, where he remains for the duration of his stay, more or less incommunicado. His residence is almost as invisible as himself, with its chimneys and red rooftops rising out of a thick surrounding screen of bushes and creepers. And, like an illustration for the wizard's castle in a fairy story, there is no access to this fantastic fortress of a house other than by a spindly suspension bridge which, in spanning the gulf between, connects it to the cliff heights above the Towan Beach; and which also, incidentally, ensures for Sir Oliver and his family a patrician aloofness from the swarming masses on the sands below.

The third of the trio of local beaches has a character completely different from either of the other two, being the exclusive preserve of those pleasure-seekers rich enough to book themselves into any one of the nearby better-class hotels. Tolcarne Beach, throughout the summer season, is hotel-land.

Whoever drives into Newquay for the first time, arriving by car and not by train, will observe on the outskirts, to the right, a bare wide undulating area of springy turf, bitten smooth by rabbits. This is Barrowfields, the burial site, presumably, of some long-forgotten ancient Cornish king, but—except by rabbits—the curiously shaped humps of grassed-over earth on the edge of the cliff have never been excavated.

No sooner is Barrowfields passed than the hotels begin, enticing new arrivals with their flagpoles and fluttering flags, their strings of fairy lights, the striped awnings and sunshades and the little tables placed outside in imitation of more exotic Mediterranean resorts. Immediately to the left is a big brash red-brick building, the Bristol Hotel, standing on its own, detached from the succeeding terrace of older prettier hotels, some of them with balconies, and all of them stucco-covered, painted in pastel shades the colours of Stafferi's ice-creams: vanilla, strawberry-pink and pistachio-green.

On the opposite side of the road to the terrace of hotels, hemmed in between a low wall and a

111

railing, is a place where pedestrians may safely perambulate: an enclosure, known as Narrowcliff, which combines the amenities of a public walkway and a viewing platform, and from the centre of which a perilously steep flight of steps descends in zigzags to the silvery sand of Tolcarne Beach.

Narrowcliff has benches disposed at intervals against its wall, and a shelter blocking off the far end. Benches and shelter could do with a lick of paint, and the macadam surface underfoot is badly in need of repair. Newquay's Council members are not, however, modernisers, and they seem to have decided that instead of smartening up their promenade they will leave it alone, untouched, to go on gently deteriorating, as it's been doing for years.

Sometimes after supper on summer evenings our parents will give themselves the treat of strolling together back and forth along Narrowcliff, mingling with the wealthy hotel guests who, wearing dinner jackets and expensive dresses, cross the road to lean on the rail and gaze out to sea, brandy glasses in hand, laughing and chatting in the loud voices of people unconcerned as to whether or not they are overheard by lesser mortals. Because our mother and father know that Narrowcliff belongs to the residents of Newquay, they feel quite at their ease in the presence of this exalted society. Sniffing the cigars of the men and admiring the jewellery of the women is as good an entertainment for our parents as a seat in the front stalls of a theatre—better, in fact: it's free! No tickets required!

To get to Tolcarne Beach from the Great Western Beach along the sands can be managed only rarely, and for brief periods. Whereas the Towan Beach and the Great Western Beach merge and become, regularly, a single vast expanse, Tolcarne Beach enjoys the priviledge of being a separate domain. The tide has to have gone very far out indeed for anyone who wants to intrude on its privacy to be able to splash round the corner, past the formidable barrier of soaring cliff and fallen rock. This may be the reason, or part of the reason, why our parents have never actually forbidden us to go there. They probably think it's impossible, or that we'd be afraid to try. It isn't impossible—not always; and as to being afraid, my sister's not afraid of anything.

Whenever Pam and I do decide to take the risk—the circumstances being propitious—we have to remember not to stay too long. For if, like Cinderella at the ball, we forget when we ought to leave, we are bound to find ourselves in serious trouble: the tide will have turned and the swiftly rising water have closed off our retreat. So it's risky—yes! But even a glimpse of this glamorous alien world, so tantalisingly close, is worth every beat of my anxious heart. Pam's heart isn't anxious. She is bold and fearless. And I, following my leader, trust myself blindly to her superior courage.

There is something excitingly decadent in the very sand of Tolcarne Beach. Owing to a veering away of the coastline here, the upper level is never reached by the sea, never washed clean and left wet, as, occasionally, are its neighbouring, more plebian beaches. Soft and dry and warm and silvery the sand remains, day after day, and week after week, piled up as fine as the face powder spilt on our mother's dressing table, and ideally suited to

113

its function of hosting a never-ending party. Every morning before breakfast the hotel staffs are dispatched down the steep zigzag cliff stairway to rake the sand over, to tidy it and pick up whatever rubbish may have been discarded during the previous evening's festivities; though even the rubbish is of a higher class than litter left on the Towan Beach: no orange peel or lollipop sticks or sweetie wrappers lower the tone of Tolcarne Beach.

On these clandestine excursions my sister and I are not accompanied by our brother Jim. He doesn't share our obsessive interest in the latest fashions any more than we are able to share in the daily worries and the nightly terrors that occupy his mind. Visiting Tolcarne Beach is a girls' adventure: infrequent and a secret. We say nothing of our trips to anyone: mum's the word! For who knows?—if we were indiscreet enough to blab about it, our parents might be jolted into uttering a veto; and that would be the end of that.

Perhaps the real reason why we've been spared an explicit Tolcarne Beach ban is because of our parents' failure to resolve their own view in regard to the giddy hotel crowd. They are disturbed, indecisive, our conformist mother and father, uncertain of just how they feel; or, rather, of just how they feel they ought to feel. Might this gay and careless throng present a threat to impressionable children? or might it not? Is the unconventional activity, speech and dress—or undress—of the Tolcarne Beach denizens indicative of loose morals, or a reflection of innocent open-air fun? Do they, or don't they, belong to a scandalously modern set—a set that is 'fast'? How can one be sure?

Our parents are in a perpetual muddle as to where to draw the line between what to label right and what to label wrong. For the line is variable. It won't stop still. It shifts and blurs. Even the terms they employ are confusing: 'fast' and 'loose', although sounding contradictory, seem to imply precisely the same forms of behaviour; both bad. To be 'fast' is the ultimate censure. In their bewilderment, however, they choose to exercise charity. Thus a girl who wears lipstick isn't necessarily 'fast', but it does suggest a deplorable leaning in that direction; and, of course— logically—the brighter the lipstick, the faster is the girl proved to be. As for peroxide blondes and plucked eyebrows, these aberrations are condemned out of hand. A young woman capable of dying her hair is capable, it goes without saying, of absolutely anything. And if she considers it an improvement to pencil on eyebrows where nature never intended her to have them—*well*! She is, quite simply, a hussy; and very likely worse. So where does this place film stars?—Jean Harlow, for instance? Hollywood film stars, our father declares flatly (he, an ardent film fan) are all hussies, and merely prove his point. Let them stay in Hollywood, or on the Victoria Cinema screen, where they belong: we don't want to have them walking about in the streets of Newquay, or on Newquay's beaches, thank you!

Then there is the vexatious matter of fingernails. A woman may, after trimming her nails, apply a thin coat of transparent flesh-coloured varnish; this is perfectly in order. It demonstrates, in fact, a proper pride in the care and appearance of her hands. But to grow her nails long, like talons, and then to paint them a lurid scarlet—no girl with long scarlet fingernails could be a nice girl, or other than extremely fast: advertising, as it were, her readiness to join on to any loose-living set available.

Divorce is a subject that must not be mentioned at all in polite conversation: divorcées are beyond the pale. We Hallsmiths would wish never to meet, or to have anything to do, socially, with a divorced person. On these, and similar issues, our parents do not waver. Their opinions are clear; and clarity, for them, spells relief. It is the equivocal, the ambiguous, the smaller cultural habits outside their limited range of experience, such as cocktails, that bother them: to condone or condemn—which? Cocktails have undeniably dissolute associations; and especially so if you yourself have never been offered a cocktail. But if there is no harm in a glass of sherry, say, or champagne at a wedding, how are you to differentiate?

Then again, take wealth, which, as everybody knows, is a two-edged sword. This being the case, it must mean, surely, that there are some people who, although rich and famous, do not pursue a rackety existence. They don't all—do they?—get divorced and gamble, and pluck their eyebrows, and smoke Russian cigarettes. They might—might they not?—have bucketfuls of wealth and still be charming and civilised, and appreciative of artists, and so on. One of them could be—would be, no doubt—a most desirable acquaintance, or friend, even, for a Hallsmith.

We listen to the coded and ambivalent arguments waged above our heads, talk not intended for our ears; listen to and judge the overheard judgements, detecting in our parents' disapprovals a wistfulness, an undercurrent of longing, a hankering after the glittering romance of the unattainable, exhibited in Tolcarne Beach's colourful carnival, its ostentatious display of the luxuries money can buy. They are drawn, our parents, as are we, to the siren song; but they are apprehensive also, drawn and repelled in equal measure, as we are not. My sister Pam and I suffer from no such doubts and hesitations. Of everything revealed to us on Tolcarne Beach we are wholly admiring, and our admiration is untainted by envy: for one day we too will wear dashing beach pyjamas and sun ourselves in scanty bathing costumes, and have neat little portable gramaphones playing dance music while we sip cocktails under the brims of shady hats. One day we will be grown up.

*   *   *

I am standing with my mother on the opposite side of the road to the line of jingles—pony-traps—that are waiting by the stone drinking-trough, ready to be hired by people who will arrive as passengers off the next train. Newquay isn't on the way to any other place: it's a terminus.

While Mummy goes on and on talking to Enid Hosking, I watch the entrance to the Great Western Railway Station, hoping to see the arrival of visitors, but no one appears. The station forecourt remains empty. It's the ponies' dinner-time, so their noses are buried inside their nose bags, and sparrows are hopping about on the ground at their feet, picking up whatever scraps and seeds have been dropped. I study the enormous picture on the hoarding behind the placidly chomping ponies and their half-asleep drivers. The picture is a very frightening one. I'd really rather not look at it, but I can't manage to keep my eyes fixed on the station entrance: they will insist on returning to this poster and staring at it, though I wish they wouldn't. It's an illustration of the film that's being shown at the Victoria Cinema. The film is called KING KONG, which is the name of the huge and terrifying gorilla snarling down at me. In one paw he's holding a tiny figure, a girl who's fainted—I would have fainted too, if I'd been her. Of course it isn't true, I know: there aren't really gorillas as big as that. But all the same, it's frightening.

Mummy is telling Enid about Pam, who isn't well: her neck is hurting again, and swollen. She may have to have another operation, Mummy says. Enid is telling Mummy that she has been staying in their bungalow at Porth for the last few days, opening it up and airing the bedrooms and preparing it for Lewarne, her brother, and also perhaps for some friends of his, who will be following her south, from Liverpool—which is where they live—next week.

Lewarne Hosking works for the family firm of solicitors, but what he enjoys more than being a solicitor is betting on horses and playing tennis and bathing, which worries Enid, and probably the rest of his family too. Actually Enid always looks worried. Her hair is short and very fair, golden, which sounds nice but isn't, because it's so dry and frizzy. Her skin burns red in the sun and her lips get sore and blistered. She doesn't wear lipstick, but probably she wouldn't anyway. Enid isn't *fast*: she's awkward and shy. We love Lewarne. He is our special friend. He likes children, which not all grown-ups do, and he gives us wonderful presents.

The Hoskings' bungalow at Porth is their holiday home, built high up, immediately above the road that traverses the head of the estuary. It's always exciting news to hear that Lewarne Hosking is on his way to Cornwall. What it means is that very soon we'll be invited—all of us—to tea at Porth, where we'll sit outside on the semi-circular steps of the bunglow, as if we were having a picnic. We aren't expected to be on our best behaviour, and it doesn't matter if we make crumbs or spill our drinks. Daddy will put on his white flannel trousers and his white shirt and white socks and white canvas shoes and a silk scarf, and be in a good temper.

The Hoskings' grass tennis court is squeezed in between the bungalow steps and the road below; and sometimes, when the grown-ups are playing tennis, a ball by mistake will be hit too high and go flying over the wire-netting enclosure and bouncing into the public road. Then they'll run down after it, laughing, as though at a great joke, out of the gate. And they may, if they're lucky, find their lost ball by the edge of the road. But if they don't, and it's gone for ever, Lewarne doesn't care a bit. He has plenty more expensive Slazenger tennis balls in cardboard boxes, new and fluffy, an endless supply of them, and he doesn't seem to mind in the least about the cost of the balls that they lose.

After tea, after the cucumber sandwiches, and

119

the cakes and the biscuits, Lewarne fetches a blanket and we three children sit on it, one behind the other, and he pulls us, bumpety-bump, down the steep grassy slope at the side of the bungalow, over and over again. You mightn't think it, but Lewarne Hosking and our Lucy Coles have something in common—a certain similarity: she's never cross, and nor is Lewarne. We love going to tea with him in Porth. And he likes having us to tea; we know that he does.

*   *   *

Because the Hoskings have a bungalow at Porth and come regularly every year to stay there, they aren't like ordinary visitors. They count as semi-residents. So do the Wilsons, who have a summer-holiday bungalow at the further end of Mount Wise. They are Australian. There are three sons in the Wilson family, no daughters: Jack, the eldest, fair and very tall, like his father, is almost grown up. It's on account of Jack Wilson that we always talk of Jack the Beachman, so as not to muddle up the two Jacks. Then there is Bob Wilson, but we hardly ever see him, and he's hardly ever mentioned. He lives in another place, in Bodmin Asylum. This is probably why Mrs Wilson, who is little and stoutish and speaks with a peculiar twang, as they all do, looks permanently anxious and miserable, thinking no doubt of Bob who isn't at home and isn't entirely right in the head. She's a nice person, Mrs Wilson, only sad. This may partly also be because her husband, Mr Wilson, drinks too much—or so it's rumoured; or even because Pat Wilson, the youngest boy—our age, more or less—is such a terrible daredevil, reckless enough in his ways to make any mother anxious, and always getting into trouble.

One afternoon Pat Wilson goes missing, and his brother Jack, and Damian Eastman—who is Jack's friend from school—search the Great Western Beach everywhere, asking everyone, until at last they spy him lying calmly spread-eagled on top of a red rubber ring, the blown-up inner tube of a lorry tyre, already some distance out to sea and being carried by the current round the corner towards Tolcarne Beach. In company with a gathering of excited spectators, we watch while Jack and Damian, who are both very good swimmers, rescue Pat and tow him safe to shore. We expect them to be angry with him, but they aren't angry, not a bit. Instead, they roar with laughter. Pat had no idea that he needed rescuing, they say. He was lying back in the rubber tyre as comfortably as though he was in an armchair, happily drifting. It's a story they tell again and again—and they laugh and laugh as they tell it.

Damian is my hero. He and Jack Wilson are best friends. They are always together, an inseparable pair. Damian's family has a big department store, a flourishing business, in Taunton, but every summer, all summer, he stays with the Wilsons in Newquay. He is very tall as well, but he doesn't have the Wilsons' crinkly fair hair. Damian is dark-haired; and beautiful. I worship him. Jack Wilson is a hero too; but not, I privately consider, as much of a hero as Damian. They are both very kind to me, and notice me, and let me play cricket with them when the tide's out, and sometimes—not often, but sometimes—Damian picks me up and I ride on his shoulders, and then I feel quite dizzy with pride and happiness.

*   *   *

I'm on the Great Western Beach one morning, wandering about by myself, absorbed in the endlessly fascinating occupation of staring at holiday-makers, when I'm stopped and spoken to by a funny sort of man. I hardly ever talk to the visitors I gaze at, and because they don't usually pay any attention to me, I have the impression I'm invisible, which means that I can stare as much as I want without being reprimanded.

This particular morning the beach is crowded; the tide, already halfway up it, is coming in. I'm surprised when the man, halting in front of me, starts to speak. At first I don't understand what it is he's trying to say. We're surrounded by so much noise: the sound of waves breaking, dogs barking, people yelling. He's a stranger, and he's wearing shabby clothes, like a tramp, and unpolished boots with the laces undone. Nobody wears boots on the beach. He takes my hand and says that if I go with him he'll show me something interesting.

I don't much want to go with him, but he has hold of my hand, and since by nature I am an obedient child, inclined always to do as I've been bidden, I go with him. I can't help wondering what he has found that he wants to show me: all kinds of things do get washed ashore. And although I'm a little—just a little—apprehensive, I'm not yet afraid.

So I allow him to lead me to this cave, with which, of course, I'm familiar. It's a very small cave, low and shallow—more of a sheltering arch than a cave. Situated under the overhanging cliff, and beyond a jutting spur of rock, it's effectively hidden from the main beach, and, owing to the rapidly advancing tide, will soon be inaccessible.

I have begun to feel afraid; and I try, without success, to pull my hand away from his controlling grasp. 'It's all right, my darling,' he says. But I've realised by now that it's not all right. I long and *long* to be somewhere else, anywhere else—*not here*; but I don't know how to escape. There's no one in sight. We're quite alone.

In order to avoid us banging our heads, we have to kneel on the sand and crawl inside the cave. I lie on my stomach and watch the sea swirling closer. He's crouching beside me, holding my leg and peering out. I'm very frightened indeed; but I think he's frightened as well. 'Don't move,' he says. 'Keep still.'

Just then, like the manifestation of a miracle, Jack Wilson splashes round the rocky point. At the same time, higher up the cliff's face, Damian appears, poised above a sheer drop and briefly silhouetted on the sky line before leaping down to join Jack on the ground.

I can't, afterwards, be certain whether or not the man does really suddenly shove me forwards, muttering in my ear, 'Get along with you—go on, push off.' Perhaps I imagined that he did. I can't be sure. But however it happens, the next moment I'm free, and stumbling out of the cold wet shadowy dripping cave into the sunshine. Damian scoops me up in his bare brown arms, laughing, and swings me aloft. I straddle his shoulders, clear of all danger. I've been saved. I'm safe—safe! Oh wonderful!—they came for me! But do my rescuers notice who is there still, behind me, crouched in the darkness of the cave? No—I don't believe they do. It was me they were searching for; and me they have found.

Later that morning, the tide being even further in, the beach even more crowded, I witness, together with dozens of holiday-makers jostling for a better view of such a dramatically incongruous spectacle, two blue-uniformed, helmeted policemen—also wearing boots; but theirs are tied and polished—marching a shabbily dressed man, their prisoner, between the deckchairs and the bathing huts towards the slipway and the road. Up the hill they go—and are gone, leaving public curiosity unsatisfied. What crime had the wretched creature committed, people ask among themselves, for him to have been arrested on the Great Western Beach this beautiful summer morning? We are left guessing: nobody knows.

As for my own involvement in the mystery, I shall never breathe a word of it to anyone; not to anyone; not even to my sister Pam. I don't want to have to think about that awful episode ever again. I mean to forget it as completely as though I were sponging ugly chalk scrawlings off a slate. I can and I shall forget it; and like that man and those policemen disappearing round the corner of the hill, it will be gone.

*　　　*　　　*

This week, as Pam isn't well, I've been let off doing lessons on my own with Mrs Oliver. Instead, while Mummy looks after Pam at home, I'm taken care of by Lucy Coles down here on the Great Western Beach, which is a lot nicer than boring old arithmetic. My sister is probably going to have to have a second operation: the previous one was obviously a failure. Mummy is making arrangements for the two of them to stay with Granny Laurie in Oxford, so that they can consult an important surgeon in Harley Street, London, called Mr Twistleton-Higgins, and ask him what ought to be done about Pam's bulgy painful TB glands.

It seems to me the Twins are very unfortunate in the matter of health, Pam with the swollen-up glands in her neck, and Jim with his double-hernia, for which handicap he has to wear the horrid-looking contraption called a truss. Jim, besides being delicate, is also considerably shorter than Pam. You'd expect them, since they are twins, to be the same height; but they're not.

Our mother has told us that Pam was born first, and is therefore, officially, the elder of the pair, although only by a quarter of an hour. Jim resents being frequently reminded that his sister Pam is the older twin. Because she's inches taller than him, he does appear to be, not merely fifteen minutes younger, but younger by *years*. He has a fragile little body, and an over-large head, and flat feet, which he turns out as he walks, and a stammer. The boys in his class at the County School, in order to tease and annoy him, chant aloud a rhyme they have either come upon or else invented that is meant to refer to and be a description of Jim: *Old Tom Toddy, All head and no body*. Who Tom Toddy is, or was, I haven't any idea, but the name has stuck, and now all the boys at school call him Toddy. He hates the name. It upsets him; so of course they're bound to shout it at him even more. I love my brother Jim and I would like to make him happy, but I can't. He's always unhappy.

He taught me how to throw a ball properly, which most girls aren't able to do. Boys have a special knack of throwing from the shoulder instead of, as girls do, from the elbow. My brother Jim showed me the way it's done, and I practised and practised until now I can throw a ball as far and as high, nearly, as he can. I'm good at running, too. I can run very fast.

Our bathing hut and the rest of the pensioned-off old-fashioned bathing huts are drawn up in a row a few yards above the slipway, close to the sea wall and to each other. Their huge red-painted wheels have iron rims and enormously big spokes, ideal for climbing about on. I pretend I'm an acrobat in a circus. By stretching my legs wide apart I can balance on the wheel hubs of two neighbouring huts, and bridge the gap. Or, if I brace myself with a hand on top of two opposite wheels, I can swing my whole body, like a pendulum, to and fro between. But that's a rather hard exercise. I can only manage to swing backwards and forwards about three or four times at the most before I have to let go. While I'm playing on the wheels I compose a list in my head and count over and over the things I can do— things I'm good at doing. This is the list: I can surf; I can run very fast; I can throw a tennis ball almost as far and as high as my brother does—and I can catch it too, almost always; I can turn a somersault; but better than anything else, I can swim.

126

I learnt to swim when we went for a Sunday picnic to Trearnon Bay. We discovered a pool that the tide had left behind, with rocks on either side, and fairly deep. And I swam—I really did. I swam from one end of the pool to the other, ten strokes, dog-paddle, without once touching my feet on the bottom; which means that now I'm a swimmer. Pam said: 'I told you it was easy.' And she's right: it is. You just have to remember to keep your fingers closed and your chin up. I had wanted to learn to swim before my birthday, the 21st of August and I have done. I can float as well. Floating, I find, is even easier than swimming: you don't have to do anything at all—simply lie on your back and spread your arms out, and look up at the sky. So that's two more things to add on to the list—if it's fair to count them separately: swimming *and* floating.

I confide in Lucy the things on my list, and then I show her how fast I can run, how far I can jump. She sits in a deckchair and watches me placidly while I demonstrate my prowess: turning somersaults, throwing a ball high in the air and catching it. 'Well done!' says Lucy, nodding approval. She is wearing her best powder-blue cotton-crêpe dress, which I greatly admire, and her hat that's like a brown plush pudding-basin, and she is perfectly content to do nothing at all herself, but simply sit and smile and watch me, with her hands folded in her lap. It could be practice for how to float, except that Lucy isn't a bather. She has never ventured into the cold Atlantic Ocean: never has and never will. Even the suggestion of it makes her shudder. The weather needs to be very hot indeed before Lucy will risk removing her shoes and stockings and paddling her feet in the water. She isn't a beach person, not by upbringing. The Coleses are traditional farm-workers: country folk. Lucy has, to some extent, urbanised herself by becoming employed in our household. But she continues to approach the sea warily, regarding it as an alien element, uncontrollable and untrustworthy.

It is, in actual fact, extraordinary for Lucy Coles to be down here, day after day, on the Great Western Beach; *and* extraordinary for her to be doing absolutely nothing, instead of busy in the kitchen at home; *and*, moreover, to be wearing her best blue summer dress, instead of a voluminous white apron—extraordinary, but nice. I'm very pleased that she is here with me, sitting serenely in a deckchair. We don't exchange much conversation, but I like just having her there. She's restful company. I'm never scolded by her. It was Lucy who gave me my painted plaster goose-girl and the flock of four plaster geese as a present on my third birthday. She'd had them, Lucy said, ever since the time she was my age. They're my favourite possessions.

One of these mornings, while I'm trying to improve on how far I can throw a tennis ball, I make a friend. He's by himself, a boy, sitting perched on a certain smallish rock that each outgoing tide uncovers. Isolated as it is in the middle of acres of flat yellow sand, this rock, from a distance, might be mistaken for a piece of driftwood, or a stranded porpoise, draped in seaweed. We Hallsmith children habitually use it as a sort of marker to aim at and sprint around when we're running races. Today I'm using it as a target for my throwing practice, trying to hit it from

128

further and further off. I'm not aiming at the boy; but he's watching, and he sees where my tennis ball lands, and he picks it up and throws it back to me. He's a very good thrower—as good, or better, perhaps, than my brother Jim. I throw the ball again, in the same direction, and he returns it again. And that's how we get to know each other, and make friends. His name is Terry.

He is the first real true special friend of my own I've ever had. I feel as though Terry is the other half of myself; the companion that's usually secretly inside my head. We spend the whole of the day together, mostly talking. He tells me about his life and I tell him about my life. He wears a plum-coloured jersey with holes in the sleeves, and a pair of grey flannel shorts that don't fit him, and he's dark-haired, like Damian—although not, like Damian, tall: he's my size. Terry, I learn, is a bit older than me, but only a little bit. When we talk it's as though we're the same age.

He arrived in Newquay yesterday, by train, travelling alone with a label round his neck as if he were a parcel. Terry doesn't have a father or a mother; not any more. He is an orphan. He was dispatched here from Paddington, London, to fill a vacancy occurring amongst the inmates of Dr Barnardo's Home for Boys. This Home, situated on a corner immediately next to the Great Western Railway Station, has always aroused the interest of us children. Whenever we're on our way down to the beach, we go past it; or at least, we pass the entrance to its gravel drive, with the big notice-board at the gate. The house itself is completely hidden by laurel bushes. Terry is the only Barnardo Boy I've ever met, or spoken to.

He's a much better acrobat than me. He can not only stand upside-down on his hands, he can walk about on them: Fancy that! I try and try to copy him. Impossible! Each time I try, I collapse in a heap on the sand. But when Terry says that he can't swim, I tell him swimming's easy: I'll teach him how to swim. I take him up the slipway to our hut, and I lend him my brother Jim's bathing costume and a towel.

'This is Terry,' I say to Lucy, who is sitting, as usual, in a deckchair on the beach, reading *The Ladies' Home Journal*. She calls it her book, but it isn't a book; it's a magazine.

She comes with us to the edge of the sea to make sure we don't get out of our depth while we're bathing. It's too rough for Terry to learn how to swim, but we splash about in the shallow waves until my brother arrives from school and it's time for our picnic lunch. Jim says he doesn't mind me lending Terry his bathing costume. I give Terry half my Cornish pasty and half my Fyffes banana and all of my hard-boiled egg because an egg's not easy to divide, and anyway I don't want it. After lunch Jim has to go back to school, and Terry and I talk and talk, and play ball, and chase each other, and I show him how you can write on bare skin by wetting your finger in a bucket of water and tracing the letters, and then sprinkling dry soft silvery sand over them so that it sticks to the wet places and nowhere else. Terry writes his name on my leg, and I write my name on his. Lucy reads her magazine. And the afternoon passes happily, happily.

It's a surprise to hear my mother calling to me from outside our bathing hut. Pam's temperature has dropped and she's feeling better, so here they both are, bringing a basket full of scones and buns and ginger biscuits and jam sandwiches for our tea. I am so delighted to see Mummy and my sister Pam. I run up the slipway to welcome them, hopping and skipping with pleasure at their unexpected appearance.

'Who is that boy you were talking to, down on the beach?' my mother asks me.

I tell her. And that's when the terrible row explodes like a thunder-clap. Mummy doesn't ever get in a rage, as our father all too often does, but she can be extremely upset and annoyed and cross, and she is very, very cross with me now. I have done something dreadful, something I never should have done; something I should have had more sense than to do. The row spills over, enveloping Lucy, who was meant to be looking after me, for goodness sake, instead of burying her nose in a trashy magazine and paying no attention to what sort of mischief her charge was getting up to.

I hadn't been getting up to any mischief, or up to anything else. I'd made a friend; that was all. My vision blurs and my ears buzz with the despair of not understanding what it is that I've done wrong. Yes—I did invite him, Terry, into our beach hut, and yes, I was inside the hut with him when he took off his jersey and shorts and put on Jim's bathing costume—I'd said he could borrow it; and Jim said that he didn't *mind* me lending it to Terry. Why was it so very bad?

I don't say goodbye to Terry. I don't actually observe his departure. My mother herself conducts him back to Dr Barnardo's Home for Boys, from which he has absented himself without leave.

131

'Why was Mummy so cross with me?' I say to Pam, snivelling.

'Well, you shouldn't have, should you?' she replies, unhelpfully; and she shrugs her shoulders. 'We don't know that boy, after all—do we?'

'*I* do—now. We made friends with each other, him and me. And in any case, it wasn't Lucy's fault. She's not a beach person. She thought he was someone we did know, already—someone the family knew.'

'You ought to have told her, then,' my sister says, severely, withholding comfort.

The likelihood of a worse row with my father tonight when he hears of my naughtiness fills me with acutest anxiety. I may even—horror of horrors!—have earned myself a thrashing with the bathroom strap, the terrifying punishment that is doled out on occasion to either one of the Twins for misbehaviour; and I shall still not have understood the reason why—what it will have been for.

However, to my infinite relief, I am spared my father's wrath. There is no thrashing, no punishment of any description, not a single angry word uttered: I have been reprieved.

Presumably the reprieve is due to my kind-hearted mother deciding, upon reflection, and out of pity for my distress, to keep her mouth shut, and, instead of reporting my transgression, to draw a discreet veil of silence over the whole regrettable affair.

I haven't seen Terry since, and probably, as the Barnardo Boys are never brought down on to the Hallsmith family's Great Western Beach, we shall never meet again. Perhaps he's been returned, with a label round his neck, to Paddington, London. Anyway, this was the first, and will be, I suppose, the last encounter we have, Terry and me—the beginning and the ending of a friendship that didn't last for very long: one day. But I'll remember it, always.

*   *   *

Jim's Newquay friends—though none of them can be described as really close friends—are Peter Mitchell, our doctor's son; Luke Gadstone, the son of another doctor; Bradford Johns, whose mother is a widow; Neville Rhys, who has several much older sisters; and Oliver Jenkins, whose well-off parents live in a big sombre house enclosed by a romantic wilderness of woods and shrubberies overlooking the mouth of the River Gannel.

Luke and Peter and Bradford all go to the same local County School as my brother Jim. Neville Rhys is sent away each term to a boarding-school. And as for Oliver Jenkins, he doesn't go to school at all: he has a tutor—or a sucession of tutors— who endeavour to educate him at home. This is because, it would seem, his doting parents believe, mistakenly, that by keeping their adored but headstrong only child under their own roof they can keep him safe and out of harm's reach.

Oliver is very good-humoured and friendly. He has red cheeks and black eyes and curly, black hair, and an impudently turned-up nose. Being entirely fearless, the rules that are intended to prevent him endangering life and limb he invariably disobeys. His exploits are legendary. He likes to climb to the top of the highest trees on the Jenkins' estate, and

133

to row across the Gannel in their dingy, which is strictly forbidden, whenever it is particularly hazardous to do so. He is determined, each and every day, to assert his independence from tiresome apron strings, and to indulge his whims, whatever they are, regardless of the consequences.

Now and again an invitation is issued to a boy, or a group of boys, to have tea with Oliver. When such a summons is received by Jim, he starts off up Mount Wise towards Pentire Head in a state of mingled excitement and trepidation. There can be no one more ill-suited to fulfil the rôle of chosen companion to a notorious tearaway than my brother Jim, who is neither robust nor athletic, and who, besides having a puny little body, is of a nervous disposition, neurotically respectful of rules and in mortal dread of the treacherous tides and currents of the Gannel. Hating heights, as well as being wholly inept at climbing trees, he is the very opposite of a daredevil. And yet, in spite of his fears, my timid brother, dazzled by the boldness and the carelessly anarchic behaviour of Oliver Jenkins, is drawn to it as a moth is drawn to a flame.

It is also a curious fact that while Jim, and other boys, go to tea with Oliver, he has never been to tea with us; nor have I ever seen him in the streets or shops of Newquay, or down on the beach, or in anyone else's house.

Mr and Mrs Jenkins rarely entertain friends of their own, but not for lack of staff or money: they have plenty of both. Simply, they don't care to socialise. They are not members of any recreational club: they don't play bridge or golf or tennis. Their lives appear to be centred, with a faint air of benign bewilderment, on their son, Oliver. The impression gained by visitors, those who do infiltrate the high red-brick boundary walls of the Jenkins' establishment, is of a zone set oddly apart from the ordinary world outside. And perhaps it's this unusual air, not of hostility, but rather of withdrawal, vaguely mysterious, that causes an invitation to Pentire House to be so appealing.

Girls never are invited. But my sister Pam and I have two or three times accompanied our mother and father when they were fetching Jim away at the end of an afternoon, and on these occasions they are politely asked into the drawing room to take a glass of sherry before leaving. We girl-children are obliged to stay with the grown-ups, and, while they are chatting, to sit still and quiet in our seats, nibbling at biscuits like well-behaved mice. Tantalising whoops of joy float in through the windows from the gardens beyond. Only *boys* have permission to rampage unsupervised about the grounds of Pentire House, engaged in the thrilling noisy rollicking games invented by Oliver. How I envy them!

*   *   *

Pam and I don't have school-friends because—as is the case with Oliver Jenkins—we don't go to school. Consequently, during term-time, we are very short of friends. We have practically none, in fact; which is why we have to depend on each other for amusement, and why, when Pam's ill, or away, I have to depend on myself. Pam has told me that the Girls' County School is horrid, and I know that for the brief time she was there, before her first operation, she was miserable.

There is another school for girls in Newquay. It's called St Kilda's, and the girls live at the school: they are boarders; but day-pupils would be accepted. The girls wear a brown uniform. Brown is a colour I usually detest. I hate having to wear brown dresses and jerseys on purpose to match my eyes. I hate having brown eyes. Pam and Jim and Mummy have blue eyes. But because I so long to be a pupil at St Kilda's I can manage to find even the colour of the uniform attractive.

Mummy says we can't go to this brown-uniform school on account of Pam's health, but I think Pam's health is just an excuse. Except when my sister's glands hurt her and swell up, which they do off and on, she's very big and healthy. I think the real reason for us not being sent to St Kilda's is because it would cost a lot of money, and we are poor, although we have to pretend that we aren't. Mrs Oliver is probably cheap, which is probably why lessons with her are so boring. Of course, doctors cost money: being ill is expensive, and the operations my brother and sister keep on having to have must be very expensive indeed. If we're so poor—and we certainly are poor—who pays for their operations? I don't know. It's one of the mysteries of our life.

As a sort of compromise Pam and I attend the dancing class that St Kilda's arranges to hold once a week in the ballroom of the Victoria Hotel. We half enjoy this, and we half don't enjoy it. We always enjoy the shining empty golden slippery space of the ballroom floor, but we don't enjoy feeling, as the only non-St Kilda's-pupils, different from the other girls, none of whom we know. We half enjoy and we half don't enjoy the new woolly dresses that Mummy has bought especially for us to wear at the dancing classes. It's exciting to have new clothes, and to have them not made by Mummy but tried on and bought in a shop as grand as Madame Hawke's. We like the fierce colour of the material: emerald green, with multi-coloured flecks all over it; and the buttons of steel in the shape of blunted Egyptian pyramids—*novelty buttons*, the shop assistant called them. The woolly stuff, though, is nastily scratchy against our skin, and when we are dancing we get too hot in these dresses. The St Kilda's girls dance in their vests and bloomers; and this is another difference between them and us.

*   *   *

Every summer brings the return of temporary friends: children, that is to say, of our parents' friends or acquaintances, who come to Newquay each year, and stay for a while, and then leave. We are expected to be friends ourselves with all of them, whether we like them or not. Sometimes we do like them, and sometimes we don't.

The Brendons are a Scottish family, now living in Plymouth. Since Mr Brendon's business affairs don't allow him to take time off for a holiday, he sends his disconsolate wife and the two youngest of their five sons to be benefitted by bracing North Cornish sea air without him. Mrs Brendon rents the beach hut next to ours, and she sits outside it, pressing her lips together and sighing as if she were suffering an unspeakable martyrdom. Her two youngest boys are twins, and as well as being the same age as our Twins, it so happens that the name of one of them is Jim. The bond of sympathy which this treble coincidence creates for our mother and Mrs Brendon is not a bond that we three are able to share. We wish we didn't have to play with the Brendon twins, Jim and Jeff. As playmates we find them insipid and uninspiring.

We feel quite differently about Rex Dyer and his sister, Eve. They turn up usually in July to stay with their grandmother. Mrs Mulroney lives in a tall gloomy-looking house, part of a gloomy-looking terrace that is said to be inhabited by wealthy residents who choose to keep themselves to themselves. The main road, on entering Newquay, passes immediately behind and above Tolcarne Beach first, and then the Great Western Beach, and this terrace of houses, having been built on the seaward side of the roadway, acts as a solid screen, blocking off the headland that separates the two adjacent beaches.

Mrs Mulroney's house, observed from the front, is unappealing, situated in close proximity to the pavement, and guarded by a pitch-black shiny spiked railing. A flight of steps leads up to a door that you might suppose, wrongly, was never opened. Because of its forbidding front aspect, what's at the back of the house has, by contrast, the unfailing effect of a delightful surprise. A long open stretch of grass, unadorned except for a raggedy tamarisk tree and a few weather tossed hydrangea bushes, reaches almost to the dangerous edge of the high perpendicular cliff. We are warned that the fence at the end of the lawn is flimsy, and we must take care, therefore, to keep well clear of it: a warning that is enough to add a pleasurable extra breath of adventure to having tea with Mrs Mulroney when her grandchildren are visiting.

We like Rex and Eve Dyer. Rex has a habit of chuckling at practically everything. He's round and fat, an india-rubber ball of a boy, while his sister, Eve, is little and thin: the exact opposite of her brother. But in character they are the same, both easy-tempered, unquarrelsome and ready to agree to any plans we suggest. So we are pleased when Rex and Eve Dyer turn up on the beach, and we miss them when they've gone.

The Dyer children are always fetched and escorted down here to Cornwall by their aunt, Audrey Mulroney, because their parents work abroad somewhere. We like Audrey very much, and so does our mother. Whenever Audrey's on the beach with us Mummy seems to change and become actually younger and happier, rejuvenated, as if she can remember how it was once to be a girl—which is a long time ago, naturally. Mummy's really quite old—older than Audrey—although not nearly as old as Mrs Mulroney, Rex's and Eve's granny.

Mrs Mulroney is an unsmiling old lady. She dresses in black, and she sits as stiff and as straight as the shiny black railings in front of her house. Her belief that manners are of paramount importance increases Mrs Mulroney's alarming air of severity. *We* think she's alarming, but neither Rex nor Eve is in the least bit afraid of their grandmother; and as for their aunt, Audrey—Mrs Mulroney's younger daughter—she doesn't give a fig for rules of behaviour. Audrey never wears a hat or gloves or bothers about her appearance—not at all! She's always laughing and joking, and her fair hair gets into a hopeless tangle, flying loose in the wind. Even Daddy, who doesn't like many people, likes Audrey. He approves of her. She teases him, but in such a way as not to make him cross, and she doesn't wear lipstick, or paint her nails, so she can't be considered *fast*. We wish all grown-ups were as much fun as Audrey Mulroney.

Some, of course, the best of them, are: the Wichelows, for instance—a family of brothers and sisters, young grown-ups, who also rent a hut in our row from Mr Poole during their time in Newquay, when they prefer the Great Western Beach—*our* beach—to the neighbouring Towan or Tolcarne beaches. The Wichelows are expert surfers. They play cricket and rounders and leapfrog, and they build immense amazing sand castles with us children, digging moats and throwing up fortifications to challenge the stormy waves, pretending the incoming tide is a furious enemy that has to be defeated. Oh yes!—life is very cheerful when the Wichelows are on holiday here.

And then there is the summer-visiting Brown family, consisting of mother and father, and their two children, Felicity and Guy, who are more or less the same age as us. Mr Brown is tall and handsome. He wears horn-rimmed spectacles, and sometimes he and our father play tennis at the Club; although not often. For, when they do, inevitably tall Mr Brown, who plays tennis exceedingly well, finishes up the victor. And the shaming fact is, our father *minds* losing a game of tennis—or any game of anything—very much indeed. He *has* to win, or he gets upset. A singles tennis match with Mr Brown is thus a predictable disaster for Daddy. Such a disaster can only be avoided by them arranging to play doubles, not singles, roping in, say, Douglas Adey and Bo'sun Hooper, or Harry North, for a foursome. Defeat with a partner is bearable. Moreover, when Mr Brown partners him, Daddy will very likely find himself on the winning side.

Mrs Brown has a dumpy roundabout figure and a temperament of overflowing kindliness. Her son, Guy, an exceptionally good-looking boy with a thin face, a pointed chin and a dense crop of curly hair, has inherited his mother's calm serenity and her sweetness of character; qualities notably lacking in the personality of his sister, Felicity, the fourth member of this family, who could be—would be—a very pretty girl if she were not so disagreeable.

On several successive Sunday excursions we Hallsmiths have taken the Browns to Porth and Holywell Bay in order to show them our own favourite picnicking spots along the coast; or, to be precise, they've taken us. We only have to guide them, sitting up as passengers in their big luxurious Daimler car. Felicity demonstrates her unwillingness to come on these picnics by refusing to join in any of our activities, and remaining as cross as two sticks throughout.

I have overheard Mummy discussing Felicity's tiresome behaviour with our father. It was really such a pity, Mummy said, such a *mistake* for the poor child's every whim to be indulged. Look at the result! To which Daddy retorted that a few strokes of the strap administered to Felicity's backside would soon have her toeing the line.

What the spoilt little brat deserved, said he, was a thorough whipping. 'Oh no, Guth—no!' my mother murmured, protesting at the harshness of the treatment he recommended. Mummy doesn't hold with beating as a corrective; but husbands, of course, know better about these matters. For me, his words conjured up a sickening vision of the dreaded leather razor-strop hanging from a hook on our bathroom door.

The fact is, Felicity despises Newquay, and everything connected with Newquay, including us children. She wishes her parents could be persuaded to spend their holidays in some more fashionable seaside resort, such as Torquay or Brighton; or better still, abroad on the French Riviera, famous for being a playground of the rich and sophisticated.

Doubtless, if Mr and Mrs Brown had wanted to have a Mediterranean holiday, they could have afforded it. But Felicity's parents, and her brother Guy as well, have simpler tastes. Instead of bragging, or showing-off about how much money they've got—although they must have plenty—they're perfectly satisfied to imitate us, renting one of Mr Poole's old-fashioned huts and eating jam sandwiches and Cornish pasties on the Great Western Beach. Nor are they drawn, any more than are the Wichelows, to the far smarter Tolcarne Beach on the other side of the headland—so temptingly close, and considered by Pam and myself to be an earthly paradise of jazzy glamour.

They do, however, on these joint outings of ours, produce an impressively expensive wicker picnic basket, such as we have never owned, or

142

even seen before, furnished with a truly awesome range of knives and forks and plates and thermos flasks and cut-glass tumblers, and goodness knows what else besides.

But the most thrilling thing about our families' friendship as far as *I* am concerned is the cardboard box which arrives by post when summer's over and the Browns have driven off, departing from Newquay in their splendid envy-arousing Daimler. Mummy lifts the lid of the box, and there, packed in layers of rustling white tissue paper, is a selection of the dresses grown out of by sulky Felicity Brown, but just exactly the size I am—clothes that are so exquisitely beautiful I can hardly believe my eyes, or believe they have been actually given to me.

*   *   *

I ponder the peculiarity of names. Brown is such a horrid colour, yet it can be the name of nice people; of a horrid person, too, of course. I remember the fat old Mrs Brown of long ago who stood me up in a hand-basin, naked, and washed me all over roughly in icy-cold water. And Felicity Brown, who has such beautiful clothes—she isn't very nice. It seems funny to me that anyone can have the word for a colour as a name. Our dentist is called Mrs Black. One of her legs being shorter than the other, she hobbles about on an ugly built-up boot; as does my godmother, our pretence aunt, Miss Isobel Clark-Ourry, who is similarly afflicted. The only part of Mrs Black that's black is her boot. She always wears a white overall, so really a better name for her would be Mrs White. Daddy has a

143

Midland Bank customer called Mr White. I wonder if there could be someone called Mr Orange or Mr Yellow.

'Have you ever heard of someone whose name is Mr Yellow?' I ask my sister.

'Don't be silly,' says Pam, not bothering to look up from her drawing book. Drawing is what Pam likes to do all the time.

I don't think I'm being silly. If a person can be called Mr Brown, why can't another person be called Mr Yellow?

Then there is the Midland Bank customer who gives us chocolate eggs at Easter. He's an elderly bachelor called Mr Woodin, which sounds as if he were made of wood. Because he's tall and very stiff indeed, I did once believe—when I was much younger—that he might actually be, as his name implies, wooden. But Pam has explained to me that his name isn't spelt with *EN* but *IN* at the end of it, which makes all the difference to the meaning. It just shows the importance of knowing how to spell properly. Pam taught me to read, and she taught me my multiplication tables; and she teaches me spelling, and sums as well. But she isn't right about everything.

Names are interesting, I do think. Our governess is called Mrs Oliver, although Oliver is really the name for a boy: Oliver Jenkins, for instance. Or it can be the name of a man: Sir Oliver Lodge with the long white beard, who has the house built on top of the Towan Beach island. Names are funny. They can belong to quite different things and to quite different people, and be rather muddling, sometimes.

When summer gives way to autumn, Newquay loses, almost overnight, its visitors, that invasive horde of outsiders. The hotels empty. The beaches again become shiningly bare, their acres of sand, each day newly washed, lying flat and smooth and—except for flocks of seagulls—deserted.

A sure sign of the summer season having been irreversibly concluded is when Jack the Beachman and his mate, Stevens, hitch their horses to the now unwanted bathing huts, and trundle them off to winter quarters, wherever that may be: an operation taking them several days to complete. I stand in the roadway, rooted to the spot, munching a pasty, or a bun, or a slice of bread and jam, silent and watchful. I have to watch; I have to see everything they do, every detail of this final farewell to summer.

They don't hurry themselves, Jack the Beachman and Stevens. Walking alongside Queenie and Bonny, they pat and stroke the good animals' necks, and click their tongues and chirrup encouragingly. And the two horses, with slipping hooves and jingling brasses, respond as best they can, straining up the steep hill again and again, until all the huts have disappeared.

Only the little boxy modern huts are hauled away. Jack the Beachman says that if any attempt was made by him and Stevens and their horses to shift the row of dignified ancient high-wheeled bathing huts, ours included, even a few yards from where they are, the poor old antiques would simply fall to pieces. So here, in a single immovable line, they must remain throughout the winter, facing

145

bravely seawards, like decrepit sentries of a defeated army: abandoned, but still faithfully keeping guard. And although this, their final resting place, is beyond the reach of enemy waves, nevertheless, whenever stormy high tides batter the low granite wall protecting them, they will be drenched in flying spray. I imagine it, and wish I might be allowed when winter comes to stand on the top step of our bathing hut, wearing my red mackintosh and sou'wester, and be drenched in spray from the wild Atlantic Ocean.

And now, lastly, the huts having gone, those piles of deckchairs that Stevens, month after month, has daily been distributing, and then collecting, and then at nightfall stacking underneath an immense green tarpaulin at the bottom of the hill—these deckchairs are now transported a short way up the road and stored out of sight in the big shed opposite our hut, together with any ropes and tackle and other gear which won't be required until next April. Once the door of the shed has been closed and securely padlocked, then summer, we children know, is officially at an end.

But when, next Easter, we hear, as we shall, in our Bay View Terrace garden, the creak and rumble of bathing huts descending on their return journey to the Great Western Beach, we will realise with joy that it's all beginning again: the summer season! There will be picnics again, and swimming and sunshine and bare feet and life out of doors. In the meantime, though, we have somehow to get through the dull dreary indoor weeks of winter.

146

We look upon winter as having to be less enjoyed than endured. But there is a sort of a pause before its onset, an in-between period known as autumn when leaves turn from green to yellowy-reds and fall off the trees, and lights go on early in shops and houses; a time when we children, coming shivering downstairs in the morning, find there is already a fire burning in the dining-room grate as well as a fire in the kitchen range; when we have porridge for breakfast instead of Force, and Lucy cooks potato cakes for tea.

Days get shorter. Habits change; and change is always, to a certain extent, interesting. Our summer clothes are put away, and in place of cotton vests we are now obliged to wear woollen Chilprufe combinations. That is to say, Jim and I are combination-clad. Pam, who is growing fast, has been promoted to the glory of a Liberty bodice, with suspenders attached to hold up her new full-length beige-coloured woollen stockings. Oh, lucky Pam!

'Can't I have a Liberty bodice too, Mummy?'

'You'll have to grow a few inches first,' says my mother, laughing. 'You're such a little shrimp, Elspeth,' she says. 'Next winter, perhaps, you'll be tall enough to have long stockings.'

I'm often called a little shrimp by Mummy. She means I'm small for my age, which I am.

The thick knee-high grey woollen socks I have to continue, unwillingly, to wear—boys' socks—are so itchy they cause my legs to be covered in a rash of painful red spots. But when I complain that my knees are cold and my pimples hurt, Mummy and

147

Lucy tell me not to make a fuss.

'Don't you come the old soldier, now,' says Lucy, mysteriously. What can she mean?

'Be a man!' says my mother, brisk and bracing.

This odd piece of advice, and her other customary injunction: *'Brave as a lion!'* are both issued with the laudable intention of helping us to check the flow of tears resulting from some slight injury. They sound in our ears as ghostly trumpets might, these rousing unrealistic admonitions, battle-cries echoing from the shadowy depths of a hideous war, recently, savagely fought, when thousand upon thousand of fearful combatants required such galvanising slogans to urge them forward into the hellish future that awaited them: exhortations quite wasted on us three post-Great War children. For whereas Pam was born courageous and has no need of exhortation, Jim and I, cowards both, know only too well we are neither of us capable of being either a man, or brave as a lion. We aspire, my brother and I, not to conquer, but wherever possible to sidestep any confrontation, and when this is impossible, then somehow merely to scrape by, to survive: no higher hopes have we than that.

*   *   *

Mummy has received a letter from the headmistress of St Kilda's School, informing her that now, with the summer holidays over, the weekly dancing lessons in the Victoria Hotel are about to be resumed. Mrs Hallsmith is therefore invited to accept the school's renewed invitation, which once again offers her daughters the unique

148

advantage of sharing dancing classes with St Kilda's pupils, even though Pam and Elspeth are not, *as yet*, pupils themselves.

My sister Pam, on hearing the contents of the letter read aloud, announces coolly, in between mouthfuls of porridge, that she is not going to go to these St Kilda dancing classes: not this term, or ever again. She doesn't say why she has come to such a decision. She gives no reason for it. Simply, she doesn't want to go, and so she won't go: that's all. She shrugs her shoulders, rudely.

'You can't make me go,' she says to her mother; more dangerously, to her father.

There is a scene; a row. And the row gets bigger and bigger, darkening as it increases, like the thunder-clouds of a gathering storm. I am horror-struck, knowing what's bound to happen. But as Pam is being forcibly dragged by a wrist upstairs to the bathroom, our mother intervenes.

'No, Guth—no!' says Mummy. 'She's not well—you mustn't. You can't! I won't allow it.' And so this time Pam is spared the discipline of the strap.

But while she has succeeded in putting a stop to dancing classes for herself, Pam has also, by so doing, put a stop to dancing classes for me. I can't attend them on my own, not without the support and protection of my older sister. And although I say nothing, I'm surprised to find how much I shall miss those weekly visits to the Victoria Hotel. For I've made a discovery: I like dancing. Actually, it's a good deal more than *like*: I *love* dancing.

At the beginning it was something of an ordeal, our weekly sessions with unknown schoolgirls in the Victoria Hotel, half pleasureable, half alarming. I can remember one occasion, very early on, when I was dressed in the costume of a bunny rabbit—a white costume made by Mummy, with pink insides to its wired upstanding ears—and I had to hop in time to the piano music being played at the end of the enormous ballroom, acres of polished floor away.

Round the floor in a circle was an audience of parents, grown-ups on chairs, waiting for the performance to start. I was supposed, as the youngest performer, to start it. But the terror that engulfed me was so overwhelming my eyes blurred and my own ears buzzed, and I couldn't hear the notes of the piano. All I had to do was to go hop, hop, hoppity-hop, keeping *in time*; and I couldn't. I couldn't get it right. I hopped all wrong. Alone and lost in the middle of that huge empty space, with people staring and laughing, I stood and wept from fear and from shame: a nightmare. But I was much younger then. It was long ago—two years at least, or even three. And hop-hop-hopping isn't the same thing as dancing—not at all the same. Dancing is wonderful!

*   *   *

With the visitors gone, Newquay's residents have become more apparent. We run into Mr Vidal-Rowe, out for an airing with his wife on one side of him and his sister-in-law on the other. Middle-aged and extremely well-to-do, they only ever appear as a trio. The ladies are so alike in appearance that Mr Vidal-Rowe could easily be thought to have two wives. They are, in fact, identical twins, with plump identical figures dressed, allowing for a slight variation in the colour of their hats, identically. Their plumply smiling faces, powdered and dimpled, are seemingly indistinguishable, and around their necks are draped identical fox furs. Each of these furs, we observe with interest, also has a face; but the little foxy faces, dangling upside-down against the warm scented ample bosoms of their wearers, are in striking contrast to the human ones above, being beady-eyed, with sharply pointed noses—and—of course—dead.

However, even more fascinating than the foxy furs is the fact that Mr Vidal-Rowe's lady-companions are *not* wholly identical. One of them—the non-wife—is deaf and dumb. She carries a small magical slate in her handbag, and scribbles messages on it at lightning speed, with Mr and Mrs Vidal-Rowe standing by, nodding and smiling admiringly. When the message has been read and fully comprehended, she pulls a slide, and at once the writing vanishes. We are enthralled by this trick, which is her method of conversing with acquaintances unable to employ sign language or to lip-read.

But what we are most impressed by is the way in which they all three of them never stop smiling, their happy smiles indicating that to be deaf and dumb, instead of a handicap, adds a delightful extra dimension to the general jollity of life. And whereas we have learned that the smiles of some grown-ups are not to be believed, in this case we do believe them. The air of innocent pleasure, of a serene satisfaction with the world and themselves, that emanates from the Vidal-Rowe threesome is as palpable as the delicious scent we inhale when the two wives—which is how we think of them—stoop to embrace us.

They have no children of their own, but to show the affection they feel for the little Hallsmith girls they have presented us with specially designed waistcoats, examples of their artistic handiwork. Pam's waistcoat is cut out of a pale blue felt, and mine, in a smaller size, out of purple felt. Each garment is embroidered with Michaelmas daisies, and its edges are bound by blanket-stitching. Mr Vidal-Rowe informs us proudly that both of his ladies are tip-top needlewomen.

'But how original!' exclaims our mother, when she is thanking Mrs Vidal-Rowe and the nearly-identical twin for bestowing these unsolicited gifts upon her two lucky daughters. 'How *kind* of you,' she writes on the magical slate. At home that evening Mummy says to Daddy it would never have occurred to her in a hundred years to use *felt* as a material for making waistcoats. 'You must be careful,' she warns us, 'to keep them clean. Felt isn't washable.'

We think our waistcoats, original or not, and whether washable or not, are very pretty. I'm glad mine is purple: a gorgeous colour, uncommon for children's clothing. As might have been anticipated, our brother Jim gains nothing from the generosity of Mr Vidal-Rowe's wives. A felt waistcoat, embroidered with daisies, would hardly, after all, be suitable for a boy.

*   *   *

This term, at the Boys' County School, Jim plays football instead of cricket, or else is sent with a string of his classmates on long exhausting cross-country runs, known as Hare and Hounds, both of

152

which compulsory activities are abhorrent to him. My brother, under-sized and suffering from a double-hernia, is in no way athletically inclined. Sporting events dismay him. He is the boy they boo at soccer matches for his failure to tackle; and the last of the muddy Hounds to straggle in through the school gates as dusk is falling will, invariably, be Jim. Our father, of course, was a champion sprinter during his schooldays. The seven gleaming silver cups on top of Daddy's desk are ever-present reminders to my brother of his father's contempt for a son displaying so deplorable a lack of physical prowess.

Since Pam and I don't play football or get sent on cross-country runs, we are forced, as an unavoidable alternative, to go on healthy afternoon walks with our mother. No matter how great our reluctance or chilly the wind, we *have* to go. Exercise is good for children, just as it's good for them to eat up their soggy cabbage, never mind if Lucy has, disgustingly, overlooked a slug or a snail.

To relieve the boredom of these dull urban walks Mummy has bought us a couple of the cheap lightweight wooden hoops hanging for sale in a cluster at the entrance to Timothy White's, the hardware shop. They are almost as big as me, coming up as high as my shoulder. And at first, never having had hoops before, we are thrilled by our new playthings, and the fun of being allowed to take them with us and bowl them along the pavements of Mount Wise or Trenance Gardens, or wherever there may be a surface flat enough. But all too disappointingly soon we realise that there's not much to be done with a hoop, once the

153

skill needed for steering it has been mastered, except to scamper in pursuit of the wobbly spokeless wheel, making sure it doesn't ever speed on ahead, out of control, and collide with indignant pedestrians.

One afternoon we happen to meet, as we are passing the stone water-trough by the Great Western Railway Station, Colonel Jones and his little old sister, he striding forward with his chin in the air, she hastening to keep up with him. They stop; and we stop too. Mummy exchanges greetings with them. We children stand in silence, clutching our hoops and waiting, expectant. We know precisely what the Colonel is going to say next; and he does.

'How's my girl today?' says Colonel Jones, speaking to Pam, and bending over his cane with the silver knob. He pays me no attention. I might as well be invisible. It's Pam he has taken a special fancy to.

Words, I've noticed, can have entirely different meanings when spoken by different people in different circumstances. When Colonel Jones refers to Pam as *my girl* it's his way of showing that he's fond of her. But when Daddy calls her *my girl*, as in, *What you need, my girl, is to be taught a lesson you won't forget in a hurry*, it's a sure sign that he isn't feeling fond of her; quite the contrary.

'I've got an idea I may have something in my pocket for you,' says Colonel Jones as though it's going to surprise her; which it isn't: she knows, and so do I, what he has in his pocket. 'You like chocolates, don't you,' he says. 'Pretty girls always like chocolates.'

From the depths of his camel-hair overcoat he

scoops up a handful of the tiny square Suchard chocolates, wrapped in red or blue paper— miniature replicas of Suchard's ordinary big blocks—that we know he carries about with him, loose in his pocket, ready for any chance encounter, such as our meeting this afternoon. Does he similarly favour other girls, I wonder, or does he offer Suchard chocolates only to Pam?

'Help yourself,' says Colonel Jones. 'Take as many as you want,' he says, encouraging her. Pam says nothing, but from his hand in its wash-leather glove she picks out three of the little blue rectangles. Blue signifies that inside the wrapping there will be a tiny slab of milk chocolate. Red paper conceals a dark and rather bitter chocolate; we prefer the milky version.

'You're Pam, aren't you—eh? I knew a Pam once. Don't be shy, Pam. Go on—help yourself. Take some more.' She takes two more.

Mummy prompts her. 'What do you say, Pam?'

'Thank you, Colonel Jones.' It's all she says: not another word. For whereas I aim to please, my sister is indifferent as to whether her behaviour pleases or whether it doesn't. The Colonel pats her head. He never looks at me. But later on Pam gives me two of her Suchard chocolates, which we agree is a fair share.

Miss Jones invites us to tea with them the following Tuesday. We enjoy going to tea with Colonel and Miss Jones. I'm sorry that Jim isn't included in the invitation, but he can't be. Besides having homework to do on a weekday, he will be dirty and sweaty from playing football—decidedly not in a fit condition to join us for polite afternoon tea with the Colonel and his elderly sister.

They live in a bungalow close by Trenance Gardens. These Gardens are open to the public, because they are the property of Newquay Council. I have had it explained to me that when a place is owned by the Council, anyone can sit or walk or play there, as people freely do on Narrowcliff and Killacourt Fields and Barrowfields—all places belonging to Newquay Council. But nobody must ever venture on to private property without permission. If they do, they are trespassing, and will be prosecuted; which means they might even be put in prison. Trespassing on private property is a very serious offence.

In the middle of Trenance Gardens there is a huge monkey-puzzle tree. I asked Lucy why it was called that, and she said it was because it would puzzle the brains of a monkey to know how to climb up it. I'm not sure this is the real reason for its name. Wouldn't all animals, not just monkeys, find it puzzling to climb? Opposite Trenance Gardens are the hard tennis courts where Daddy plays tennis with Bo'sun Hooper, and Mr Harry North, and Douglas Adey (and sometimes Pig-faced Ralph), when our private members-only grass courts are closed, as they are now, the season having ended. Beyond the Gardens, further on, the famous viaduct, immensely high up, spans the valley; and further on again the River Gannel flows down through its widening estuary, leaving Crantock village out of sight over to the left, and Pentire Head over to the right, until it reaches the sea.

Mummy says that before Colonel Jones retired he was an officer in the Indian Army. He doesn't have a wife. Miss Jones, his sister, travelled out

156

from England, half across the world, in order to look after his welfare in India, and now she looks after him back here in Newquay, Cornwall. India is full of palm trees. I expect that's why Colonel and Miss Jones have planted palm trees on either side of the steepish path leading up to the steps of their bungalow, as a reminder of where they once lived.

There is always a plate of macaroons for us on the table, and also a plate of chunky individually wrapped expensive Club chocolate biscuits, orange-flavoured. Nowhere else do we get given the treat of expensive Club chocolate biscuits: only here. I would like to ask if I might be allowed to take away a Club chocolate biscuit for Jim, but I don't ask. Mummy would consider it was rude of me, and when Daddy was told he would be furious.

Usually a person, if she is in her own home, will remove her hat. Miss Jones, however, keeps her summery straw hat on in the house. It has a shady brim and is trimmed with a pink velvet ribbon and with pink artificial roses. The brooch that she uses to pin the lace bunched up round her neck is a copy, she tells us, of her brother's regimental badge, but made in gold and enamel and twinkly diamonds. She pours the tea out of a silver teapot, and in addition to the teapot she has a silver kettle on a stand, which isn't at all like Lucy's kitchen kettle, or like any other kettle I've ever seen. Underneath it is fixed a little silver basin. Sticking up at the centre of the saucer-shaped lid that covers the basin is a cotton wick surrounded by purple methylayted spirits, the colour of my new waistcoat.

The Colonel, striking a match, lights the methylayted spirits for her, and the warmth of the flame from the burning wick is just enough, she says, to keep the water in the kettle hot. It's probably something Army officers do in India. I think it's a clever invention.

What with one thing and another, going to tea with Colonel and Miss Jones is most instructive and interesting. Their bungalow is full of curious furniture and objects that I presume they must have brought back from India. It wouldn't be good manners, I know, for me to ask questions about them; which is a pity. But it's all right if I *look*.

*   *   *

The fifth of November is Guy Fawkes Day, and for more than a week the shop windows have been displaying fireworks. Usually Daddy buys a boxful from Timothy White's, and after tea, when it's dark, and if it's not raining, we all go into the backyard where he arranges for us to have our own fireworks entertainment.

I don't like the backyard, a long narrow weedy dismal enclosure. I never have liked it; or anyway, not since the time I saw a scruffy-looking man out there, talking to Lucy, and holding a dead rabbit up by the hind legs. While I was watching, he suddenly, horribly, stripped the soft furry skin clean off the rabbit's carcass, toes to head. The backyard is the sort of place you might expect to see such a disgusting sight: not a suitable place for the enchantment of sparklers.

Last year's display was a very short one, because we didn't have many fireworks: a Vesuvius, and a few Roman Candles, and a couple of Catherine Wheels which had to be hammered into an upright piece of wood, and a rocket propped in an empty milk bottle, and a packet of sparklers. The Catherine Wheels got stuck and wouldn't whirl around, having been hammered in too tightly, and the rocket shot off at a wrong low-down angle and disappeared into somebody else's backyard. The sparklers, though, were lovely. We were allowed to hold them ourselves, wearing gloves: four sparklers each.

But at breakfast this morning Daddy makes an announcement. We are not, it seems, going to have any fireworks tonight. Fireworks, he has decided, are a waste of good money; and especially so when they turn out to be duds, and get stuck. He might as well, says he use his ten-shilling note as a spill to light his pipe with, and see it go up in flames!

He's exaggerating, of course. Daddy hasn't ever spent as much as ten shillings on fireworks. What an idea! It would have been half-a-crown at the most—and probably less. He has to pretend it was a ten-shilling note that he spent a year ago because a note is made of paper, which burns, and you can't set fire to coins. But he's telling the truth when he says it's the same thing as burning money: it is— exactly the same thing. *Good money*, he always calls it. I never heard him speak of money being *bad*.

Besides the folly of chucking away good hard-earned money on something that will be gone in a few seconds, with nothing to show for it afterwards, fireworks are dangerous. They can, and they often do, cause terrible accidents. The only sure guarantee of safety, he declares this morning, is to avoid handling them at all: better to be spectators. Which is why tonight, instead of us huddling together in the dankly dispiriting backyard, we shall be standing out, he tells us, in No. 9 Bay View Terrace's little patch of a front garden to watch, from this high vantage point, as from the gallery of a theatre, the display of rockets other people will be squandering their good money on.

Our father's change of programme is actually quite a relief to me; although I'm sorry if it means us having to miss the sparklers. Rockets will be panoramically beautiful, I know, arching up into the wide open sky above Newquay's descending rooftops, the terrifying sound of their explosions reduced by distance and space to far-off harmless crackles.

But when Daddy arrives back from the Bank in a tearing hurry this evening, his breakfast-time plan is immediately scrapped. Someone he met in the street on the way home has just informed him of a gigantic bonfire already alight in the grounds of the Council School, with a tarred and feathered effigy of Guy Fawkes—which Lucy explains to me is a kind of scarecrow—perched on the summit of the blazing pile. Apparently the spectacle—a real corker—has been organised by the Council for the enjoyment of the general public, and is absolutely free of charge.

'Quick!' our father cries to his three children, astonishing us as he bursts into the hall, 'Get your coats on—quick! We'll have to run!'

And run we do, out of the house, helter-skelter, with Mummy and Lucy chasing after us to wind about our necks the woolly scarves we haven't waited for, and to button our overcoats.

Down the hill, turn left, and along Mount Wise we gallop, the four of us, our father running

160

eagerly, leaning forward with shoulders hunched. He has me so tightly gripped by one hand I almost fly through the air, swung off my feet at every stride. The Twins keep up as best they may, Pam easily, fleet as a deer, Jim struggling, all of us excited. We arrive, panting, at the gates of the Council School. A great crowd of half-seen figures is milling round the bonfire, an immense construction on top of which can still be seen the remains of the Guy Fawkes effigy, a charred and sagging scarecrow.

Merely to be here, mingling unchallenged with the rest of the public, gives us a thrill. Never in normal circumstances would we have dared to enter the Council School forecourt, or dared, indeed, to approach anywhere near the big iron-barred gates of a school that has such a fearsome reputation. It is the haunt of those rough ill-mannered boys with dirty faces, who fight each other in the roadway, and snatch off one another's caps, and don't care *how* they behave. Council School pupils are judged to be as different from pupils of the vastly superior County School as inhabitants of an uncivilised bloodthirsty foreign country, and in our eyes are more dangerous for well-brought-up children to risk encountering than exposure to any amount of Roman Candles in the backyard of No. 9 Bay View Terrace.

But today is the fifth of November, and we have nothing to fear. For a few hours the enemy's territory has ceased to be out-of-bounds, and the threat is suspended. Besides, are we not, we three, under the leadership and protection of our hero-father, holder of the DSO medal for gallantry on the field of battle?

The unequal status of the Council School and the County School is made apparent by their being situated at opposite ends of Newquay, practically the entire town lying between and effectively separating them. The older Council School is located in Newquay's oldest quarter, which clusters round the harbour, with the original jumble of little shops, and intricate hugger-mugger lanes and steps and passages, rising steeply above it; whereas the County School belongs to a later era of residential and hotel development, the buildings of which reflect a solid advance in prosperity, and were clearly not designed for the housing of either fishermen or small shop-keepers.

Belching out flames and smoke, the colossal bonfire is roaring with the fury of a captured wild animal, and, to add to the infernal atmosphere, squibs and firecrackers are being let off without warning all round us in the shadowy crowded forecourt. I keep both hands clamped over my ears, thankful to be saved from mockery by the darkness. Loud explosions hurt my eardrums, but nobody ever believes me. They think I'm a baby to mind the bangs, and I feel ashamed.

Although unusual, treats improvised unexpectedly out of the blue by our father do occur from time to time, and tonight is one of those times. Generally we are wary of Daddy, rather afraid of him, in fact (or Jim and I are; not Pam), on account of never knowing when he is going to lose his temper; and often, when he does lose it, we don't know why. But this evening he seems actually to want to have us with him, and to be enjoying himself in our company.

Mostly we feel that our father wishes he didn't have children; we are a nuisance to him, as well as an expense. Earning enough money to support a family, enough to clothe and feed us and pay the rent, *is no joke*! His bitter complaints have made us aware—guiltily, uncomfortably aware—that it is we, his children, who are to blame for Daddy's misery. Because of us he is obliged to slave away, cooped up behind the counter of a beastly bank: no fit employment for a gentleman in any case, and particularly not for a gentleman whose true vocation is to be—or was to have been—an artist.

When the Great War drew finally to a close in 1918, 2nd Lieutenant Guthrie Hallsmith (promoted to Captain) was released from a German prisoner-of-war camp, liberated into a newly born undiscovered world of limitless horizons. There he stood, poised on the brink of it, a young man of twenty-four, alive, when millions were dead, with his miraculous future stretching out in front of him. What went wrong? How can it have come about that he now finds himself back again in prison?—for this is the view our unhappy father takes of his present inescapable daily drudgery. He suffers, and we suffer too. The miasma of his gloom, his disappointment, spreads through the whole of the Hallsmith family.

But then, as he did tonight, he will suddenly spring a surprise on us, changing all at once into quite another person, a grown-up friend, like Lewarne Hosking; or like somebody else's father, not ours. And when this happens it's as if we can stop holding our breath in his presence; as if we've been granted a brief holiday from the constantly nagging worry of whether or not we might be going, unintentionally, to displease or upset him. Brief it will be, but for as long as it lasts we are safe, and there is even the hope, the chance of us having fun with Daddy.

As a matter of fact, we had a similar spur-of-the-moment outing with him fairly recently, on a Saturday afternoon in October, only then, instead of a bonfire, it was the tempestuous Atlantic Ocean we set forth to see. A sight worth seeing, said our father; and so it was. Mummy didn't accompany us. She had one of her headaches. To find ourselves, as we do at these headache times, handed over to Daddy, put in the sole charge of our usually awe-inspiring parent, undoubtedly lends an extra whiff of risky adventure to whatever the enterprise he is conducting us on.

That afternoon we were full of glee at the prospect of being outside in weather most people were staying indoors to avoid. Running, skipping, hopping, off we went with him, to join a group of other hardy mackintosh-clad souls gathered on the Towan Beach esplanade. From their dripping bedraggled appearance they could well have been the survivors of shipwreck, rather than having chosen—as had we—to brave the wild elements for the sake of entertainment. At our backs we had the Pavilion Theatre, its posters already advertising a Christmas presentation of *Ali Baba and the Forty Thieves*; but infinitely more dramatic than any pantomime, or than any stage production, was the sea we faced.

The tide that October day was exceptionally high. A gale-force wind, blowing from a northerly direction, drove the waves on-shore, whipping them into a frenzy of attack. Crested with white and yellow foam, they were crashing against the sea wall, drenching the railings and flooding the roadway beyond, even reaching as far as our feet and wetting our shoes. Fountains of spray, flung yards up into the air, came cascading down, splattering on to the concrete. Our cheeks were stung by it; our lips tasted salty. Weeks before, when summer was over and the beach huts were rumbling up the Great Western Beach hill to their winter quarters, I had imagined being close to such a tempest; and yes!—it was as exhilarating an experience as I had supposed it would be.

Our father stood wordless, perfectly still, holding my hand and gazing out across the surging heaving tossing savage ocean, smiling dreamily, almost as though mesmerised by the storminess of the scene confronting him. I knew how he felt. His mood was peaceful because, for a short while, here and now, there was no need to be angry. The

165

violence of wind and waves was expressing on his behalf, more vividly than he ever could, the rage that had to be kept, as a rule, bottled up inside him.

*　　*　　*

Soon it will be Christmas. Every year Pam and I make presents for our aunts, and for Granny Hallsmith and for Granny Laurie. We have our own ideas of what to make, but Mummy has suggested gifts of calendars for all the elderly relations listed, and she has bought us a number of inch-sized calendars which we are to glue on to the bottom of our pictures, with a loop of ribbon stuck on at the top. We don't say so to Mummy, but we aren't enthusiastic about her idea. Home-made presents are supposed to be home-made—that's the whole point of them; and if she goes and buys us these calendars from a shop, then the present won't be properly home-made.

The dining-room table where we are sitting has been covered in protective sheets of newspaper. Each of us is equipped with a paintbox, and an egg-cup full of water, and a paintbrush, and a pencil, and an india-rubber. Pam hardly ever uses her india-rubber. I am trying to copy a fairy-story illustration of a gnome wearing a pointed red hat, sitting cross-legged on a toadstool. I draw him, and rub him out, again and again, until there's a hole in the paper. When I start to paint him, hoping that colour will improve matters, the brush is far too wet. Tears of mortification, mingling with the watery brush-strokes, reduce my red-hatted gnome to a messy splodge.

166

'It's awful, Ellie,' says Pam, not unkindly, but with truth. 'You can't give Aunt Molly *that*!'

Her fairies have beautiful multicoloured wings, like butterflies. I'm no good at drawing and painting, but my sister Pam is very good. You might think that our father would praise her for the pictures that she's always drawing and painting. After all, it's what he likes doing. But he never praises her for anything. He looks at her pictures and tells her what's wrong with them. She doesn't reply.

Our mother has taught us how to do cross-stitch embroidery on canvas. She says that once upon a time it's what all little girls of our age learnt to do. We think cross-stitch is boring, and it takes too long, and is too finicky, and I keep pricking my finger.

Mummy has also, recently, taught my sister how to knit and how to crotchet, and Pam has taught me. Knitting and crotcheting are much more fun than cross-stitch embroidery, and a great deal quicker for getting results. A cross-stitch bookmark, although it was the smallest embroidery present we could think of, still takes ages, whereas a perfectly acceptable bookmark can be made in practically no time at all out of cardboard. So it seems a pity, really, for us to have to waste hours on doing fiddly cross-stitch.

The fact is, we both enjoy the feeling of being industrious that we get when we're making Christmas presents; but we like to be able to dash them off at top speed, and with a minimum of bother. Furthermore, our pleasure in the creative process depends on us making what we make *in private*, secretly, in a corner, without any help or

167

advice from anyone, even if we have to explain, when the thing's finished, what it's meant to be and the purpose of it. *This*, for instance, is a table mat, and *that* is a hair-combings tidy; and this box, decorated with swirly patterns, is for putting pencils in; and that's a comb case, or it could be a spectacle case. We can crotchet a woollen hat for a boiled egg, to keep it warm, in an afternoon; and a pen-wiper—one of our best inventions, only requiring a few scraps of material, fastened together by a button sewn in the middle—can be completed in *half* an afternoon.

Our Christmas present for Daddy is a dozen or so of the spills that he uses to light his pipe with: strips of coloured paper folded, over and over, lengthwise, and then tied in a bunch with a piece of knitting wool—easy! The handkerchief I've made as my present for Mummy is hemmed round the four sides with disgracefully big stitches, and the corners, which were very difficult, are lumpy; but she won't mind. She'll be pleased, I know; especially as I've succeeded in embroidering a cross-stitch M on it, which was more difficult even than sewing the corners. M is for Mummy. Pam says it should have been a J, because her name is Janet. But we don't call her Janet; we call her Mummy.

On Christmas Eve we all three of us hang up one of our father's discarded, washed and mended socks—our socks are too small—knowing we shall see a transformation immediately we open our eyes on Christmas morning. Instead of hanging limp and empty, every sock will be stuffed full and bulging with mysteriously exciting shapes. It will have a cracker sticking out at the top, and a tangerine and a silver threepenny-bit concealed in the toe. Sticking out at the top of my sock, as well as the cracker, there will be a rolled-up copy of *Chicks' Own* and a copy of *Tiger Tim*.

Usually it's only when I'm kept in at home, bedridden, running a temperature and afflicted by chickenpox or mumps or a snuffly cold, that I'm given the rare treat of *Chicks' Own* or *Tiger Tim* to read. And I daresay it's the companionship they provide me with when I'm isolated and ill that accounts for why I still find everything about these juvenile publications enthralling: the brightness of their colours, their stories, the puzzles, the competitions, the Editor's Letter—which I am almost convinced is a personal message addressed to me—everything! Nor has it ever struck me as peculiar that Mrs Bruin, a stout and kindly brown bear on the front page of *Tiger Tim*, should act as mother to such a very odd assortment of Boys, (they are all boys): Joey the Parrot, the cheekiest of her Boys, and Oswald Ostrich, and Georgie Giraffe, and of course Tiger Tim himself, their leader. Mrs Bruin's Boys never quarrel or behave roughly, never dispute. And it's maybe because they are always in harmonious agreement that their mild exploits continue to delight me, even though I'm shamefacedly aware I ought by now to have outgrown them.

We know who fills our stockings. We know it isn't Father Christmas. Our own father has been at pains to explain to us there isn't any such person, and that the entire notion of Father Christmas is a load of superstitious nonsense. We strongly suspect he holds much the same view of God, which may have some bearing on why we are inclined to

169

confuse the two personalities. But while accepting unequivocally that the tale of Father Christmas climbing down children's bedroom chimneys and filling their stockings with toys in the dead of night is pure bunkum, we are less positive when it comes to other manifestations. Might not God be either a superior version of Father Christmas, or else a sort of twin brother to him? Whether real or not, both God and Father Christmas have many characteristics in common. Both are acknowledged to be old, and they both have long white beards. Both are invisible, with extraordinary powers, managing to be everywhere at the same time, and to travel about up in the sky without us ever catching a glimpse, neither of one, nor of the other. It might be—could be—that God and Father Christmas are indeed the same person, one who simply finds it convenient for some reason to use two names, except for Daddy's categoric declaration that Father Christmas doesn't exist. Why, then, do so many people believe he does?

When it's a case of believing or not believing in God, our father keeps his mouth shut, and won't say what he thinks. This may be in order not to offend our mother, since Mummy does believe in God. She would like us to believe in God as well, and in Jesus too. Jesus was a real man, but also somehow God, only young, not old, who lived hundreds and hundreds of years ago in Palestine, which is hundreds of miles off on the other side of the world; and this poor Jesus got killed, in some sort of way so very horrible we don't ever talk about it, although we can't help noticing crucifixes in churches and drawing our own conclusions.

We don't often go to church, nor have we been

to many different churches. The one which is nearest to where we live is St Michael's parish church, a massive grey building situated a short distance up Mount Wise. Our mother has taken us there on several Sunday mornings in the past, if it happened that the morning was free of other plans—which is to say, if it wasn't the right season or the right weather for picnicking. But St Michael's is so huge inside, and so cold and dismal and echoing, we didn't enjoy it at all. Consequently, after those few trial attempts at local church going Mummy hasn't taken her children there again.

I went again, though, once. It wasn't on a Sunday, and it wasn't with my mother. I went with Lucy, to see her sister Lily getting married. Pam could have come along with us if she had wanted to, but she wasn't interested. I was very interested, never having been to a wedding before. It was a disappointment, however. There was nobody in the church, apart from Lily herself, and Albert, the man she was marrying, and Lucy's gigantic brothers, Dick and Frank, and Dick's wife Ada, whose front teeth are missing, and Mr and Mrs Coles, and me and Lucy; and, of course, the clergyman.

Lily is blonde, like our Lucy, but in other respects, being much bigger and heftier, she more resembles their brothers. For her wedding she was dressed as a proper bride should be dressed, all in white, with a white veil, and carrying a bouquet. Albert was wearing a tight brown suit. He didn't have a top hat, but he had a white carnation in his buttonhole. I particularly noticed how well-shone his boots were. When I was younger, and Lucy took me to visit her parents, Mr and Mrs Coles, in their country cottage, I had been surprised, I remembered, by how small they were. They looked even smaller now in the front pew of St Michael's church: tiny, and with a bewildered air, as if they were lost.

The ceremony was over very quickly. There was no singing. Outside in the porch Lucy gave me a paper bag and told me to throw handfuls of confetti at Lily and Albert, which I did. And that was the end of that. Lily kissed me, and the two great hulking brothers, Dick and Frank, were cracking jokes and laughing, but it still seemed to me a saddish occasion, not the way a wedding ought to be; not what I had expected. Lucy Coles's family is a country family, and I wondered why Lily and Albert didn't get married in a country church like, say, the one we sometimes go to in the village of St Columb Minor.

It's where we go on this Christmas morning, after the ritual of opening presents, followed by a sustaining breakfast, first of porridge as usual, then of sausages, eggs and bacon. Thus fortified, and wrapped up warmly, we set off on foot for the church of St Columb Minor. If there is any church that we think of as being *our* church, this is it.

We discovered it by chance, more than a year ago, when we were driving through the village on the way to a picnic at Porth. In those days we still had a half-share in Mr Cooper's car. The Fiat we later acquired only remained ours for the summer. That autumn it was returned ignominiously to the accommodating garage-owner who had agreed to sell it to Daddy, little by little, on the instalment system, the regular monthly payments having proved to be, as Mummy had foreseen, a strain too great for the Hallsmith family's meagre resources.

'We don't need a car during the winter, Guthrie,' our mother had said, consolingly. And she had employed our father's own argument to help him swallow his pride and accept the inevitable. 'It's a waste of good money, Guth, to have the Fiat parked outside the door, month after month, when we're not using it for expeditions at weekends.'

This is why we are walking to church today, instead of driving. The bus that runs a week-day passenger service from Newquay to St Columb Minor—and from there to Porth, and then along the coastal road to Watergate Bay, and then on to goodness knows where—doesn't operate on Sundays or on Christmas Day.

Luckily, by taking a short cut, which branches off the main road a quarter-mile or so beyond Barrowfields, through farm lanes and over stiles, it's not too far to walk. This church is quite little, with a low roof, as different as it's possible to be from gloomy St Michael's. And since today is Christmas Day, there are flowers in abundance and sprigs of holly adorning every pillar, every window sill, and all its dim recesses are lit by the flickering golden glow of many candles. It's also, today, crowded with people, which proves how popular it must be with families who don't live in St Columb Minor but who come, like us, from somewhere else.

The church is so little and the crowd is so great we are obliged to sit on chairs at the back, which pleases me because it means we are close to the crib of the Jesus baby arranged on the cover of the

173

stone font where they christen real babies. We don't care to enquire into the death of Jesus, but his birth is a lovely story, much appreciated by me and my sister Pam. A real live baby of our own would be the height of bliss, infinitely better than the dollies—pretence babies—we've always been forbidden to have.

I screw myself round on my chair to look up at our father standing behind us, to find out if he's joining in the prayers and the singing of the congregation. I thought he probably wouldn't be, and he isn't. He has his chin raised, and his eyes fixed ahead with the same expression I've seen on his face when he passes us by in the street, marching up to the windy headland and its granite cross on the 11th of November, Poppy Day. He's wearing his DSO medal, too.

We make a point of also traipsing over to St Columb Minor for the cheerful festivals of Easter and of Harvest Thanksgiving. We like the singing and the decorations. On Harvest Thanksgiving Sunday the church smells of apples. There are sheaves of corn propped up round the base of the pulpit, and fruit and vegetables everywhere, either in piles or else laid out in rows, and the hymns we sing, as loud as we can, are all songs of rejoicing.

Easter Sunday is almost equally enjoyable. But what neither Pam nor I can understand about the Friday before Easter—which, as we know, although we'd rather not have to think about it, is the day that poor Jesus was killed—is *why* it's called Good Friday. What it should be called, obviously, is Bad Friday. The good bit is on Sunday, when Jesus came alive again and made everything all right; and this is the reason St

Columb Minor church on Easter Sunday is full of daffodils. I did ask our mother to explain the mistake, but she pretended not to hear my question. I could tell she was flustered by it, so I didn't ask her a second time.

On Easter Sunday and on Harvest Thanksgiving Sunday our father walks over to St Columb Minor with us, but when we arrive at the door of the church he leaves us there, and walks away by himself, to spend the next hour watching seals bobbing about in the deep ocean swells off the tip of Porth Island. Only on Christmas Day does he come actually inside the church, and remain for the service.

Daddy isn't religious. Except for accompanying us to church on Christmas Day, he won't have anything to do with religion. He doesn't approve of it. This being his inflexible opinion, our mother has a struggle to fulfil, unaided, what she perceives as her parental duty, which requires us, her three children, to be instructed in at least the rudiments of a Christian faith. She had once, after all, when she was very young, expected to become the wife of a clergyman; an expectation only dashed when the man she was engaged to marry, Basil McNeile, died early of tuberculosis.

It is Cousin Edith Martin who sends our mother necessary support in the shape of a big heavy brown volume entitled *Stories from the Bible*. Stories! That sounds promising! Encouraged by our reaction, Mummy hopes to establish a regular routine of reading aloud a chapter to us every Sunday night, as soon as we have undressed and are snuggled up in bed.

For a while, the scheme works well. We are

175

delighted by the full-page colour illustrations, although we wish there were more of them. Some stories are better value than others. A particular favourite of ours is to do with an old man, Elijah, who lives in the wilderness. He has nothing to eat, and is dreadfully hungry, but the ravens bring him food in their beaks, and save his life. It's nearly the same as the story of Hansel and Gretel, but without the witch. When Hansel and Gretel were lost in a forest they were looked after and fed by robins. In stories—not in real life—birds can be very helpful, because they are able to fly.

But then, on a certain Sunday evening, it all goes terribly wrong. Pam has grown bored and impatient, and she interrupts Mummy at an especially serious moment in order to make a joke about the mess there would be if *her* cup overflowed.

Mummy stops reading, and closes the book, and tells my sister it's very *very* naughty of her to joke about Holy Bible matters. Our mother's cheeks have gone pink, and we realise that she is truly deeply upset. Jim and I wait, aghast, open-mouthed, wondering whatever in the world will happen next. But Pam doesn't care, not in the slightest. She doesn't mind our mother telling her that she's a naughty girl. She squeezes her lips together mutinously tight, and shrugs her shoulders, and refuses to apologise. Isn't she sorry for her rudeness—her shocking behaviour? No, she's not. And then Mummy begins to cry, which is so awful, I start to cry as well. And still my sister doesn't care. We never have another Bible-story-reading session after that.

Pam and I say our prayers, though, every single

night, kneeling on the hard floor beside our beds, while our brother Jim is doing the same in his own separate bedroom. First, I listen to my sister reciting her prayers, which are sometimes lengthy and sometimes brief, according to her mood and her immediate needs, but always airily inventive and made up on the spot.

Then it's my turn. My prayers are short, and they never—unlike Pam's—vary: 'Please God, bless Mummy and Daddy and Pam and Jim—*and Lucy*—and make me a good girl. A-men.' Pam says that I ought not to include Lucy in my prayers because she isn't a member of the family; to which I reply, with uncharacteristic stubborness, that they are my prayers, and I *want* to have Lucy in them—so there!

Just occasionally Pam and I are already cosily in bed before it dawns on us that our prayers have been forgotten.

'We shan't have to get out again, Ellie,' my sister decides. 'We can say them in bed.'

I disagree. 'Prayers don't count unless we're kneeling down.'

'They will count, Ellie,' she assures me, 'if our eyes are shut, and if we lie flat on our backs, and keep absolutely still while we're saying them. That's what I'm going to do.'

But this is one instance when I mistrust the judgement of my leader. Prayers demand a kneeling position, of that I am certain, otherwise they never reach heaven and God, and are simply wasted; or are worse, perhaps, than wasted: may even result in a God-given black mark. Argument with my older sister being of no avail, I risk her scorn and slide back out of bed. Pam stays where she is. But in all decisions, whether spiritual or temporal, she is bolder than me.

*   *   *

Love for my mother is a constant inner agony; an agony hidden inside me because I never can express this love of mine in words. I can't ever declare it to her, openly. I don't know why I can't, but I can't. When I hear or see her weeping, I feel anguished. I want her to know that although our father may give her cause to weep, and sometimes Pam will too, I never will. I will never ever make my mother cry. I love her; and if only I could pluck up enough courage to tell her so, she would surely be comforted, and I be eased of my pain. But I can't manage to speak of it. I can't pronounce the words. I am struck dumb. It is the secret burden I carry with me at all times.

'Oh, what a funny little face you have, Elspeth,' says my mother, laughing.

Is my face funny? What is wrong with my face? Funny? I gaze at it anxiously in the mirror. Is the funniness of my face—which must be why she laughs at me—the obstacle that blocks my way and prevents me telling my mother that I love her?—prevents me giving her what I yearn to give her, yearn to have her accept as a gift of unique value from me, her daughter?

What I really want is for Mummy to say that she knows perfectly well how much I love her, and that this knowledge compensates for all the sorrow she suffers, healing the wounds inflicted by others, curing her grief. And if I tell her, then I shall know that she knows. Why is it so impossibly difficult for

me to tell her? But it's not impossible. I can do it—
I can!—I will! I take hold of her hand, urgently.

'Mummy—'

'What a funny little thing you are, Elspeth,' says my mother, laughing down at me—laughing, laughing. The confession of love dies at source, unuttered, unutterable; and the awful ache in my bumpety heart is still there, still unrelieved.

*   *   *

The Hallsmith family doesn't have a turkey or a goose for Christmas dinner. Instead we have a roasted chicken, which our mother says is quite as delicious. After the chicken's been eaten there will be mince pies to follow. Pam and I have helped her to make the mince pies by rolling the pastry out on the kitchen table, thin and flat, and then cutting it into circles. We were allowed to stir the mixture for the plum pudding too, and also the mixture for the Christmas cake, but that was in November. They've been waiting till now on a shelf in the larder, the pudding tied up in a china basin, and the cake in a tin. Generally cakes would go stale if they were left for so long before we ate them, but a Christmas fruit cake, Lucy tells us, gets better and better the longer it's left. It was iced at the weekend, and I fastened the gold-and-silver paper frill round it, and placed the snowman and his toboggan on top, exactly in the middle.

The snowman and the cake-frill were presented to me by Miss Dorothy Stevens, free of charge, as a reward for having stood on a stool all through Monday afternoon, behind the counter of the Dorothy Café, which is a confectionery shop at the bottom of Bury Road. It sells cakes and sweets and biscuits and boxes of chocolates at the front, and cups of tea on trays at the back, where there are three small tables.

The café belongs to Miss Dorothy Stevens, who is very dainty and ladylike and who has taken a fancy to me. This is why I had to wear my best clothes and spend a whole afternoon pretending to be her shop assistant. Mummy said how kind of Miss Dorothy Stevens to invite me, and what a lucky little girl I was to be given such a very special treat; but it wasn't a treat at all. That Monday afternoon was most *excruciatingly* dull, and it seemed to go on and on, for ever and ever; and the snowman and the cake-frill that I took away with me at the end of it weren't enough—not nearly enough—to make the dullness worthwhile.

Miss Dorothy Stevens is very chatty to my mother, but not to me when we're on our own together; and there were hardly any customers to provide an interest. I think that it isn't really true that she's taken a fancy to me. It's Mummy she was trying to please, for some reason. The trouble with being a child is, you are never asked what you want to have, or what you want to do: you're simply told. You're even told that something is a treat for you, when it's not.

Most of the Newquay families have a fir tree in their sitting room during the Christmas holiday. We can see them through the windows when the lights are on, decorated with tinsel, and with miniscule candles, and glass balls dangling, and on the point of the highest branch there is always a silver star. We Hallsmiths don't have a tree, but whether because our father considers that for us to have one would be pandering to the superstitions of the season, or whether because he thinks it would be a waste of good money, I'm not sure.

In the month before Christmas the greengrocers, and other shopkeepers too—even the butcher and the fishmonger—had fir trees of all shapes and sizes on the pavement for sale. I sniffed the strange bitter smell of their prickly foliage as we went by. I wish we could have a fir tree for Christmas. We would hang it with paper-chains not costing anything, made from painted newspaper strips, as described in the *Daily Mail*'s Teddy Tail section for junior readers, and with a star cut out of cardboard, also painted, to go on top. We did make a few of the Teddy Tail paper-chains, but they weren't a great success. They kept getting unstuck and falling off the picture rail, which irritated our father. If we had a tree ourselves, though, we would be more careful and make better paper-chains for it.

As we are not being taken to *Ali Baba and the Forty Thieves* at the Pavilion Theatre (Daddy was told it's quite unsuitable for children—much too vulgar), my sister and I had had a plan to write our own pantomime, and act it at home on the evening of Christmas Day, as soon as tea was finished. But we needed our brother Jim to help us by taking part in the story we'd made up, and he was unwilling. And Pam and me couldn't, on our own, just the two of us, act the King and the Queen, *and* the Princess who was going to be stolen by a band of wicked robbers, *and* the Prince who rescues her. So after one rehearsal we decided to give a carol concert instead.

We haven't had to memorise the carols, not

entirely. We can read them from the printed carol sheets which Pam grabbed hold of as we were leaving St Columb Minor church this morning, and stuffed into her coat pocket. I wasn't absolutely certain if it was all right for us to take them, but Pam said it was. And having listened to different groups of carol singers who go from house to house before Christmas, knocking at doors and asking for money, we know some of the tunes fairly well. We've been practising in our bedroom: 'While Shepherds Watch Their Flocks by Night', and 'Away in a Manger', and the first verse of 'Hark the Herald Angels Sing'. The second verse has got words in it we don't understand and that might be rude, and anyway one verse is enough.

Of course we shan't expect to be paid any money, not like the door-to-door carol singers. It's a free entertainment, intended exclusively for the Hallsmith family—almost exclusively. Lucy Coles has been invited to join us from the kitchen, and she's to come along without her apron. Daddy and Mummy and Jim and Lucy are the concert audience. They sit on the chairs we've arranged ready for them in a row, and we stand in front.

'Oh, well done!' says Mummy, clapping and clapping. And since the concert is over rather quickly, she asks us to sing the carols again. So we do; and then a third time. We both feel pleased that our performance has been such a success, and that it was a good sort of ending for Christmas Day.

*   *   *

Christmas-holiday time is the time for childrens'

parties. Mostly they are held in hotels—the Victoria Hotel, or the Headland Hotel; and once, a year or two ago, in the crimson-carpeted impressive Great Western Hotel, which belongs to our friend Bo'sun Hooper, when he gave a party for his little girl, Sheila, who lives there with him.

The rooms in private houses, being full of furniture, don't have space enough, generally, for the games we play: Hunt the Slipper, and Twos and Threes and Musical Chairs, and Postman's Knock. I remember playing Oranges and Lemons when I was younger, and Here We Go Gathering Nuts in May; but those were babyish games. The parties we go to now, and the games we play at them, are for older children. Sometimes I am the youngest person at these parties. The grown-ups who organise them for a nine- or a ten-year-old son or daughter must feel that when the Hallsmith twins are invited it would be a pity not to ask me too; so my name is added to the invitation card.

This year, on Boxing Day, we went for the first time to a party in the big red Bristol Hotel at the far end of Narrowcliff. The manager of the Bristol Hotel is Mr Francis, a Midland Bank customer, and his two boys are pupils, as Jim is, at the County School. I don't think my brother Jim likes the two Francis boys. I think, although he has never actually said so, they are amongst those of his classmates who have nicknamed him Toddy, and who chant that nasty rhyme at him: *Old Tom Toddy, all head and no body*; and who bully him for being bad at sports and always coming last in the cross-country races. But anyway, this year they invited him to their party, and me and Pam as well; and Mummy wrote back, accepting for us all; and so we went. It was an unusual party: not much fun, we thought. Instead of games there was a film-show of Felix the Cat, and afterwards a conjuror, doing tricks. We had to sit still, and watch. No rushing about and biffing each other with balloons, or any of the rowdy behaviour expected at childrens' parties.

But this winter the most exciting invitation we have ever had has come from the rich eccentric owner of the black three-masted schooner moored permanently in the River Gannel. Just before Christmas, apparently, he walked into the Midland Bank, and said to our father:

'You've got some little kiddies, haven't you, Hallsmith?'

And even though Daddy disapproves of the word *kiddies* (we've been taught it's a word we mustn't say; we mustn't say *pardon*, either; or *perspire*; or *lady*, unless she's an old one, when it changes into being polite, somehow)—Daddy replied that yes, he had. Which is how it was we received an invitation to the party this notoriously reclusive elderly man, indulging a sudden inexplicable whim, is giving for children on board his piratical schooner, the fabulous great sailing ship we've so often stared at and wondered about on our ramblings along beside the Gannel.

In the latest consignment of Felicity Brown's outgrown clothes for me there were two party dresses, both exquisitely beautiful. My mother's favourite is made of thick heavy lace, like clotted cream, lined with chiffon, hanging perfectly straight, and loose, with no sash or belt. I've overheard it being said that I look so sweet in it— so quaint. I don't know what *quaint* means. I ask

184

my mother.

'Does it mean funny?'

'No, Elspeth, no—not *funny*,' she answers. 'Charming!' So I don't have to worry about the lace dress.

But *my* favourite is the other one. It has a tight-fitting waist, and a sticky-out skirt, and puff sleeves, and is a dream of prettiness in rustling rose-pink taffeta silk.

On the morning of the schooner party I wake up with a sore throat. I try to conceal my sneezes and my runny nose from Mummy, who is luckily so preoccupied in getting herself ready to escort us that she isn't noticing much else. It's Lucy who slips the creamy lace dress over my head, and Lucy who says to my mother:

'Excuse me, Mum, for troubling you, but in my opinion this child is in no proper state for party-going. She did ought to be in bed, Mum—I do believe as she's running a temperature.'

And I am: the thermometer proves that Lucy is right. Off comes my lovely lace dress, peeled back over my head, and in five minutes I'm stretched out between the sheets, underneath a pile of blankets and an eiderdown, a hot-water bottle tucked in alongside, listening to Pam and Jim and Mummy being fetched by Mrs Mitchell, our doctor's wife, the mother of Peter Mitchell, and driven away to the schooner party without me.

The tears roll down my cheeks into my ears and on to my pillow, unstoppably. So terrible is the disappointment, so indescribably bitter, I think I shall die of it. More than anything in the whole world I had wanted to be able to clamber at last up that gangplank, up its dangerous tantalising

185

previously forbidden slope, step by step, to the top—I had imagined myself doing it; and then— *then* I would discover what was waiting out of sight, below decks, in the bowels of the black three-masted schooner. It was to have been the most romantic experience of my life. Why, oh *why* do I have to have a sore throat, a runny nose, a temperature, sneezes, today of all days—why *today*? It's not *fair*!

And when my sister returns from the party, the unfairness does really become almost unbearable.

Before leaving his vessel, the children invited aboard it by the retired sea captain had each been given a present, a parcel, from under the Christmas tree. Jim was given a set of lead soldiers wearing scarlet uniforms, which our father, on the party-goers' return, immediately confiscates and puts into the dustbin out in our backyard. Several years earlier, when we were living in the Bungalow, the gift of a toy fortress bestowed on Jim by some friend or relation in a mistaken act of generosity, was likewise impounded and disposed of. The ban extends to any and all toys connected, however remotely, with warfare. Having regard to our father's personal involvement in scenes of bloody battle, the ban is understandable. More understandable than Daddy's total prohibition of dolls, which as playthings could never surely be suspected of promoting bloodthirsty tendencies in his two daughters?

My sister's present from the old sea captain is a doll. Her name, printed on the cardboard box that she reclines in, asleep, is Rosie. She has curly hair, and her eyes—blue eyes, that open and shut—are fringed with lashes. Her satin dress is the same

186

colour as my favourite new party dress: rose-pink, to match her name. If I had only gone aboard the schooner too, might I not also have come away with a dolly of my own as wonderful as Rosie?

'You can borrow her,' says my sister; '—sometimes you can, when I'm not playing with her.' She means it kindly, to assuage the misery she knows I'm suffering. But borrowing isn't the same—not the same at all—as *having*.

'I'm going to knit a blanket for her,' says Pam, 'to keep her warm. And you can knit one too, if you want. Or you could crotchet her a hat—same as the hats we make for boiled eggs. We'll share her, Ellie,' she promises me hastily, observing the tears that are beginning to roll down my cheeks and into my ears again.

Our father is, as yet, unaware of his law being flouted. Pam had whisked upstairs with Rosie under her coat, as quick as lightning, the moment they reached home. She intends to hide her in a drawer, beneath a layer of vests and stockings.

'But what are you going to tell Daddy if he asks about the present you were given at the party? He probably will ask,' I warn her.

Pam considers this. We tell the truth, always, my sister and I, because lies are wicked, and God, who—unlike Daddy—knows everything, would be sure to punish us if we were to tell lies; and so we don't.

'I shan't answer,' says Pam.

Not answering is my sister's best and strongest weapon against her father. It drives Daddy absolutely mad.

But whose side will Mummy be on? Can we trust her not to betray us and our guilty secret?

187

'That's all right,' says Pam, carelessly. 'Mummy hasn't seen Rosie—she doesn't know what I was given. She'll probably think I was stupid, and forgot, and left my present behind.'

And then there's Jim. But whatever Jim knows, he won't say a word. Like me, his guiding principle is never to stir up trouble. He's in trouble enough himself, daily, my poor brother, without having to do any stirring.

*   *   *

Spring has returned. There are primroses in the hedges again, and cowslips growing in the field beside the grass courts of the Tennis Club, where rows of cars will park when the season opens.

The fact that soon the weather will make possible a renewal of our picnic excursions at weekends, and that we have no car with which to make them, weighs heavily on our parents, Daddy especially. But then, out of the blue, Fate intervenes. We hear that Mr Cooper has approached our father, wanting to heal the breach between them, and offering, moreover—a thunderclap!—to sell him outright the car we used to share, and that had been the cause of their quarrel. Mr Cooper, who is not young, has decided, it seems, to cease altogether from driving an automobile, and is giving Daddy, despite their previous hot exchanges, the chance of first refusal. He has a week to consider the proposal.

Daddy agrees to shake hands across the counter. Whereupon Mr Cooper says that he has further decided to move his account once again back to the Midland Bank, of which he has always, until

188

their regrettable falling out, been a customer.

'Oh Guthrie!' exclaims our mother, on being told of this astonishing conversation, 'I am so glad the two of you have made it up. And what splendid news that Mr Cooper has offered to sell you his car.'

Her response is impulsive, uttered before having paused a moment for reflection; but our father turns on her savagely.

'How can you be such a fool, Janet, when you know—you *know* we don't have the money. For God's sake, where are your brains, woman? I couldn't tell him—could I?—the snivelling little pipsqueak, that we don't have money enough to pay for the groceries even—'

'Oh Guthrie, we do—oh hush!—the children—' She is in tears.

'—let alone to buy his rotten car.' He is ranting, raving. 'Splendid news! Is that what you think? A week to consider it! A week!'

He has shouted—is shouting—at Mummy; has called her a fool—a dreadful swear word, as bad, or worse than *damn*. We are shocked, ashamed, horrified. Lucy must have heard as well. She appears from the kitchen and hurries us off up the stairs to bed.

Subsequent discussion concerning Mr Cooper's proposal to our father is conducted more guardedly, and out of our earshot. Consequently we remain ignorant of exactly how it happens that our father, who so frequently within the sacred confines of the family (not, of course, ever beyond them) bemoans the hardship of being penniless— how does he come to be the possessor, as he now is, of the familiar shabby old putty-coloured Ford with the removable side-windows made of talc which we were accustomed, when it started to rain, and after the canvas roof had been raised and extended to its full length and fastened down with butterfly screws, to slot into place?

How indeed has it come about? We children are naturally not informed of the secrets of the transaction, but from the scraps of private talk we manage to pick up and to piece together, we draw the conclusion that it must be Mr Knight, owner of the Beachcroft Hotel, who has wrought the miracle.

Mr Knight admires our father for being a hero of the Great War, and has often expressed this admiration in the warmest of terms. We know he has, having heard our father repeat his gratifying remarks to Mummy at home. Although Mr Knight, as an older man, was himself denied by age the opportunity to fight for his country, he has declared on a number of occasions that in his opinion the Government has been woefully deficient in adequately rewarding our brave serving officers. And to redress in some small measure the balance, he has lately presented Daddy with a subscription to the Golf Club, and an expensive set of golf clubs.

Our father, while thanking him, admits to not being a golfer: his game is tennis. Mr Knight says that in that case he will pay for Daddy to have lessons from the Club's professional. Golf, he breezily states—and probably without wholly comprehending how this will be sure to clinch the argument—golf is a magnificent game for gentlemen to take up. Every gentleman should play golf. The Prince of Wales plays it.

There is, though, a further snag. The golf links are a considerable distance away from the Midland Bank, overlooking Fistral Bay, and our father, at the end of a long exhausting day's work as the one and only cashier in the Bank, would be unable to drive up to the links for a recuperative round of golf. And why is that? Because he has no car.

We think that Mr Knight must have arranged for the solution to this problem also.

But our father's profound relief at the change in his fortunes is none the less tinged with uneasiness. He finds it hard to accept with uncritical gratitude these tributes from his new patron. On the one hand there is the pleasure of being treated by Mr Knight as a holder of the DSO *ought* to be treated—and it *is* very pleasant: not many people seem to realise that such is his due. Mr Oxley, for example, his Manager, skulking nervously behind a door forever shut, has never accorded him the respect he deserves. On the other hand he chafes at and is suspicious of Mr Knight's benevolence.

'What's he getting out of it, I wonder? What's he up to? Clearing his conscience, I daresay.'

'Oh, Guth—no! He just wants to be helpful, and to show how greatly he honours you for what you did in the War—for your gallantry.' Daddy is mollified; but then she spoils it: 'He's a very kind-hearted man, Mr Knight.'

'Well, it doesn't cost him much, his kindness—does it? He's not going to miss a few quid—the old chap's got bags of money,' says our father, who is in a unique position to know precisely how many bags of money Mr Knight has. 'Probably made it out of selling tanks and guns—that's how these Jews got rich in the War.'

191

'Why do you say that, Guthrie?' Mummy protests. 'Mr Knight isn't a Jew.'

'How do you know he isn't? You can't tell with these Jew-boys. They change their names.'

But whatever nagging doubts our father may have in regard to his benefactor's motives, he stifles them, for the doubts are plainly outweighed by the ineffable value of the favours received. These favours are, quite simply, priceless. On being elected a member of the exclusive Golf Club (his membership, sponsored by Mr Knight, is carried through without a hitch), he not only enters a social circle that was closed to him before, but under the protection of his champion he enters it on an equal footing as an officer—or an ex-officer—and a gentleman, rather than as an insignificant and inferior bank clerk. Indeed, had he been rated merely as the latter lowly creature, our father never would have gained admittance to membership of the Newquay Golf Club or even been allowed to set foot across its discriminating threshold.

And for him to be able to seat himself behind the steering wheel of a car again—a car, not partially, but fully owned by himself—is a blessing, a glory, Daddy revels in. On Saturday afternoons he motors up, alone, enjoying a bachelor freedom, to the windy sea-bordered golf links and plays an exhilarating round; preferring, after the first couple of lessons, to dispense with instruction, which he has decided is superfluous. Daddy believes he was born with a natural gift for golf; and perhaps he was.

On Sundays he packs his family into the Ford, and we set off once more on countryside jaunts, or explorations of the coastlines, north and south. Now, instead of weekend outings fraught with nail-biting anxieties, we can sally forth in a mood of hopeful expectation under the auspices of a father whose gloomy spirits have soared and whose temper has amazingly improved. Thus are we all the beneficiaries of Mr Knight's generosity.

It is too early still in the year for bathing, so when Holywell Bay is our chosen destination, being spared the wearisome necessity of trekking a mile across the beach to far-off rocky pools, we picnic amongst the nearer sand dunes. On the way home our father will stop the car for Mummy to climb out and gather armfuls of tall foxgloves from the hedgerows with which to beautify the sitting-room fireplace, camouflaging its empty grate where, since the advent of spring, a fire no longer burns.

And while Mummy is picking flowers at the roadside, more likely than not along will come the friendly A.A. man on his motor-bike with the buttercup yellow sidecar attached to it. Finding the Ford stationary, he too stops, and engages our father in a conversation agreeable to both of them. We meet him quite often on this run, and Daddy is actually persuaded to fork out the fee required to join the club of the Automobile Association.

It may very well be that Daddy is not so much ensuring assistance in the event of a breakdown as buying himself the salutes of the nice A.A. patrol man. This particular A.A. man is the only person left in the world who never fails to salute our father smartly, and address him as *Captain*. Daddy sometimes does get letters with *Captain G. Hallsmith, DSO*, typewritten on the buff-coloured envelopes. He doesn't throw these envelopes away. He keeps them, clipped together, inside a drawer of his rolltop desk.

*   *   *

Pam's neck isn't getting better. Throughout the winter and into the spring it's been getting worse and worse. The surgeon who operated on her before couldn't have taken enough of the TB glands out, and her neck on that side has been swelling up again, bigger than ever, and it hurts her. So Mummy and Pam are going to go by train to London for another visit to the specialist in Harley Street to find out what has to be done.

We shan't have anyone coming to look after us while they are away because Mummy says she doesn't know how long they'll be gone: perhaps it's only for a few days, three or four. And Daddy says we can manage perfectly well on our own without any interfering busybody being brought into the house to boss us around, thank you. And Lucy says: 'It'll be all right, Mum. I can see to Jim and Elspeth, and to Mr Hallsmith. I know how you like things done.' And so our mother cooks an oxtail stew to be eaten hot for one dinner, and a ham to be eaten cold for the next; and in a flurry of haste, off they go.

Pam's doll, Rosie, has gone as well. She's not a secret any more. Daddy's been told of her presence, and perhaps because my sister is really ill, or because of the tactful way our mother told him, he hasn't made a fuss or said anything about dolls having nasty cold faces. He hasn't mentioned Rosie at all, in fact.

194

Mummy and Pam are staying with old Mrs Bazin in a part of London that's called Finchley. Mrs Bazin is rich. I think she's as rich as Cousin Edith, and much nicer. She's very fond of our mother. Every July she sends Mummy a pair of gloves for her birthday present; the sort of gloves that Mummy couldn't afford to buy for herself. The reason why Mrs Bazin is so fond of our mother, and gives her gloves, is because Mummy *was* going to marry her son, Geoffrey Bazin, but unfortunately he was killed in the Great War at the start of the week when he should have returned on leave from the trenches in France to England, and married her. It was a very near thing, when you come to think of it, and the third time she would have been married if the person hadn't happened to have been killed, or died.

First, there was Basil McNeile, who died in Switzerland of tuberculosis. Then there was Will Lawrence, a pilot in the Royal Flying Corps: shot down and killed. Then there was Geoffrey Bazin, killed while fighting with the British Army. And so, in 1919, quite soon after the Great War ended, she married our father, who hadn't been killed, or died, or even been wounded. He was twenty-four and she was thirty-two. Basil McNeile's tuberculosis was a bit of bad luck, I know, and can't be blamed on the Great War; but that War, it seems to me, has a lot to answer for.

The news from London is disturbing. Mr Twistleton-Higgins, the Harley Street specialist, has said that Pam must be operated on immediately, and by the time our father gets Mummy's letter telling him this, my sister will already be in hospital, preparing for her operation tomorrow. So they'll be gone for more than just a few days; they'll be away for three weeks at least, which sounds almost as long as for ever. Daddy says this is an emergency, and it's important that we sit tight, and pull together, and that we don't rock the boat. He appears to be taking it in his stride, whistling and swinging his stick as he sets off for work. An emergency, we therefore decide, is a sort of adventure.

Lucy writes a letter to our mother. She doesn't have to rule the lines to keep straight, as we do. Her sheet of paper is from a pad, the pages of which are already conveniently lined. Jim and I are impressed by how neat and how small her writing is. It's much neater and smaller than ours. We had no idea that Lucy is so good at writing. After she's finished her letter she shows it to us:

Dear Mrs Hallsmith, Madam, she has written. (When she talks to Mummy, she calls her *Mum*; but in the letter she writes *Madam*). *This is to put your mind at rest, Madam. You don't have no need to worry yourself about us we are all doing fine here. Jim and Elspeth say their prayers regular I see to that and are eating well. The stew was enough for two dinners and still plenty of ham left it was a big one. God bless you Madam our thoughts are with you and Pam and hoping all goes well and you both back soon. Yours faithfully*
Lucy Emma Coles.

'You never told me you've got another name,' I say to her, astounded. 'Are you really called Emma, besides Lucy?'

'Why, certainly I am,' she retorts, with some spirit. 'I don't have to tell you everything—do I?— Little Miss Know-It-All!'

She allows us each to enclose a note in the envelope with her letter, sending love and kisses to Mummy and Pam, and promising to write to them properly tomorrow.

At the beginning, when our mother and our sister—nearly half the family—are somewhere else, the house feels peculiar. I'm not used to being without Pam. Of course they were away that other time, for the first operation, but I was younger then. It's different now. Everything's different. Some of the difference I like. For instance, I don't have to go to lessons with Mrs Oliver while Pam's away, which means I spend all morning in the kitchen with Lucy. I make up sums to pretend I'm at a real school, and I practise writing, and reading aloud, and telling stories to Lucy, who is a good listener.

On Saturday I have a very special treat. I'm allowed to go with my brother Jim for a picnic in Fistral Bay with his friends, Bradford Johns and Oliver Jenkins and Peter Mitchell. The arrangement has been made by Mrs Mitchell, and our father says that if Dr Mitchell has given permission for the boys to go picnicking on their own without a grown-up, then that's good enough for him. And when I ask Daddy if I can go too, he agrees; which is a great surprise—I thought he was sure to say no. He tells my brother Jim it's his responsibility to look after me and see that I come to no harm. Usually it's Pam who looks after me; it's never been Jim before.

Lucy makes up two packages, one for Jim and

one for me: sandwiches and hard-boiled eggs and a Fyffes banana each, plus two medicine bottles, thoroughly rinsed and then filled with lemonade and firmly corked. I can tell by the way she screws the corks in, as if she were screwing her mouth shut, that she thinks I ought not to be allowed to go off with the boys when there is no grown-up in charge. Mummy, she knows, would never let me go; but my father has said that I may, and she dare not speak out against Mr Hallsmith. She doesn't like it a bit, though. I, on the contrary, like it very much indeed. I think it's absolutely thrilling to set off on a picnic with a bunch of boys, and no grown-up. It hasn't ever happened before, and almost certainly it won't ever happen again.

We walk up Mount Wise on either side of a silently disapproving Lucy to the Mitchells' house, where she leaves us. Bradford Johns and Oliver Jenkins are already there, as well as Paul Hewish, whose father is the manager of Barclay's Bank, and we all cram into the Mitchells' big black saloon car, and Mrs Mitchell, sitting dwarfed behind the wheel, drives us up to Fistral Bay. Out we scramble, and off she goes. Peter is the possessor of a wristwatch, and our instructions are to be back at the same place by precisely half-past three, when she will pick us up and drive us home.

Why Paul Hewish has joined our expedition today I don't know. Nor do I know why he is so unpopular. Nobody likes Paul Hewish. He isn't a regular member of the gang, any more than I am. The other boys, whenever they assemble on a Saturday, do so by custom in the extensive grounds belonging to Oliver Jenkins' parents. The Fistral Bay picnic is Mrs Mitchell's notion of varying this custom.

Mrs Mitchell is lively and small (I have heard someone describe her as *petite*, which is a French word, meaning small), and very pretty. Her husband, Dr Mitchell, twice her size, wears horn-rimmed spectacles and has a baggy, sagging face, heavily creased. He is the ugliest man I have ever seen, but nice. Their only child, Peter, is small, like his mother and, also like his mother, good-humoured and jokey.

Even if it wasn't too early in the season for bathing, which it is, we wouldn't be allowed to bathe here: it's far too dangerous in Fistral Bay, which is famous for its invisible currents and strong undertow and its enormous crashing waves. We've been forbidden to paddle, or to go anywhere near the sea. We take our shoes and socks off and play hide and seek, bare-footed, amongst the sand dunes. And presently, as nobody talks to Paul Hewish, he wanders away, awkward and stiff, by himself; but I am not made to feel unwanted or a nuisance. Jim and Bradford Johns are very kind and attentive to me, and pull me down the dry soft silvery slopes of sand again and again, using my coat, which I've removed, as a sort of toboggan. The sun shines, and the sky's blue, and the wind is blowing, and the larks are singing, high up above, and it's the best and most enjoyable picnic I have ever had in my life.

We don't see much of our father during this period when Mummy and Pam are in London. Where he has his lunch, I've no idea: he doesn't come back to Bay View Terrace for it. In the evenings, when the Bank has closed, he does return, but only for a quick snack, which he eats alone, and then immediately drives off to the Golf Club and doesn't get home until after we are both in bed and asleep. Lucy lays out a cold supper ready for Daddy in the dining room. Then she goes to bed as well. She doesn't wait up for him.

Jim and I have our high tea, which is a mixture of tea and supper, with Lucy in the kitchen. We spend most of our spare time now in the kitchen with her. Jim does his homework here. He lets me sit beside him while he's doing it, and sometimes I can even be a help. His favourite subject, and his best, is geography. It's his favourite and his best because our Uncle Malcolm, the older of Daddy's two half-brothers, who are both doctors, gave Jim, some years ago, a stamp album and an envelope full of foreign stamps and an atlas, and now Jim knows where heaps of places are in the world: Rome and Singapore and the Suez Canal and the Cape of Good Hope. I like to ask him, and he likes to show me, where they are. Most evenings, when Jim has finished his homework, and we've had our high tea, we play games on the kitchen table with Lucy. We play Snap and Old Maid, and Ludo and Snakes and Ladders, and just before going upstairs to bed, last thing, we have a cup of cocoa each. I miss Pam, and I miss Mummy too, but I have to say that these hours we spend, my brother and me, with Lucy Coles in the kitchen are times we enjoy and look forward to. It's very peaceful, and cosy. There are no rows. No one is cross with anyone. Nobody shouts; no one is made to cry.

Lucy never goes shopping in the town. I don't know why she doesn't, but she doesn't. In the morning our father gives her some money, and she writes a list of what we need to buy, and then I go with her to the shop in the road at the back of Bay View Terrace which is so conveniently close to where we live. Here we can buy most of our provisions—what are called *dry goods*: that is to say, sultanas and sugar and flour—plain and self-raising—and pats of butter and loaves of bread and slices of bacon and bottles of tomato ketchup, and squares of yellow cheese cut from a bigger block with a wire, and little pots of anchovy paste, and tins of cocoa and tins of golden syrup; and candles and porridge oats and boxes of matches. These are the sort of provisions we are able to buy in Mrs Clements' General Grocery Stores. It isn't a big shop. It's long and it's narrow, and most interestingly crowded, with a delicious smell that makes my nose tingle.

Lucy writes down how much every item costs while we are still in the shop, and then at home she writes out the list again, carefully, on to another piece of paper, and hands it over to Daddy that evening, together with any loose change there may be.

He praises her for the exact account she keeps of our shopping. 'Well done, Lucy,' he says, reading the list and nodding as he reads it; checking her figures. 'No mistakes—well done!' And Lucy ducks her head, smiling, proud that Mr Hallsmith, her master, is pleased with her. She likes to please our father.

He doesn't say *well done* to Jim when inspecting the sums that my brother brings home from school and has to wrestle with in hateful arithmetic exercises. But then Jim, who can locate Calcutta or the Straits of Gibraltar instantly on a global map, all too often fails to get his homework sums right;

in particular he gets wrong those sums involving a decimal point. Our father will fly into a rage of contempt at Jim's total inability to grasp the simplest rules of addition and subtraction, as manifested by his incorrectly positioned and miserably muddled up decimal points. Daddy's rages are terrible.

During our mother's absence, fresh vegetables, at first, are a problem for us. To start with, we eat a great many potatoes: boiled or baked or mashed or roasted. There are strings of onions hanging up in Mrs Clements's shop, and she also sells potatoes from a barrel standing on the floor in front of the counter, but no other vegetables. Then one evening Lucy's brother Dick arrives at the back door with a whole sackful of Brussels sprouts and cabbages, as well as a cauliflower and some carrots and a bunch of beetroots.

'That's very good of your brother,' says our father, but sounding rather huffy. Why is he huffy? I don't understand why. This is a puzzle I shall have to consider. 'He must be paid, of course—well, of course he must. How much? Did he say how much?'

'Oh no—there's nothing to pay, Mr Hallsmith, sir. It's all veg out of Dad's garden. He sent it along to help us—with the meals, and that—knowing as how Mrs Hallsmith is away from home, like, and poor little Pam ill, in hospital—' Lucy, embarrassed by the realisation of having somehow committed a blunder, lapses into her original rough Cornish accent. Normally she doesn't speak as the rest of her family do. I've often noticed the way she tries to imitate our mother's voice, and even to copy, or try to copy, the way Mummy

202

laughs.

'Of course I shall pay your brother, Lucy—for all the stuff—all these—these vegetables he's lugged up here,' insists our father, frowning. He appears, instead of feeling grateful to old Mr Coles, to be increasingly irritated. Generosity from the lower orders, quite simply, isn't acceptable. It turns everything back to front and wrong way round, and might even be construed as an insult. But eventually, when money has been forcibly paid—I don't know how much money—Mr Coles and Lucy's brother Dick are forgiven. Next day we have cabbage for lunch, and I find a snail from Mr Coles's garden, cooked, in my plateful of greens.

Daddy brings us the supplies we need, at intervals, from the butcher in town—a leg of mutton, say, or a dozen sausages—and from the fishmonger, a piece of cod or some finny haddock. One evening he arrives back with a dead cock pheasant which a wealthy land-owning customer has given him. This gift of a pheasant is, it seems, perfectly acceptable—flattering, indeed—having nothing in common with Brussels sprouts from Mr Coles's vegetable garden. While Lucy is busy plucking the bird's beautiful feathers, and pulling out its bloody insides, I sit at the bottom of the staircase, until the job has been done and it has ceased to resemble a bird.

Every morning the postman delivers a letter from Mummy, conveying her latest news with regard to the invalid. Pam's operation is over, successfully. She's not very well. She's very weak, and has a cough. She's better. She's sitting up in bed. And finally she's out of bed, and on her feet, and able to travel; and they are coming home.

'I want to meet them off the train, Lucy,' I say, hopping with excitement.

'Well, you can't,' she replies. 'You're too young to go down to the station on your own, Elspeth, and it wouldn't be right for me to leave the house empty.'

There is no one this afternoon to take me to the station. Jim is at school, and my father at work in the Bank. 'Please, Lucy!' I beg her to let me go. I argue with her. It isn't far, I say. I don't have to cross a road. Daddy allowed me to go on that picnic without a grown-up. 'I do so want to be there to meet them, Lucy—please! *Please!*'

But Lucy is adamant. 'I've said *no*, Elspeth—no!—and that's that. You're to stop here and wait at home with your Lucy, as you've been told, like a good little girl.'

I look at the kitchen clock, and the train is due in. I think I hear a whistle. Just for once, I, who am always obedient, will *not* be a good little girl and stop here at home with my Lucy. I run out of the kitchen, and out of the house, as fast as my legs can carry me, down Bury Road, past the privet hedges, the hydrangea bushes, the shop on the corner that has a scarlet pillar box outside it; on and on, past the entrance to Dr Barnardo's Home for Boys; past the line of expectant jingles with their glossy long-tailed ponies patiently waiting by the stone water-trough; past the towering Victoria Cinema hoarding advertising its current film, *Bitter-Sweet*; swerving in across the Great Western Railway Station forecourt: I've done it!

The train has already arrived: there is a plume of smoke puffing up above the station roof. And emerging from the station entrance, surrounded by a straggle of other passengers, are my mother and my sister—actually Mummy and Pam! Behind them comes a porter, laden with their luggage. Pam is holding Rosie, tight against her chest. But what I notice, more surprisingly, is that my sister has grown pigtails. Two short, thick pigtails, tied with blue ribbon, stick out above each of her ears. Pigtails! I throw myself at Mummy and hug her hips.

'Why, Elspeth!' exclaims my mother. 'What on earth are you doing here, all by yourself? Where's Lucy, for goodness sake?'

I can't explain. I've no breath left. I take her hand. I skip along beside her. And Mummy is so occupied in tipping the porter, and then engaging the driver of a jingle and giving him our address, that she forgets in the flurry to ask any more bothersome questions.

A jingle! We are to ride home in a jingle— something I have never before experienced! What unutterable bliss! There is a single round step protruding at the rear. The jingle driver has gripped one of my mother's gloved hands to steady her balance as she mounts; and then he helps my sister to climb aboard. But before I can put my foot on the step, he catches me under the armpits and lifts me clean in; which is a disappointment: I have yearned for ages to have the chance to place my own foot, as I've watched other people do, on a jingle step, and feel it bounce a little, like a spring, under my weight—a regret, though, unimportant, and quickly forgotten. The drive back to Bay View Terrace is triumphant, a dream come true, perched alongside my sister, with Mummy opposite us, behind a smart little trit-trotting pony. I want it never to end.

And here is Lucy, standing, distraught, at the gate of No. 9 Bay View Terrace, strands of her pale thin wispy hair, torn free of the meagre bun that fastens them, blowing untidily over her anxious face. I'd worried her sick, she says, running off out of the house like that. She hadn't known what to do for the best: whether to follow after me, leaving the house for burglars to ravage, or to stay.

'Never mind, Lucy,' says Mummy, consolingly. 'I shan't mention a word of it to Mr Hallsmith, now that we're all home again, safe and sound. And oh!—what a long *long* time we've been away.' She doesn't scold me. And if she had done it would still have been worth it for the ride in the jingle.

Pam is undressed and put to bed at once, even though it's a sunshiny afternoon, and hours before our proper bedtime. The journey has exhausted her. For the next few weeks she will have to rest every afternoon, says Mummy, and not get overtired. I'm allowed to stay with my sister, sitting on a chair that's drawn up close to her pillow by her bed. The new scar on her neck looks like a miniature pink banana: not nearly as big as a Fyffes banana, but the same shape. You can see the prick-marks where the stitches had been. But what makes her so different, almost like a stranger, is not the new scar, but the new pigtails. When Pam's hair has grown longer it will hide the banana scar. I wish I could have pigtails. But I don't have a scar on my neck that needs to be hidden.

*   *   *

It's the summer again, and Mrs Oliver, our teacher—or governess, as she prefers to be called—has acquired a new pupil. So now there are three of us children boxed in together every morning; and our mornings, as a consequence, have become a great deal brighter, and much less boring.

Ada Møeller is the niece of Mrs Miller who lives halfway down Trenance Hill in a big house entirely concealed from the view of any passers-by on the sunken roadway that skirts its high surrounding walls. Growing at the very edge of these walls, the tops of which are several yards above the level of the road beneath, an almost impenetrable barrier of dense bushes and overhanging trees ensures complete protection for Trenance House and its inhabitants from the inquisitive gaze of the general public. But now my sister and I, we two, have been singled out from that unwanted anonymous public, and find ourselves made uniquely welcome. And the magic password allowing us entrance into Ali Baba's cave and its hidden hoard of treasures, isn't *Open Sesame* but *Ada Møeller*.

What is immediately intriguing about Ada is her nationality. She comes from Denmark. We have never encountered a foreigner before. This is the reason why her surname is spelt so funnily, and why it is so hard for us to pronounce it correctly. Her first name has to be pronounced *Adder*, as if she were a snake. Ada Møeller doesn't look like a snake. Far from it. She has a mop of curly golden hair, and very blue eyes, and she wears pinafore dresses, hand-embroidered, and she can speak hardly a word of English. But although she isn't able to say much except 'Oh yes', and 'Oh no', and

'Thank you', which she says all the time, she laughs often, and smiles whenever we happen to glance in her direction, and everything pleases her.

Probably because we don't go to a real school, Pam and I have very few friends; practically none, in fact, apart from the summer season holiday visitors. So it's an exciting surprise to be suddenly presented with this nice new friendly companion. And if everything seems to please Ada, everything about her pleases *us*. She has extremely good manners and is very polite, especially to grownups. Whenever a grown-up person comes into the room, Ada stands up and curtsies. English girls don't curtsey—not unless they are being introduced to the King or the Queen. But we like to see Ada do it: a quick little bob. It shows how foreign she is.

Ada Møeller has been sent over to stay with her aunt, Mrs Miller, at short notice, on account of her mother falling ill and having to go into hospital. As soon as her mother gets better, Ada will go home again, back to Denmark. Her aunt is also Danish, only she altered her name to an English version of it when she came to live in this country. It's easier for people like us to pronounce *Miller* than *Møeller*; which is why, we suppose, she decided to change it.

Before Ada joins us for lessons with Mrs Oliver, we overhear our father talking to Mummy about Mrs Miller, and what she said to him that afternoon in a private conversation: nothing to do with money. Mrs Miller seldom, apparently, sets foot herself inside the Midland Bank, choosing to transact her business instead either by post or by telephone. She is nonetheless one of the Bank's

208

most valued customers. Valued means that she is rich. On this occasion, however, she did visit the Bank *in person* to ask our father if, as a favour, he would allow her niece to be included in the private tuition arranged—according to her information—by Mr Hallsmith for the instruction of his two little daughters, who are, she understands, about the same age as her little Ada.

Their conversation took place when there were no other customers in the Bank. We imagine Mrs Miller leaning towards our father across the huge expanse of the counter, and discreetly, sweetly, murmuring her confidences to him. Daddy, in repeating them to our mother, is at pains to emphasise that Mrs Miller has approached him as a supplicant seeking a *favour*; which, in the circumstances, is appropriate, but gratifying all the same. What circumstances? We stretch our ears.

Mrs Miller is believed to be a widow. Presumably to lessen the loneliness of widowhood—for as she is wealthy already there can surely be no need to supplement her income—Mrs Miller shares her large mansion, and what would otherwise be a sadly solitary existence, with a pair of elderly gentlemen, described as her Paying Guests, or PGs for short: a term our stretched ears have never heard of before.

The tentative—but gratifying—request made by Mrs Miller is discussed by our parents throughout the evening in lowered voices. Why are their voices lowered? Our mother has never met Mrs Miller, who doesn't care to mingle in Newquay society, but lives very quietly, secluded from the outside world, with only Dr Hankin and Mr Rainsforth, her two elderly lodgers, for company.

'Nobody we know has ever met her, Guth—except for Mrs Mitchell—and she told me—' Whisper, whisper: we can't be sure of what Mrs Mitchell told our mother, but we catch the words *beautiful* and also *charming*. 'Is she, Guthrie?'

Our father finds it a difficult question to answer. When Mrs Miller was younger she might have been—he daresays she would have been—considered a beauty: yes! And he further admits that in his opinion she would be a good subject for a portrait; he would be glad—yes, he would—of the chance to paint her. What age is she? Daddy can't be certain: neither young nor old, but somewhere in between. As for charming, he would agree that she does have a superficial charm of manner. And in any case, whatever the rights or the wrongs of it may be, Mrs Miller is a valuable customer, and he doesn't want to risk offending her.

'Besides, Guth,' says our mother, forgetting to keep her voice low, 'the poor child isn't to blame for—you know; it isn't her fault if—well, anything—'

And this is how it comes about that Ada Møeller is one day driven up in a big black old-fashioned high-off-the-ground vehicle like a hearse, and delivered to Mrs Oliver's front door; and how my sister and I, by gaining a new fellow-pupil, gain a whole new dimension to our lives, indescribably thrilling in its novelty.

*　　　*　　　*

Our first invitation to tea with Ada Møeller has

developed into a regular Thursday afternoon custom. Thursday is early-closing day for the shops in Newquay, and it is also half-day for the entire staff of Trenance House. In the absence of servants to minister to their needs, Mrs Miller and her two bachelor PGs find it convenient to remove themselves likewise, and to pass those hours between lunch and their evening dinner, when they would be unattended at home, elsewhere. In order to avoid having either to take Ada along as well, or to leave Ada behind in the big empty house alone—alternatives equally undesirable—Pam and I are invited to spend the whole afternoon at Trenance House, thereby solving Mrs Miller's recurring weekly problem of what to do with her niece on Thursdays. And as for us, we are only too blissfully happy to be the means of solving her problem.

No form of entertainment is provided for us; nor do we wish for any amusement other than the ineffable pleasure of being free to wander, unsupervised wherever the fancy takes us in the sloping sunny gardens belonging to Ada Møeller's beautiful Aunt Astrid. For although our father may have hesitated in describing her thus, Pam and I have no such doubts: Mrs Miller, whether young or old or in between, is *beautiful*! We are in love with her, and with her clothes, and her scent, and the roses in her garden, and the alabaster ornaments in her house—with very nearly everything to do with her. Everything connected with the dreamy atmosphere of this enchanted kingdom, unlocked especially for us, into which we have been beckoned by Mrs Miller, the Fairy Queen herself, is beautiful; excepting for Dr Hankin and

Mr Rainsforth, her two lodgers, who are, undeniably, the very reverse of beautiful. But we glimpse them only briefly, when they are setting forth on their Thursday outings and sometimes, not always, when they return.

Trenance House is close enough, and Pam is thought to be old enough now, for us to cover the short distance from Bay View Terrace unescorted. Hand in hand, we run down the steep hill to the bend in the road. Here, tucked unobtrusively into the leafy corner where stone hedge ends and brick wall begins, is the small scarcely noticeable wicket gate intended, as we really know, for the use of tradespeople. But ever since the start of summer we think of it as being ours, put there on purpose for us—our own private entrance. We could not have invented a more romantic approach than this for all that lies beyond. Our little gate, pushed open, lets us into a narrow sunless tunnel of clipped evergreens, which leads directly to the kitchen quarters at the back of Trenance House— on Thursday afternoons, a deserted area.

Round at the front of the house, parked on the gravel, ready to leave, is the big black saloon car, with Dr Hankin waiting impatiently beside it, watch in hand. To our relief—for we are somewhat in awe of Dr Hankin—he ignores us. A tall, bulky, bumbling bear of a man who smokes a cigarette as he walks to and fro in a quick fussy shuffle, he wears half-moon pince-nez spectacles, and a grey hat the shape of a trilby—but hard, instead of being soft like Daddy's—and a watch-chain looped across his beige buttoned-up waistcoat. On Thursdays he takes the wheel of what is, we have learned, *his* Daimler car. The Daimler may be old-fashioned, but then so is Dr Hankin. It has beige velvet corduroy upholstery, the same shade as Dr Hankin's waistcoat, and silver vases, like ice-cream cones, for nosegays of real flowers, and a speaking-tube, so that anyone sitting on a back seat can communicate with the driver through the glass partition.

Each morning, however, Ada is delivered to Mrs Oliver's door, not by Dr Hankin, but by Trethewy, the gardener (a relation of Trethewy, the fishmonger) doubling as chauffeur in a cap with a peak and a bottle-green jacket and leather gaiters. Dr Hankin is too busy writing in his study every day to conduct Ada to her lessons. What he is writing about—what keeps Dr Hankin so very busy, shut into his room all day, every day—Ada either doesn't know, or hasn't yet acquired enough words in English to explain.

Here she comes—Ada—running out, smiling, to greet us, followed by Mr Rainsforth, a little grinning wizened old man, as different as can be from his friend, the doctor. We think he resembles a monkey—an amiable monkey. Mr Rainsforth doesn't ignore us. He pats my head. 'Hullo, hullo—' And then, with remarkable agility in spite of his age, he clambers up on to a back seat of the Daimler.

Dr Hankin goes inside the house. We hear him shouting. 'Astrid!—Astrid!—what *are* you doing? It's three o'clock!'

And finally Mrs Miller appears in a floating cloud of pale-blue and pale-pink chiffon scarves—her favourite sweet-pea colours—pulling on her gloves while managing somehow, simultaneously, to hold on to a parasol, an embroidered handbag

213

and a straw wide-brimmed hat. Unhurried, she stoops to embrace us, first Pam, and then me. We are enveloped in the delicious aura of her scent. She kisses our cheeks. Close-up we observe that she has lipstick on her mouth. Scarlet lipstick is a sign, we know, of being *fast*, but very pale pink lipstick is quite all right, we are sure. Mrs Miller is almost as tall as Dr Hankin. Her eyes are large and blue, and her curly hair, a faded greyish blonde, must once have been as golden as her niece Ada's.

'Dear children—I am so pleased you are here,' she says to us. She always says it, every Thursday, and she always sounds as if she really is pleased. 'You will have a nice time together—yes?' Another kiss.

'Astrid!'

She settles herself on the passenger seat in front, and they are off. We watch the Daimler slowly, slowly descend the wide curving sweep of the drive, down, down to the main gates at the bottom, which Trethewy has opened in readiness this morning, and away: they've gone! Our task is to chase across the lawn after them, to close the gates. They close with a satisfying clang. It is the equivalent, we feel, of raising the drawbridge of our castle which, now that we are truly alone, belongs entirely to us three: Pam and me and Ada.

How do we pass those empty sunshiny hours ahead of us? They simply evaporate. We don't do anything very much. We explore, lazily, over and over again, every nook and cranny of our domain, becoming familiar with the wild and the cultivated parts of it: the area of woodland; the moist and mossy, squashy patch that suggests a hidden spring, or even, perhaps, a subterranean stream. We find the place where Trethewy dumps his grass-cuttings; where he grows vegetables; his hothouse, his tool shed.

Most remarkable to us, though—to Pam and me—is the silence, the huge living silence of flowers, trees, bushes, grass, broken only by musical bursts of birdsong, or the drowsy incessant cooing of pigeons. We are not used to a garden at all, and we are certainly not used to being alone in the silence of one. The noises that usually fill our ears are the splash or the roaring of waves, the screech of seagulls. For as long as we can remember the Great Western Beach has been our summer playground, and our days on it are ruled by the ceaseless restlessness of the ever-changing tides. Here there is utter peace, a timeless tranquillity that must be what is meant by Heaven.

We lie on our stomachs, and the tiny movements of insects journeying close to our noses through the grassy blades absorb our attention; or, when we lie on our backs, the shifting of leaves against the blue sky above our heads; or the sudden alighting and equally sudden taking-off of butterflies, and their erratic flight. We sit, cross-legged, on Ada's tartan travelling rug, making daisy chains, until she jumps up, daisy-crowned, announcing:

'And now we shall be having tea—yes?'

In the conservatory, amongst the potted palms and ferns, we find the feast prepared in advance for us children, laid out on a rattan table under protective muslin: cucumber sandwiches wrapped in a damp linen napkin, plates of shortbread biscuits and sponge cake, Danish pastries, bowls of fruit, a jug of raspberry cordial. We can decide to have our lavish tea in the cool of the conservatory, or we can transport a selection of it carefully outside on trays to eat on the lawn, in the sunshine, sitting on the tartan rug. When the clock in the marble-floored hall strikes half-past five, Pam and I bid a polite farewell to Ada, and thank her for our Thursday visit, matching her good manners with a practice demonstration of our own. Usually by then the Daimler can be heard crunching slowly back up the drive.

* * *

Does the sun always shine on Thursday afternoons? Not always: once it pours with rain—a summer thunderstorm. Are there always just the three of us, Pam and me and Ada? No—there is a day when our brother Jim, who for some reason hasn't gone to school this Thursday, comes with us: a dark day, best forgotten, were it only possible to forget it.

Jim has never, until now, been to Trenance House. We are taking him on a guided tour of *our* garden—*our* personal paradise—when we stumble across the body of a blackbird lying on the ground, its claws in the air, lifeless and stiff: dead. The discovery shocks us. Blackbirds are meant to flit and swoop from tree to tree, entrancing us with their silvery trills and ripples of song, not to lie dead on the ground. We cluster about it, staring, fascinated, repelled: so this is death—it's horrible. But worse, much worse, is to follow.

We have pushed our way through the close barrier of bushes to the top of the high wall. Pam is cradling the corpse of the blackbird. We plan to give it a ceremonial funeral, so as to make ourselves feel better about its death. But when we peep down from the top of the wall into the road below we are transfixed by the sight of a roughly dressed man who is gazing up at us children, and wagging his head like an idiot. He is wagging something else as well as his head. His trousers are undone, gaping open in front, which is wrong—it is dreadfully *wrong*. We huddle together, horrorstruck; then turn and thrust our way back through the scratchy bushes in a panic, fleeing from what is not understood, is frightening, beastly. We will not speak of it to one another, then or later, or to anyone else, ever. We avoid looking at each other, ashamed to acknowledge what we have shared. The blackbird's funeral, which we hurriedly organise and occupy ourselves with, doesn't succeed in obliterating, as we had hoped it would, the one blindingly vivid sickening moment indelibly stamped on our mind's eye. We may say nothing, but we can't forget what we were forced to see. We will never go near the top of the wall again.

What happens on the Thursday afternoon of the thunderstorm is more of a misfortune than a calamity, and is not to be compared with the stark awfulness of the man-in-the-road episode. We three, Pam and me and Ada, are playing hide and seek in the garden when a sudden deluge of rain, accompanied by thunder and flashes of lightning, obliges us to scurry for shelter, transferring our game from outside to inside.

We are well aware of the house-rule for Ada's visiting friends: the rooms with doors that are shut are rooms we mustn't go into. Downstairs we are allowed in the hall, and in the cloakroom off the hall, where there is a lavatory and a washbasin, and pegs for coats, and where umbrellas and Mr Rainsforth's galoshes are kept. And on a rainy day, as it is today, we can tiptoe through the drawing room to reach the conservatory, instead of entering it by the French windows from the garden. The kitchens, the dining room, the library and Dr Hankin's study are out of bounds.

Upstairs, we have only ever been into Ada's bedroom and a bathroom. But today Pam twists the handle of the door into Mrs Miller's bedroom—whether by mistake or on an impulse of devilment, I can't be sure. Within lies the territory that is, we know, sacred, inviolable. We ought at once to retreat. I tug at Pam's gingham skirt. She yanks me forward. Curiosity overcoming my timidity, as it does my sister's prudence, we are both drawn, fatally, towards the dressing table, which is draped all round in a fragile pink-and-blue material, and laden with crystal jars and bottles of scent, and silver-backed hairbrushes, and alabaster bowls inlaid with multicoloured marble designs— ravishingly pretty, I think. My sister dabs at her face with a swansdown powder puff. She aims a dab at my face, but I dodge.

Ada is shouting from below: 'One hundred—I come now.'

It is too late for us to find another hiding place. Pam drags me behind the dressing table. We squeeze in together beneath it, and crouch there, concealed by the drapery, breathless with guilty giggles that we try to suppress.

We don't hear the disastrously early return of the Daimler, the gravel crunching, the car doors being slammed. But we do—aghast—hear, faintly, voices in the hall. Trapped—we are trapped! Whatever shall we do? We are paralysed by fear. Pam presses her fingers over my mouth to stifle my whimpering. We can only wait, our hearts thumpety-thumping.

The bedroom door, which we had left ajar, closes softly. Mrs Miller is humming a song as she sits down on the stool at her dressing table. But her foot, in its glacé-kid shoe with the pointed toe and the cut-steel buckle, pokes in under the draperies and touches Pam's knee; and Pam, losing her balance, topples over.

Mrs Miller screams.

We reveal our presence, crawling wretchedly out from behind the dressing table's flimsy curtains. I am crying, and have wet my knickers. Pam is muttering: 'Sorry, sorry, we're very sorry—we were hiding from Ada—sorry, sorry—'

Mrs Miller, who had sprung up when she shrieked, sinks down again on the stool.

'You were playing a game?' We nod. I am hiccupping. 'In *here*?' More nods, more hiccupping. I can't stop crying. The punishment we expect, and undoubtedly deserve, is too apalling to contemplate. Will she send for Dr Hankin to whip us with a strap like the one that hangs on the back of our bathroom door?

Mrs Miller puts an arm round each of us. 'You are very naughty children—you know that?' She is laughing. Laughing? 'I had such a fright—such a terrible fright. I thought a wicked big man was going to murder me. But no—you mustn't cry—no more crying. It's over—see? I am alive!' She kisses us: Pam on one side of her, me on the other. 'Little girls must never cry. They should be smiling.' She wipes the tears off my cheeks with a scented handkerchief, and then gives it to me. 'There, Ellie my darling, blow your nose—keep it, keep it. No more crying—you promise?'

She lifts the lid of an alabaster box and pops a sugared almond into each of our mouths. 'Come— hold out your hands, Pam,' she says; and into my sister's cupped palms, laughing as though at a delightful joke, Mrs Miller tips the whole contents of the box of sweeties.

So of *course* we are in love with Ada's Aunt Astrid. How could we not be? Such kindness is past belief. We would die for her, willingly.

*   *   *

I'm balanced on the cold iron rim of one of our beach hut's enormous wheels—a good place to isolate myself when I want to think without being interrupted. Between me and the next hut—empty just now—is a gulf of deep cool shade. I'm thinking about the holidays: about what has happened, and what is going to happen, or may be going to happen; about what is the same this year as last year, and what isn't the same. Things change; or some things do—not everything.

Our Cousin Mildred Martin has been to stay. She comes every summer. Last year she gave us a blow-up floatable rubber duck, big enough for me and Pam to sit on astride, one behind the other; although we were no sooner on the duck's back than it would roll over and tip us off into the sea— but that was part of the fun. It was the sort of unusual bathing toy you might expect to see on Tolcarne Beach, where the smart hotel visitors

congregate, but never on the Great Western Beach; which is probably why we only had our inflatable duck for a few days before somebody stole it. One night a thief broke into our beach hut by unscrewing the fastenings of the padlock. When we told Cousin Mildred this year what had become of her expensive present to us, we did hope, secretly, that she might give us another blow-up duck, a replacement; but if she had done it would very likely have been stolen too. And anyway, she didn't.

After Cousin Mildred had been and gone we had our Granny Hallsmith to stay with us on her regular summer holiday visit. She brought a number of books with her—books that had belonged, she said, either to our father, or to his brother, Martin, who was killed in the War, or to his younger brother, Harvey, who died in the 'flu

221

epidemic. She had made up her mind that as we three are her only grandchildren, we should have them.

I can remember hearing Granny say to our father on her visit last summer that she was surprised the children weren't being provided with more books to read. She had noticed, she said, how very few books there were in the house. He—Guthrie—and his brothers had always had plenty of books to read when they were boys; and so had his sisters, Dorothy and Rosemary. I could tell how much her remarks were irritating Daddy. He often is irritated by his mother, who is our Granny. We love her, but I don't think Daddy does. Didn't she realise, he replied, crossly, that books cost *money*, and that money didn't grow on trees?

So ever since then the presents we get from Granny Hallsmith have been books. On the Twins' birthday Pam had *Little Women* and Jim had *The Last of the Mohicans*. For Christmas she had *Anne of Green Gables*, and he had a copy of *Moonfleet*; I had *What Katy Did*. And when Granny Hallsmith stepped down off the train this July she asked the porter, in her lovely lilting Scottish accent, if he would be so kind as to load a rather heavy box of books on to his trolley, as well as her suitcase.

The books that she sends to us for birthday and for Christmas presents are brand new, straight from a bookshop, but these books have had other owners before us, and some of them have—obviously—been read and reread, time and time again, by people we don't know, and will never know. *Prisoners of the Sea* is a blood-curdling adventure story, given to Martin by a friend of his, Douglas. Their names are written in ink on the

222

flyleaf, and the date it was given underneath: 1908. The title of another yarn, *The Silver Hoard*, by Harold Bindloss, refers to salmon fishing off the coast of Nova Scotia. Jim has shown me where Nova Scotia is on a map in his atlas. There is also a large red volume, *The Arabian Nights Entertainments*, packed with hair-raising tales of magic flying carpets, of mosques and minarets and Caliphs' palaces, of Djinns and Viziers, and Sinbad the Sailor.

In Granny's box of books is a collection of poems written by Omar Khayyam, which belongs to our father. Mummy, curiously enough, already has a copy of this volume, with her name in it and the date—1916—which is when she must have acquired it, I suppose. You might think that, considering how strongly she disapproves of Omar Khayyam's poetry, she would have thrown the book away, instead of keeping it in a drawer, with a lot of old photographs, for so long. I'm glad she didn't throw it away. But this latest copy belonging to Daddy, and left lying about, provokingly in view, has had the effect of stirring up a positive hornets' nest of argument and recrimination. Mummy declares that in her opinion the poems are not only depressing, they are downright *immoral*.

'Oh, Janet, what idiotic nonsense,' retorts our father, beginning to lose his temper. 'The trouble with you is, you've no ear—no eye—no appreciation of beauty: none. It's magnificent stuff!' And at mealtimes, to annoy her, he recites lines from Omar Khayyam: '*A loaf of bread beneath the bough, a flask of wine, a book of verse—and thou.*' She reproaches him, bitterly. They quarrel; and the quarrelling, as so often, ends in Mummy's

223

tears.

I have read all of Omar Khayyam's poems. A few of them I've learned by heart. *'The moving finger writes . . .'* They are very strange indeed, often incomprehensible, but thrilling, and the illustrations, in luminous colours, of starry moonlit landscapes, are dream-pictures, and—yes!—indescribably beautiful.

Books have entered our lives, and we are swamped by floods of glorious fantasy. Fiction or fact, imagined or real—shall we ever be able to disentangle them again? In the privacy of my perch on the wheel of our beach hut, I ponder this, and various other important questions.

For instance, was it as a result of our father being so nettled by Granny's critical comments that he and Mummy returned one evening several weeks ago from an auction sale with a bookcase stuffed full of books? And was the bookcase, which is quite small, made especially, I wonder, for these books to fit into?—because they, too, are small: pocket-sized. Most of them are part of *Nelson's Classics*, a series of books, all covered in scarlet cloth and looking, on the outside, exactly the same. A uniform edition, is what it's called. *Nelson* is the name of the publisher. And I wonder—is the publisher of these books a relation of Lord Nelson who won the Battle of Trafalgar? He might be. I ask my brother Jim, but Jim says he doesn't know.

The contents of our new auction-sale bookcase, in addition to the books that our Granny Hallsmith is giving us, means that I shall be able to read and read and *read* for years to come. From now on I shall be surrounded by a story—sheltered by it—every minute of my life. I'm not going to try to

224

remember the names of the different authors, except for Charles Dickens. The stories he's written—six or seven of them—aren't published in the series of *Nelson's Classics*, but they are the same size and the same colour, which is no doubt why they have been included in this bookcase.

My parents haven't forbidden me to read the books they've brought home from the auction sale, but it's probably better if I don't ask for their permission. I shall just read them, one after another, from the left-hand corner of the top shelf, down to the right-hand corner of the bottom shelf. There are four shelves, each as wide, or nearly as wide, as my ruler, and I've counted how many of these handy little books there are stacked in them: forty-four altogether. What a treasure lies waiting in store for us! Me and my sister will never have to be bored again.

Pam is reading a book called *The Man from America*. I am reading *Oliver Twist*. I've almost finished it. This afternoon I was sitting on the smooth slope of rock, on the other side of which is *that cave*, when I came to the page telling of Nancy's murder. It was such a dreadful thing to happen—dreadful, dreadful! I could hardly bear to think of it, to see it written on the page. It seemed to be actually happening as I read. But at the same time in my ears I was hearing the cries of seagulls, and the shouts of children playing on the beach, and dogs barking. And when I lifted my eyes they were dazzled by sunshine, by the glitter of the sea, the tide coming in, waves breaking. Nancy wasn't being murdered here, on the Great Western Beach. Everything here was real, and it was all right. And I told myself: the Great Western Beach and me are fact, and poor Nancy and the wickedness of Bill Sykes are fiction. So it is possible, after all, to disentangle them—fact and fiction—and be rescued from nightmare.

*   *   *

It's my birthday, the 21st of August, and I open my presents immediately after breakfast. I open Daddy's present first, before he goes off to work. He has given me a book of poetry that was written on purpose for children, called *A Child's Garden of Verses*. I like having a poetry book of my own, but the poems—the ones I've read so far—seem to me to be a bit babyish, although I shan't say this to Daddy. I like Omar Khayyam's poetry better.

Jim has given me a yo-yo. It's a *de luxe* model, thin and flat, a shiny varnished bottle-green colour, and it runs up and down, up and down, easily, without the string getting into a tangle of knots, as the cheap little knobby one I've had until now does. This summer everyone is yo-yoing. It's a craze. Our father informs us that the Yanks invented it. Yanks are Americans. They say *O.K.* when they mean *Yes*. *O.K.* stands for *All Correct*. Why doesn't anyone tell the Americans that their spelling is wrong? I'm very pleased with my new luxury bottle-green yo-yo. It's nice to look at, and it feels nice as well. I think it probably cost my brother all of the pocket money he's been saving since our mother's birthday in July.

Pam has given me two presents: a bouncy multicoloured india-rubber ball, *and* a flicker-book. You hold the flicker-book, which is only about a couple of inches big, in your left hand, and

226

with the thumb of your other hand you flick-flick-flick the pages over, terrifically fast, and if you do it properly it appears as though Charlie Chaplin is actually moving—as if he's walking along. This is how they make films for the cinema. Millions of snapshots (or if it's a Felix the Cat cartoon it would be drawings) follow one another as quick as lightning. Of course, when it's a film in a cinema there's a machine that whizzes the pictures around, instead of somebody's thumb having to do it.

My present from Lucy is a box of seven cotton handkerchiefs. Each handkerchief has a garland of flowers and the day of the week printed on it. But the present I like best of all is from Mummy. Unfortunately, she isn't here to give it to me herself. She's in Anglesea, Wales, on account of her Uncle Stuart having died. He's been ill for quite a while, and he was old—he must have been very old indeed—so although it's a sad event for Mummy, she was expecting it to happen before the telegram came. As soon as the telegraph boy delivered the telegram, she packed a bag and was off in a hurry to the funeral. The present she left behind for me, wrapped up, with a card saying *Happy Birthday, Elspeth*, is a junior-size—my size—deckchair. I love this new deckchair of mine. It has white-and-orange-and-blue stripey canvas, and is exactly the same as a grown-up's deckchair, only smaller.

Lucy brings home-made pasties down to the beach for our lunch, and in the afternoon we play French cricket with the bouncy ball Pam's given me. Rex and Eve Dyer, who are staying with their grandmother, Mrs Mulroney, join in, and so does Muriel Bennett; and even Lucy agrees to play for a bit, although she refuses to chase after the ball. When Rex and Eve hear that it's my birthday they buy me a Mars Bar from the kiosk, and Muriel Bennett buys me an ice-cream cornet from one of the Stafferi brothers in his prettily painted little jingly-jangly cart. It would be rude of me to tell Muriel that we Hallsmith children aren't allowed to have Stafferi ice-creams, and so I take it, and say 'thank you very much'—and it's absolutely delicious! I've come to the conclusion that it isn't really true about the Stafferi family keeping their stock of ice-cream underneath their beds at night. It's just one of those fibs that grown-ups fabricate as an excuse for putting you off things.

This summer is the first time there's been a kiosk on the beach selling chocolate and sweets and cigarettes. It sells beach balls too, and buckets and spades. We've been told by our parents that we're not to spend our pocket money on buying sweets from this kiosk. We wish we could; but that's not what pocket money is for—and anyway, sweets are bad for our teeth. The sweets we're allowed to have are bought by our father, and doled out to us on Sunday mornings: two sweets each. But I can't say 'No thank you' to Eve and Rex, when they've been so kind. Mars Bars are new in the shops this season. I let Pam and Jim each have a bite of mine. So now we all three know what a Mars Bar tastes like: very very good!

The fact is, you think that things are going to go on being the same as before for ever; but changes are always happening. You can never guess in advance *what* the next change will be. The kiosk, for example, was a complete surprise. One morning, when we arrived on the Great Western

Beach, there it was, planted in the soft sand at the bottom of the slipway, ready to sell Mars Bars and slabs of Cadbury's Milk Chocolate and Capstan cigarettes, and goodness knows what else. It doesn't sell ice-creams, though. I daresay the person in the kiosk is afraid if he did it might upset the Stafferi brothers. And it wouldn't be fair of him to deprive them of their customers: after all, *they* were here first. They've been trit-trotting about with their pony and cart on this beach and on Towan Beach, selling vanilla ice-creams, either cornets or wafers, for as long as I can remember. The kiosk is fitted with wheels, so that when the tide is very high, it can be dragged up the slipway by Jack the Beachman and his horse Queenie, and parked overnight on the road, out of reach of the waves.

Today the tide is very high, crashing and splashing against the wall. With no sand remaining dry for us to sit on, no beach not covered by the furiously incoming sea, we retreat to the road above and sit outside our beach hut—me in my new deckchair—to eat my birthday tea. We invite Eve and Rex Dyer and Muriel Bennett to have a slice of the birthday sponge cake which Lucy baked, and iced, with my name on it, and brought down here in a tin. They tell me to make a wish while I'm blowing out the candles, and I do; but I mustn't say what the wish is.

Things change. But I'm glad something that doesn't ever change is my birthday being always in August, during the summer holidays. August is absolutely the best month in the whole year, *I* think, for anyone to have a birthday.

229

It's a Saturday morning and I'm skipping along beside my mother, going shopping with her, when we are met and stopped by Mrs Have-You-Heard in the steep and narrow pedestrians' lane that is a short cut to the centre of town. We can't avoid her. 'Oh dear!' says Mummy to me, very quietly; and she squeezes my hand to show that we're sharing a joke.

'Mrs Hallsmith! I am so *delighted* to have run into you,' says Mrs Have-You-Heard, blocking our way down. 'I've been hoping for a chance to offer my *sincerest* congratulations. You are an heiress, I'm told—you've inherited a fortune! What simply *wonderful* news for you, and your dear brave husband, and your lovely children!'

'Oh, good gracious me, no!' my mother answers, laughing lightly, as though Mrs Have-You-Heard has made a silly but trivial mistake. She sounds both amused and annoyed. But there is also an undercurrent of jubilation in her voice. 'Not a fortune by any means—what a ridiculous rumour for people to spread around. I'm lucky to have had a little windfall—yes!—from my late uncle's estate—a very small legacy: that's all.'

How quickly a story does get about! The entire population of Newquay seems to have learned of the money our mother has been left by her Uncle Stuart in his will. It's called a bequest. Nobody knows, except for our parents, the precise amount of money he left her, but it is enough to make a great many differences, apparently, to the way we shall live in future.

No wonder I detected a note of excitement in

Mummy's voice—despite her irritation—when we were stuck in the lane with awful Mrs Have-You-Heard. The differences are so immense, and so unforseen, and so incredible it's hard to know where to begin—which item to put at the top of the list in my head. I might as well start, I suppose, with the car. We have a new car. Our father had discussions, numerous and lengthy, with the garage-man; and Bo'sun Hooper offered him advice, as also did other friends at the Tennis Club and the Golf Club; and he and Mummy talked it over and over at home, and then, finally, they decided to use up some of her Uncle Stuart's money (only, of course, it's her money now) on buying a large absolutely *new* Austin tourer. This new car of ours is a shade of dark red, which the garageman says in known as maroon. Daddy drives our new car; but Mummy could if he let her—she knows how to drive. After all, she drove an ambulance in the Great War.

Even more important than buying the Austin, however, is what we become aware of by overhearing our parents' private conversations when they think we aren't listening. We are going to pack up and leave No. 9 Bay View Terrace, and move, lock, stock and barrel, into another bigger better house, just as soon as our father and Mummy have found the right one to suit us.

It is as if a thunder-cloud, forever hovering above the Hallsmith family, casting a shadow and threatening catastrophe, has blown away, been dispersed. In its place is clear blue sky; and instead of shadow, sunshine. The constant requirement for us to conceal, not merely our poverty, but the shame attaching to genteel poverty, has gone, and we are freed, at a stroke, from the obligation to consider always the cost of everything; freed from the dull tyranny of having to remember that every penny counts, is valuable, and must not be wasted. Bills can now be paid without anxiety. This is—it surely is—for all the family, a miraculous turning point. Our mother's Uncle Stuart has guaranteed us, we do believe, a future of happiness. We can depend upon it—can we not?

*　　　*　　　*

The various pieces of furniture chosen by our mother from Plas Magen—which is the name of the house in Beaumaris, Anglesea, where her uncle lived until fairly recently with his two sisters, Jessie and Annie—were today delivered to our address by carrier-van, and dumped in the patch of front garden, surrounded by hydrangea bushes. They were dumped here because Lucy, being on her own, was flustered when the van arrived and couldn't decide what room she should tell the carrier-men to put the furniture in. We've been helping her to transfer indoors the folding table and the firescreen, and several foot-stools, and a taller square stool for sitting on, and a chair without arms, and a crate of china labelled FRAGILE. It was Mummy's Aunt Jessie who died a short while after we had moved from The Bungalow into No. 9 Bay View Terrace, and Miss Annie Laurie—our mother's other aunt—is now in an old people's home, where she presumably doesn't have need of these things any more.

When our mother was young she often went and stayed at Plas Magen. Her Uncle Stuart had no children; he never married. I expect he was especially fond of Mummy on account of her father—his brother, James—being drowned in Southampton Water when she was only twelve. Mummy has an album that she keeps in a drawer, full of brownish faint photographs. A few of the photographs record a visit she made with Basil McNeile, years and years ago, to her uncle and aunts in Anglesea.

There they stand, the three of them, Basil McNeile and our mother, and her elderly rather stout Uncle Stuart, outside the ivy-covered house, pausing together for an everlasting moment by the pony trap in which they are about to set forth on an afternoon's drive, while someone unseen—Aunt Annie perhaps, or perhaps Aunt Jessie—takes the snapshot. Mummy is wearing a skirt that comes right down to her ankles. Of course, she wasn't our mother then: she wasn't Mrs Hallsmith—not *then*. She was Janet Laurie, aged eighteen or so, a very pretty girl with goldy-red hair, who thought she was going to marry Basil McNeile and be a vicar's wife. She was wrong about that, as she was wrong subsequently, about marrying Will Lawrence, and after him, Geoffrey Bazin.

But here, now, in Bay View Terrace, Newquay, to remind her of those early far-off days, are these bits of furniture, every inch of them—except for the table—decorated with needlework designs on canvas: the chair, and the stools, and the clever octagonal firescreen that can slide conveniently either higher or lower on a pole, and be fixed according to where you want it, so as to shield your face from the heat of the flames. Her aunts, Annie and Jessie, must have spent hours and hours—a

233

lifetime—slaving away at their tapestry wool flowers. And the resulting pictures, embroidered in cross-stitch, are further garnished by dozens of tiny sewn-on beads. Did they enjoy doing it, I wonder? Or did they long, as I would have longed, to be reading books and playing in the garden amongst real roses and forget-me-nots instead? I should have *hated* to spend my life doing flowers in cross-stitch and sewing on teeny-weeny beads.

Lucy was on her own when the furniture arrived from Wales because Daddy had asked his Bank Manager, Mr Oxley, to let him off working on Saturday morning, so that he and Mummy could catch a train on Friday evening up to London's Paddington Station, to celebrate what our mother had described to Mrs Have-You-Heard as 'her little windfall', meaning the legacy from her Uncle Stuart. Having booked in as soon as they arrived on Friday at the smart new Cumberland Hotel, on Saturday evening they took a taxi-cab to a theatre in the fashionable West End of London where a popular musical comedy called *The White Horse Inn* was being performed.

Daddy has brought us back a gramophone record of the songs they heard being sung on the stage, so that we can enjoy hearing them too. One of the songs, 'Goodnight Vienna', he puts on repeatedly, winding the gramophone up again and again; and he also sings it at the top of his voice, when he's in the bathroom, shaving. The only gramophone records we've had up till now have been Offenbach's 'Tales from Hoffmann', and Alexander's Ragtime Band, and 'If You Were the Only Girl in the World', with 'Tea for Two' on the other side. Daddy sings these songs as well when he's shaving, and if he's in a good mood, which used to be not very often. And there's another song he particularly likes to sing, 'The Maid of the Mountains', from a musical show, that he and Mummy went to see together before I was born. Mummy never sings, except for hymns in church, and she doesn't sing them very loudly.

'Your poor mother isn't musical,' we are told by our father. 'She's tone-deaf—can't sing a note in tune.'

Daddy is proud of his own singing voice, even though he practises using it exclusively in the bathroom. Since the London trip he's been whistling and singing in the bathroom almost every morning.

Our parents would never normally have dreamt of spending so much money—*wasting it*, they would have said—just for entertainment: staying the weekend at a swish new London hotel, and buying tickets to a London theatre, and driving about in taxi-cabs. It's what we imagine other people doing, not us. When Mummy and Pam had to travel up to London for my sister's operations it was out of necessity, and they stayed with friends or relations, so it was only the train fares that cost anything. I have wondered sometimes who did pay for Mr Twistleton-Higgins' fees and the hospital bills, because the Twins were ill before our mother had her windfall, and doctors' visits and bottles of medicine are very expensive, I know. It might, I suppose, have been—could have been—Cousin Edith Martin or Mrs Bazin, who are both rich; or even Mummy's Uncle Stuart: he was alive still, then.

Ever since our mother inherited her legacy it's curious how she seems to be much more visible in Newquay. People she hardly knows, mere acquaintances, will stop her in the street, just as Mrs Have-You-Heard stopped us not long ago, and offer congratulations on her marvellous good fortune, as though it has made our mother, quite suddenly, a figure of importance. She and our father receive numerous invitations to bridge parties, which gatherings take place generally on Saturday afternoons, or, occasionally, more grandly, on week day evenings. They have been invited to join the Newquay Amateur Dramatic Society, and elected—an even greater compliment— to the Cottage Hospital Committee, a limited group of distinguished personages.

Newquay has a nursing home up at the far end of Mount Wise, but no local hospital. Plans to construct one have been progressing slowly for years. The building, which will be approached by an improved version of the present not-much used road running past the back of Bay View Terrace, is to face across the valley of the River Gannel, on a level with Newquay's famous viaduct, and will eventually, when completed, be opened by His Royal Highness, Prince George of Kent.

Due to the flurry of interest aroused in connection with our mother's reported legacy, it has come to the attention of the Committee's members that Mrs Hallsmith was once upon a time, during the Great War, Commandant of King Edward's Convalescent Home for Ex-Servicemen. Who more appropriate, therefore, than she to join the Cottage Hospital Committee? And of course her husband, who was awarded the DSO for gallantry, must be invited to join the Committee along with her.

And so join they do. Every invitation extended to our parents, after being scrutunised and passed by them as worthwhile, is accepted. In a very few weeks their social circle, and with it their social standing, has enlarged out of all recognition. Our father no longer depends on the patronage of Mr Knight, proprietor of the Beachcroft Hotel, to give him a leg up. Mr and Mrs Hallsmith are widely regarded now as persons of substance in their own right, and, as such, deserve respect and admiration, mixed with a dash of envy from the less fortunate. No wonder Daddy whistles and sings 'Goodnight Vienna' in the bathroom while he's shaving.

It's extremely unlikely that Mrs Miller, when she sends our parents a note inviting them for a glass of sherry at Trenance House one Sunday morning, is influenced in the slightest degree by the story being circulated concerning Mummy's windfall. Living, as Mrs Miller does, entirely removed from Newquay society, she will probably have missed hearing this current item of Newquay gossip; and would have remained unaffected by it, probably, even if she had heard. But although Mrs Miller may be unaware of any change occurring since the day she spoke to Daddy in the Midland Bank about her niece, Ada Møeller, sharing lessons with his two little daughters, everything regarding our parents, their state of mind and view of themselves included, has been in the meantime transformed.

They accept the invitation with a calm self-confidence they would not previously have had.

Also, although they will never admit to it, they are agog with curiosity. Mrs Miller, the beautiful widow—if widow she is—doesn't entertain; doesn't go out in the world. Practically no one has ever met her. She leads a life of affluent mystery, alone in her big house, with a bevy of servants, and the two old bachelor PGs. Why has she decided to break her rule and invite our parents into her fortified castle? Is it in order to beg, as before, a favour? What sort of a favour could it be? Apart from which, might this not present our parents with an opportunity to learn the truth, or otherwise, of the tittle-tattle whispered by Mrs Mitchell into Mummy's ear?

Favours and tittle-tattle are of no interest to me and Pam, and have nothing to do with the acute anxiety we suffer, watching, expressionless but worried sick, our mother and father drive away from Bay View Terrace—they don't walk: they drive—in the brand-new Austin tourer. Ready for anything, a match for anyone, off they go, dressed in clothes carefully chosen to convey an impression of perfect ease, as befits honoured members of the Cottage Hospital Committee and the Amateur Dramatic Society, not to mention our father's familiarity with the rules of the Golf Club.

My sister and I are worried sick from fear that the privilege we have been granted of free access to the Trenance House gardens is about to be withdrawn, and that we shall for ever be cast out of Paradise as punishment for some offence forgotten, or unwittingly committed. What did we do? We rack our brains. Mrs Miller, we know, is an angel of forgiveness. But Dr Hankin? Has he—not an obvious child-lover—expressed to Mrs Miller a

238

wish for her to get rid of us?

We could have spared ourselves the worry. Our parents return, flushed with sherry and the happy glow that irradiates people newly bewitched. They have fallen beneath the spell of Ada's Aunt Astrid, and we are saved! It is not Pam and I who are to be cast into outer darkness, but instead—hurray!— our teacher, Mrs Oliver.

We have endured, with silent stoicism, for goodness knows how long, the daily boredom of term-time sessions under the supervision of Mrs Oliver, never breathing a word of complaint to the grown-ups, our parents. But Ada Møeller, friend and fellow-pupil, has confided, it seems, to her Aunt Astrid a dismal tale of woefully wasted hours. The standard of Danish schooling bears no resemblance, clearly, to crumb-spattered readings from *Letters to Hilary* and one-finger renderings of '*Au Claire de la Lune*' on the piano.

Ada went home to Denmark at the beginning of August, as we had known she would when her mother came out of hospital. But her mother's health isn't yet, alas, fully restored, and Mrs Miller is expecting to have Ada back staying in Trenance House again soon. She has therefore been making discreet enquiries for a teacher better qualified than Mrs Oliver to undertake her niece's education while in England; and these enquiries have resulted in her being given the name of a certain Miss Howard, the daughter of a grammar-school headmaster and possessor of a diploma in teaching, who already instructs two or three other little girls, approximately our age.

Mrs Miller didn't attempt, we understand, to force her opinion on our parents. Not at all! She merely suggested that if Mr and Mrs Hallsmith were themselves not wholly satisfied with the lessons being administered to Pam and Elspeth by Mrs Oliver—doubtless an admirable old lady, but hardly, according to her niece's account, an educationalist—they might consider interviewing this Miss Howard, a teacher most highly recommended. And might they then perhaps further consider conducting the interview on Mrs Miller's behalf as well as on their own?—the experience and the judgement of Mr Hallsmith and his delightful wife being, naturally, far greater than the experience and judgement of somebody who was English neither by birth nor by upbringing. If they could agree to do this for her, she—Astrid Miller—would be infinitely obliged to Mr and Mrs Hallsmith.

'Please—you will believe me, I hope,' she had said, disarmingly, charmingly, while Dr Hankin refilled their glasses with his excellent sherry (Mummy, in high spirits, re-enacts the scene for us, mimicking her hostess; Mummy has a gift for mimicry). '—I am not wanting to upset the apple cart—only to make improvement for the education of our children. They are so darling and so clever and so pretty, your Pam and your little Elspeth—and my Ada, too. We have to try the very best for them, do we not?'

How could Mummy and Daddy resist the subtle blandishments of Mrs Miller, or refuse to grant the favour—the second favour—she has requested? To resist or refuse her simply doesn't occur to our parents. They are completely won over.

'He seemed a nice enough fellow, I thought, that Dr Hankin,' remarks our father, summing things

240

up in Bay View Terrace, under the safety of his own roof. 'And the other chap—Mr What's-His-Name—very friendly, didn't you think so, Janet?'

'Yes—and Guthrie, you were quite right,' our mother declares, '—she's not young, Mrs Miller, but she really *is* beautiful!'

Our father hotly denies ever having said that Mrs Miller is beautiful. Then he rounds on us, standing alongside, listening, open-mouthed. 'This woman, this Mrs Oliver woman—it turns out she's a prize idiot—a nincompoop. Why on earth didn't you tell us—your own father and mother—your own flesh and blood—instead of leaving it to some little foreigner to spill the beans to her aunt? And she's a foreigner too, come to that—they're Danish, both of 'em. Why didn't you speak up— eh? You're not dumb—you've got tongues in your heads, haven't you?'

We hang those heads; but we stand our ground. Daddy isn't, we know, seriously angry: he's blustering—even, unusually, a bit boisterous. They've enjoyed their visit—the first time they've been to Trenance House; enjoyed the glasses of sherry, and being asked a favour—the second favour—by beautiful Mrs Miller.

As for Pam and me, today we have nothing, after all, to worry about, but on the contrary, a reason for rejoicing. We are going to have a new teacher, someone who will actually teach us. This is what we have wanted for ages, and now, because of Ada Møeller and her Aunt Astrid, we will have it.

*   *   *

We are on our way, late one afternoon, to

interview Miss Howard, the prospective replacement of Mrs Oliver; or to be interviewed by her—we are not sure which. She has indicated that she will have to meet not only the parents of the children she is being asked to teach, but the children also, before she can decide whether or no she can accept them as her pupils. Daddy and Miss Howard have exchanged brief exploratory letters, but neither he, nor any member of the family has, to date, seen her.

Leaving Jim in the kitchen doing his homework, with Lucy for company, Mummy and me and my sister Pam walk sedately down to what, although cramped and crooked, is in fact the central and usually crowded jostling thoroughfare of the town, now emptied of daytime traffic. The pavements too are clear, and all the shops we pass have their blinds drawn and are shut till tomorrow morning. Outside the Midland Bank, its massive doors likewise closed, we are joined by Daddy, and the four of us proceed in a solemn silence to keep our appointment with Miss Howard.

She lives, Miss Howard, on the side of town furthest from where Mrs Oliver resides, in the older and rougher, less genteel, and therefore, to us, more interesting quarter of Newquay. Centred on the harbour, which was once the focus of a thriving pilchard-fishing industry, the district has to a great extent—allowing for a few modern innovations, notably the Victoria Cinema— retained its original workaday character.

The Victoria Cinema is the source of thrilling, if rare, treats, the latest being when Mummy was away in London with Pam, and our father took me and my brother Jim to see a film, *Evergreen*, in which there is a famous actress, Jessie Matthews, who dances and sings. It's lucky for us that Daddy happens to be a film-fan.

A very narrow street without pavements, hardly wider than a lane, runs uphill between the blank side-wall of the Victoria Cinema and the largest grocery shop in Newquay. Behind the grocery shop is a big yard crammed with a jumble of crates and boxes and barrels; and in a corner of the yard we discover an unobtrusive green-painted door which, when opened, gives access to an exceedingly small, dark, almost vertical staircase. This ill-lit stuffy little staircase proves to be the entrance to Miss Howard's apartment: her balcony-type upper-floor flat.

It seems to me and Pam a surprising sort of apartment—or flat—for a teacher to have; not in the least what we were expecting. A closed-in gallery, supported on a row of solid wrought-iron pillars, it overhangs the whole length of the cluttered backyard, and was doubtless formerly used by the grocery shop's owner as extra storage space before being converted into living rooms and rented out to Miss Howard, probably very cheaply, for her bizarre home; nearly as bizarre as—and resembling closely, we realise—the ex-railway-carriage in Porth inhabited every summer by Miss Veah and Miss Isobel Clark-Ourry.

For us, the oddity of Miss Howard's address is an immediate and sufficient recommendation. How truly wonderful if this is where we are to be allowed to come for our lessons every morning. It wouldn't even matter if the lessons themselves should turn out to be as boring as those we've had to suffer with Mrs Oliver. But will our parents find the oddness as delightful as we do, or just the reverse? The idea of their daughters being tutored in such peculiar surroundings may very well appal them.

As we fumble our way upstairs we are greeted by a terrific outburst of barking. Having a deeply rooted terror of dogs, I am thankful to be at the rear of the Hallsmith delegation. When we reach the top of the stairs, however, the barker, to my huge relief, has been banished, and we are confronted by Miss Howard alone. She conducts us through the first room, past a long table, wooden chairs, a blackboard, into the room beyond, which is furnished adequately if somewhat sparsely, as a sitting room.

As soon as the polite how-d'you-do and hand-shaking ritual is over, Miss Howard fixes her full attention on the Hallsmith children, me and Pam. She asks us our names and our ages: information we are able to supply without any difficulty. What—she next enquires—do we consider to be our favourite subjects? This is harder to answer. *Subjects* at Mrs Oliver's establishment were as good as non-existent. We glance at each other for inspiration.

'Books,' we declare, simultaneously.

'Stories—and poems,' my sister adds. Then, wishing to be more helpful, she enlarges her reply: 'Ellie likes writing things, and I like drawing—and painting pictures.'

'I see,' says Miss Howard, with a nod. And we have the impression that she does indeed see.

Miss Howard isn't exactly old, or not very old; but nor is she young. We have learnt that it's possible to be, as Mrs Miller is, not young but still beautiful. Miss Howard, who isn't young, isn't beautiful. She is, we think, extremely ugly. But funnily enough, we aren't put off by her ugliness. She obviously doesn't take any interest in her clothes. They are brownish cover-up, never-mind-they'll-do garments. Her hair is worn unbecomingly in what we call snails: the two plaits are coiled around and then pinned, like lids, or like snail shells, one over each ear. What we notice above all else, though, is her jaw, which is big and square, and thrust forward like the jaw of a bulldog. It is a stern unsmiling face, such as you might imagine would strike terror into the hearts of little girls; but for some inexplicable reason it doesn't alarm us. We look up at it with confidence, unafraid, my sister and I, waiting hopefully for a verdict.

While the grown-ups are talking about us, and deciding our fate, we prospective pupils are instructed to wait in the schoolroom. The door, which was left ajar for a while, has now been firmly shut, and even if we strain our ears we can't hear a single word distinctly, only a low mumble of voices. So we spend the time inspecting our novel environment, taking particular note of the shelves and the piles of neatly arranged exercise books and textbooks on them: no visible copy of those dreary *Letters to Hilary*! Tacked up on the wall are several shiny maps: one of the world, one of Europe, one of the British Isles, and one of the stars in the sky at night. In the middle of the table where we are sitting there is a globe, also illustrating the world, but in the shape of a ball which can be spun with the tip of a finger: Pam's experimental finger.

'Look, Ellie!'

Anxious, I beg her in a whisper to stop twiddling the globe, for fear Miss Howard should catch us playing with it.

'I'm not playing with it, Ellie,' she says, whispering in return. 'Don't worry—it's meant to be twiddled. That's what it's *for*.' But to please me, she stops the globe spinning, and we sit still again, idle, gazing silently around us.

Because of the blackboard we feel as if we are in the classroom of a real school. I've never actually seen a blackboard before. Everything is very clean and orderly. We can glimpse through the window brightly coloured posters on the far side of the road, advertising films, either showing this week or coming shortly. Fancy us being so close, here, to the glamour of cinema films and Hollywood film stars!

Walking home we are told absolutely nothing of the conversation which has taken place between our parents and Miss Howard. But this evening, by employing the long-practised art of eavesdropping, we gather that Miss Howard's considerable teaching qualifications outweigh, in our parents' estimation, the unusual features of her accommodation. She is obliged, we understand, to live so wretchedly above the backyard of a grocery shop on account of her unfortunately straitened circumstances: a cause for pity, not for scorn.

Straitened circumstances means that Miss Howard is very poor.

Being poor is no crime, our father says to our mother; and Mummy agrees. But being Roman Catholic—which apparently Miss Howard is—does come very near to constituting a crime. It is this vexed question of religion, and not her eccentric

246

address, that creates the doubt and hesitation in the minds of our parents. Undeniably Miss Howard's Roman Catholicism is a stumbling block; but how great a stumbling block? Two of her present pupils, Kathleen and Miriam Kiley from Crantock, a village across the River Gannel, are Roman Catholics, but the widowed mother of Mollie Purchase, her other pupil, is said to belong to the Church of England. As to Ada Møeller, nobody can be sure what kind of religion Danish people are in the habit of subscribing to; but Mummy thinks that it isn't R.C.

Our father, although he doesn't believe in God, is profoundly suspicious of Roman Catholics, rating them as only slightly less of a menace than Jew-boys, darkies, and the defeated but still malignant Hun. Would it be right to entrust the education of their daughters to a person whose avowed affiliation is to the Pope in Rome? Right or wrong? One has to take a moral stand in these matters. Education, says our father, is a serious business.

'But Guthrie,' we hear our mother protesting, 'religion simply doesn't come into it. She said herself, it isn't a subject she teaches, or would ever dream of teaching—or would even touch on. She said so, positively—twice—when you asked her. Don't you remember?'

How our mother manages to dispel his fears we never know, since we are sent off, up to bed, while the advantages and the disadvantages of engaging Miss Howard as a teacher continue to be argued back and forth. Pam's wishes, and mine, are not, of course, consulted; but perhaps the desire to conform to the wishes of Mrs Miller has something

247

to do with their final decision to risk the contamination of popery. Next morning at breakfast we are informed that Miss Howard is going to be our new teacher. We are overjoyed.

*   *   *

So much that we hadn't expected has happened this year; so many surprising happenings—nice ones, mostly. There was the arrival of Ada Møeller, our new friend, and us being invited by her Aunt Astrid into the private gardens of Trenance House for tea on Thursday afternoons. And there was the cigarette-and-sweetie kiosk on the Great Western Beach; and Mars Bars, and yo-yos; and Mummy's inheritance, and our new car, and a new house to look forward to; and best of all, no more lessons with Mrs Oliver!

It wasn't very nice, I know, for Pam to have to have a second operation, but she's quite recovered now, and her hair has grown longer and been permanently waved, so that the scar on her neck is practically hidden by a mass of curls. I don't say so to Pam, but in fact I think the pigtails, which she had before, suited her better than the perm.

There have been enough unexpected changes recently to last us for the rest of our lives. Until tonight we were certain there wouldn't be— couldn't be—any more surprises. But tonight, after we've undressed and brushed our teeth, Mummy comes upstairs, and instead of tucking us in and kissing us goodnight, as she usually does, she sits on the foot of Pam's bed and summons Jim to join us from the next room, which is what he did when she was reading Bible stories aloud on Sunday evenings. It isn't Sunday tonight, though, and she isn't carrying the big brown book, either.

'I'd like you to be in here, with me and the girls, Jimbo,' she calls out to him. *Jimbo* is the name that only Mummy uses for him, and only occasionally. It's a sure sign, when she does use it, of her having a reason to feel especially fond of Jim just then. 'I've something to tell the three of you—something quite amazing. A wonderful piece of news!'

He comes obediently into our bedroom, wearing his pyjamas, and sits on my bed; and we wait. Mummy is laughing.

'Go on—what is it, Mummy?' says Pam, impatiently. 'Tell us, can't you—'

So our mother tells us. And what she tells us is indeed amazing: even more of a surprise than all of this year's other surprises put together.

'Next year—sometime in the summer,' says Mummy, speaking slowly, and trying to sound solemn, although she's laughing still, '—you three children are going to have a baby brother or sister. What do you think of that? Isn't it wonderful?'

We stare at her in silence, dumbfounded— incredulous—not at first comprehending.

'You mean—you mean that you're going to have a *baby*?' Pam asks her, after several moments, astounded. We are all astounded. Our mother? It's impossible.

'Well, yes—yes, I am,' says Mummy. 'I'd supposed I was much too old to have another baby. But today—today I went to see Dr Mitchell, and I'm not, after all—apparently—too old.' She isn't laughing because it's a joke, but because she's happy. 'So it seems, children—my dear children— Pam and Jimbo, my Twins—Elspeth—we shall fairly soon be having an addition to the family.' And she says again: 'A baby!—isn't that wonderful?'

Jim bursts into a torrent of tears. He sobs and sobs, hysterically. 'But I don't *want* us to have a baby. We're all right as we are, the three of us. Why do we have to have somebody else in the family? There's no *need* for anyone else—' The news that Mummy has presented to her children as being wonderful upsets Jim dreadfully. He weeps angrily, miserably, and he can't be comforted.

But for Pam and me the news is—it really is— incomparably wonderful: a miracle, if ever there was one! We, who have been forbidden dolls, are to be given a proper live warm breathing baby of our very own to dress and undress, to bath, and to cuddle and fuss over. Dollies?—pouf! We can do better than that! Even Baby Jesus in his crib at Christmas was a pretence baby. Our baby will be real.

*　　　*　　　*

Today is a Sunday, the day our parents are to inspect at their leisure, without the tiresome presence of an escorting estate agent to distract them, the house, unoccupied and empty, which they have settled on as being suitable to rent from the beginning of February for our new home; and we three children, after promising to restrain our excitement, and to be as good as gold, are going with them on their tour of inspection.

It's not nearly as large and as grand as either Mrs Miller's Trenance House or Mr and Mrs Jenkins' Pentire House, nor does it have extensive

250

gardens and grounds, as they do, but in comparison to where we have lived until now it is undeniably a palace of a place. Can it be true that the five—soon to be six—members of the Hallsmith family will very shortly themselves be inhabiting this palace? Wonders will never cease!

Built on a corner, at the near end of Mount Wise, Grosvenor House is in command, as it were, of Grosvenor Road, which drops down fairly steeply to one side of it. Because a high brick wall, topped by a railing smothered in climbing plants, effectively screens off its front entrance on Mount Wise from the terrace of humbler dwellings jammed up against its other side, Grosvenor House has the misleading appearance of being fully detached, a gentleman's residence that stands proudly apart from its immediate neighbours, like a rich relation at pains to disown impoverished hangers-on. We shall indeed have a not-very-desirable neighbour living a few yards away in this terrace, the elderly Mrs Wray, a widow known ungratefully to us children more for her awful smelly breath than for her charitable gift at Christmas some years ago of party clothes for the two little daughters of Mrs Hallsmith: the green chiffon handkerchief dress for Pam, and for me the brown velvet dress which I hated.

Our father pushes crossly at a tall imposing red-painted wrought-iron gate. His crossness is due to John Julian, the estate agent, having given him the back door key, instead of, as he should have done, the key to the front door: a deliberately insulting gesture, according to our father, who keeps a sharp look out for insults. Mummy tells him that it wasn't intentional—wasn't, she says, an

251

insult, but a mistake, simply. In addition to his estate agency business, John Julian owns the furniture store where later on our parents will be buying new armchairs, and new beds and wardrobes, and whatever else may be required to make the palatial Grosvenor House's roomy interior habitable. And it is one of John Julian's fleet of removal vans which will eventually transport our miscellaneous goods and chattels— or as many as we decide to retain—on their quarter-mile journey down from Bay View Terrace to Mount Wise. In these circumstances, and despite the fact that John Julian has chosen to have his money taken care of by a rival concern instead of by the Midland Bank, for Daddy to feel affronted now and to kick up a fuss would be, as our mother is aware, unhelpful. Prosperous and affable, and ambitiously set on succeeding, John Julian has a son who goes to the County School and who is about the same age as my brother Jim. Why this handsome boy and Jim are not friends, I don't know, but they aren't; which I regret.

Daddy's irritation is increased by the iron gate resisting his initial shove. I hear him muttering under his breath: *'Hell's Teeth!'*. This is the nearest he ever does get to swearing. Even when he loses his temper completely and becomes enraged, hauling my brother off to be thrashed in the bathroom, his eyes will blaze and he clenches his own teeth, but still he doesn't use bad language. Both our parents disapprove strongly of swearing. Our mother, at moments of great stress—failure, for example, to thread a needle—will burst out with 'Oh, drat it!', and I've seen her stamp her foot. But to swear is an unforgivable sin, worse than the excessive drinking of alcohol, and much *much* worse than girls who are fast and who paint their nails and wear lipstick. Swearing is downright wicked, and our parents exercise extreme self-control in order to avoid this wickedness. Mummy can say *Drat*, but Jim earned himself a flogging for *Damn*, a word that certain of his schoolfellows had assured him was permissable, geography having taught them to admire the officially sanctioned civil engineering feat of damming up rivers.

My sister would never have fallen so easily into a trap so infantile. But neither did she let herself be cowed by the fate of her unhappy twin. Not she! Outraged at the injustice of his punishment, Pam proceeded to draw a graphic illustration of a barrier built across a swirling river, and to label it, in capital letters: A DAM. She showed her picture to Daddy, daring him to punish *her*; and in spite of her boldness—or perhaps because of it—was spared the discipline of the leather razor-strop.

Here we are, outside Grosvenor House, and our father pushes the gate again, harder. It yields with a squeak, scraping rustily over the black and white tiles that lead up to a glass porch of a size almost sufficient for it to be termed a conservatory. To the right of the porch is a square patch of gravel, surrounded by scrubby flower beds. To the left, and also gravelled, a squeezed-in path runs round the house in the shadow of a dense laurel hedge, path and hedge terminating at a short flight of steps that bring us down to the level of the back garden, with a small wooden gate for tradesmen opening on to Grosvenor Road. This back garden, so-called, consists of an area of grass considerably bigger than the patch of gravel in front: big enough for us to be able to play French cricket on it, and to practise with my skipping rope.

Having circled the house, we continue to follow in our parents' wake, up two steps, past the coal-hole and what will be Lucy's lavatory, up two more steps into the scullery, on through the kitchen—always my favourite room—and from there into the hall: a hall magnificently spacious, as judged by us. Opposite the kitchen is the dining room, twice the size of our Bay View Terrace dining room, and next to that an even larger sitting room. We are rendered speechless. Our house-to-be is *huge*!

As we tramp up the stairs, from which the matting has been stripped, our feet, as we mount, produce a hollow echoing sound. On the half-landing we pass by the bathroom. Goodness! What an enormous bathroom! And here is the bedroom that will belong to our parents. It has the fascinating feature of a projecting triangular window, such as we have never seen before. If there was a watchman on duty, guarding Grosvenor House from enemies, he could spy out in both directions: either up Mount Wise, or else towards Bury Road and the bottom of Trenance Hill, and be warned of who was approaching.

The other main bedroom, with windows that face on to the steep slope of Grosvenor Road, is for me and Pam to share. Fitted in between these two big bedrooms is a very narrow little room, not much wider than the width of a single bed, which will be for Jim to have. There is a room for visitors, too—a spare room for Granny Hallsmith, or Granny Laurie, or Cousin Mildred Martin, or Aunt Molly, whenever one of them arrives to stay. And there is also a sort of a boxroom—more like a biggish cupboard than a real room—that will do for Lucy on those occasions when we shall need her to sleep the night here.

For I've learnt, upsettingly, that after we have moved, Lucy Coles—our Lucy—will no longer be living with us, not properly. Lucy, it seems, will come and go, returning most evenings, when she has finished clearing away and washing up the supper dishes, to her own home in the country; and then getting up very early in the morning so as to catch the first bus back to Newquay in time to cook us our breakfasts. I'm not sure quite why this different arrangement has been made. Perhaps it's because the boxroom is only fit for occasional occupation. Or perhaps it's a consequence of Lily, Lucy's older sister, having married Albert, which means that Mr and Mrs Coles, who are old, would be left all alone in their cottage if Lucy didn't go home to them. This may be the reason, but I don't really know if it is. I haven't been given an explanation, only told. It will seem very strange, and very worrying, not to have Lucy available, close at hand, overnight. She did, I remember, disappear mysteriously for a week or so once when I was much younger, and I can remember missing her then, and the disagreeable sensation there was of emptiness. But that was long ago. Lucy has always, otherwise, been with us; always.

Except for this one anxiety of mine, though, every future change will be for the better; with, of course, the most miraculous change of all ahead: a baby soon to be born! Now that we have seen and explored the inside of Grosvenor House we wish we could instantly, without further delay— tomorrow!—take possession of it. No. 9 Bay View

Terrace has become, in a matter of hours, almost unbearably drab and poky. But Mummy says we must try to be patient. There is a great deal to be done, she says, before the 1st of February—carpets to be chosen and curtains to be made, and goodness knows what else besides. A vast amount of our mother's Uncle Stuart's money is obviously going to have to be spent on furnishings, and equipment in general. We children realise it's more, far more, than a splendid new home we are about to enter into: it's a whole new era of plenty. No more scrimping and scraping! People who have Grosvenor House for their address can afford to buy whatever they fancy from the abundance of modern first-hand furniture on display in John Julian's well-stocked emporium.

*   *   *

We have to be patient, our mother has said to us. Patient, yes—but for *how long*? As time passes, and we find we are still living at the old familiar Bay View Terrace address, our hopes gradually fade, and we cease to wake up in a daily state of high expectancy. We begin to doubt that the exciting removal we were promised is ever going to happen. A sense of uncertainty, of insecurity creeps over us, like a cloud obscuring what was a clear horizon.

Christmas is approaching, but this year its approach is barely noticed. Our parents are not able, it seems, to focus their minds on anything but samples of material for curtains, and patterns of wallpaper; on measuring floors to be covered, and comparing prices of stair-carpet. Their unending discussions and arguments are so excrutiatingly dull that in order to spare ourselves having to listen to such boring talk we try to block our ears, instead of stretching them to overhear, as we are accustomed to doing. And Mummy and Lucy, down on their knees on the floor, busily packing and sorting, and throwing away all kinds of objects we would much rather that they didn't throw away, have no attention left for us, or for what we are attempting to tell them. Various items they describe as rubbish we are obliged to retrieve surreptitiously from the dustbins.

Life grows increasingly muddly and uncomfortable at Bay View Terrace, so that when the day arrives for us to embark on lessons administered by our new teacher, Miss Howard, it is a distinct relief to me and my sister Pam. We had thought we would once again be sharing lessons with Ada Møeller, but Ada is remaining for the present in Denmark, her mother's health having improved, and we don't know when she may be returning to stay with her Aunt Astrid in Trenance House. Her visit has been postponed indefinitely. Pam and me, therefore, have to face up to the new teacher, Miss Howard, unsupported by our friend Ada Møeller.

We knew, of course, that Miss Howard was already giving lessons to other pupils. One of them, Mollie Purchase, we had met before, but we hadn't met the Kiley girls, Kathleen and Miriam. Kathleen is the same age as I am; her sister is younger. Mollie, who stammers dreadfully, worse even than Jim, hasn't any brothers or sisters. She is large and fat and fair-haired and red-faced, like her mother, Mrs Purchase, and a bit older than me. The Kileys we know are Roman Catholic, the same

257

as Miss Howard. They have a great many brothers and sisters, all a good deal older.

The three girls are very polite and very friendly towards us, and seem to be pleased that we've joined them. So now, as well as a new teacher, we have three new friends.

As a result of our mornings being satisfactorily settled into a regular routine, we have found the disorder in Bay View Terrace much less disturbing. Week succeeds week in a steady rhythm, and we almost begin to forget what all the upheaval and preparations are for. Christmas comes and Christmas goes. January slips away. Then, without any previous warning, Jim is informed at breakfast that today he's not to come straight home after school, as he normally does, but to go back with Bradford Johns to *his* home; and my sister and I are similarly told that at 12.30 a.m., when our lessons finish, we will be conducted by Mollie Purchase back to *her* home for lunch, and later for tea.

Mollie Purchase and Bradford Johns each live up at the Pentire end of Mount Wise, each with a mother, but no father. According to arrangements made between their parents and ours, we are to wait there, Jim with his friend Bradford, and me and Pam with Mollie and Mrs Purchase, until such time as Daddy arrives by car in the evening to collect us; which he does.

We left Bay View Terrace this morning without knowing it was to be for the very last time, and without knowing, or even suspecting, we should be sleeping tonight in our new John Julian beds, in our new Grosvenor House bedrooms.

So we needn't have given up hope after all. It finally did happen: we've moved!

III

Grosvenor House

Since old Mrs Oliver, the retired governess, has been replaced by a proper teacher, the walk my sister Pam and I take every day to school—for *school* is how we like to think of our lessons with Miss Howard—is much more colourful and interesting than once it was. To reach Mrs Oliver's little house we used to set forth in an out-of-town direction. Now the direction has been reversed, leading us down into the narrow twisting street that is Newquay's main shopping centre, its veritable heart.

There's a hint of adventure about the route which we now follow on our way to school. We are seeing the shopping quarter as we have never seen it previously, at an hour when it belongs entirely to the commercial fraternity: before, as it were, the curtain rises. It is the hour when shopkeepers are getting ready for their day's custom, pulling up blinds or shutters, laying out boxes of fruit and vegetables. The fishmonger stands in a clean white apron, hooking strings of dead upside-down hares and rabbits round his doorway. The butcher, and the stationer who sells newspapers, and the haberdashery assistants—all are engaged in preparing for the day ahead. Presently their customers will start to arrive: in a trickle at first, but soon in a steadily increasing stream, until so many of them are jostling together that some people, if they are to make any progress, have to step off the pavements into the road, where vans and lorries, toot-tooting, and the occasional horse and cart, negotiate with difficulty a slow passage through the general congestion.

This will be the scene that meets our eyes later on, a scene utterly transformed, in which we too shall be engulfed when returning from school. But for now—going to school—the air we breathe is fresh and invigorating, and the atmosphere, while remaining tranquil, is quietly businesslike. The shopkeepers, intent on setting out their merchandise to its best advantage before the hubbub of buying and selling begins, turn their heads to nod and smile at us. We pick a way past them with care, trying not to impede their activity. Pam and I feel a small glow of pride, convinced that their nods and smiles are an indication of us having been accepted as honorary members of an early morning society of tradespeople.

Wishing to avoid the uneasiness of finding ourselves in a possible danger zone at the foot of the hill on which, halfway up, the Boys' Council School is threateningly positioned, we take the precautionary measure, when we have reached a point opposite to the Midland Bank, of crossing over. The Bank isn't yet open, but we know that our father, who leaves home before we do, is already at work inside, an invisible presence. We hurry on, past the Bank, and past Timothy White's the Ironmonger, with its tempting and quite un-ironmongerly pavement display of beach balls and flowery cretonne sun hats. Much as we should like to dally, lingering is out of the question. We mustn't be late for school. Breaking into a trot, we round the bend, and a wonderfully raw fishy smell wafts up to us from the harbour below. We come to a halt, momentarily, beside the plate-glass windows of the gents outfitters. There's hardly any traffic yet. I take my sister's hand.

'Now, Ellie,' she says; and we cross again.

The Victoria Cinema's posters are advertising Grace Moore in *One Night of Love*—alluring pictures: no lingering, though! We hasten on, and into the grocery store's backyard, where the smell that assails our nostrils isn't a local fishy smell, but a strongly spicy, exotic, foreign aroma. Oh, delicious!

As we climb the dark little enclosed staircase, I clutch at the skirt of my leader Pam for reassurance. Folly, Miss Howard's big brown-and-white spaniel, is barking, barking, barking—an awful sound that makes me shudder with fear. But his mistress calls Folly away from the top of the stairs, and the barking ceases. We have arrived.

We are not late. We are never late; but the Kileys, Kathleen and Miriam, and Mollie Purchase too, are always sitting in their places at the schoolroom table when we get here. This is because Kathleen and Miriam live in the village of Crantock, and must therefore be rowed across the River Gannel by a grown-up brother or sister; and whoever rows them over has to do it before going to work. They cross the river as naturally as we cross a road; and then, having crossed, the Kiley children, aged eight and six, toil up a steep lane to Mount Wise, the summit, where Mollie Purchase joins them for the final stage of what we regard, with envy, as their inexpressibly romantic journey to school. Fancy being rowed every day, to and fro, across the wide mouth of the Gannel! Something of the lustre of that envied romance rubs off, we feel, on us, adding an extra dab of colour to the kaleidoscopic pleasure of the mornings we now spend as pupils of Miss Howard, our new stern ugly Roman Catholic teacher.

She is stern, yes, a strict disciplinarian, but calm. She will not ever lose her temper and fly into a rage: we can rely on it. And although she may be unsmiling, she is absolutely fair. We can rely on that as well. Above all, she *teaches* us. She loves to teach. We can tell she does. And so, from her— Miss Howard—we love to learn. To be taught and to learn is an experience my sister Pam and I have hankered after for ages.

Music, art, and of course religion, are not subjects taught by Miss Howard, but every other subject commonly included in an educational establishment's curriculum is dealt with, plus a few random extras; astronomy, geology and oceanography may well be touched upon from time to time in passing, as may also wild flowers, the Northern Lights, the annual migration of swallows—nothing is ignored if a connection should happen to arise.

Arithmetic is explained to us—the intricacies of long division and fractions—with the aid of clear white chalk figures on the blackboard. We are introduced to algebra as if to a puzzle, a game, that has its logical solution: *let* x *be the unknown number*. Can we find the number? Have we understood the reasoning? No? Then a duster wipes the blackboard clean, and Miss Howard explains again; and if that isn't enough, again. We must never say we understand if we don't. She knows when it isn't true.

Using compasses and rulers we copy into our geometry exercise-books the diagram she has chalked on the blackboard of an isosceles triangle. We learn the Latin meaning, and its English translation, of the neat little symbol with which Euclid's geometrical theorems, originally demonstrated to students in Ancient Greece, are concluded. Any argument that crops up at home now between Pam and me can be clinched by the same device: '*Q—E—D!*' we shout in triumph at each other. She who shouts it out the loudest, wins.

Geography: the Sahara Desert was once upon a time, amazingly, an ocean. Yes, indeed, it was— imagine that! History: the Romans invented central heating and piping hot baths; they paid their soldiers with dollops of salt; the roads they built for their conquering armies to march on were as straight as a ramrod. ('What is a ramrod, Mollie? Miriam? You'll find it under R in the dictionary—'). And although my sister and I can't any longer amuse ourselves by poking at the keys of a piano with an index finger to conjure up the melody of '*Au Clair de la Lune*' (Miss Howard doesn't have a piano), we can chant with unhesitating gusto the present tense of *Être*: *Je suis, Tu es, Il est*.

Each of us compiles her own spelling book. A spelling book is lined, like an ordinary exercise-book, and it's the same length as an ordinary exercise-book, but no more than three inches wide, with stiff glossy maroon-coloured covers. We enter, in a single carefully written column, the corrected version of the words we've spelt wrong, and every Friday Miss Howard tests us individually, to be sure that we really have learnt how to spell them right.

We have become aware that language is made up of words, and that these words, which we unthinkingly scribble and speak, are distinguished

265

by names of their own: a noun, an adjective, an adverb; and that the proper construction of a sentence depends on the proper use of grammar, in the same way as our legs and arms, in order to function properly, depend on the bony framework of a skeleton.

There is no end at all to the quantities of fascinating information waiting for us to discover, and no end either to us discovering more and more and *more* of this treasure-trove of knowledge if we only, like detectives, follow the clues. Miss Howard, our teacher, is providing us with clues. She is educating us.

Suddenly, shattering the industrious quietness of our schoolroom, an enormous voice booms out from the other side of the street. 'One night of love . . .' sings the disembodied, immensely magnified voice of Grace Moore. And then, as abruptly as it has blared forth, it breaks off; only to resume after a minute or so of deathly silence. It starts, and it stops, over and over, louder, softer; and louder again. The Victoria Cinema's management is adjusting the volume of sound effects in readiness for its evening film entertainment—a weird and wonderful accompaniment to our earnest attempts at solving knotty mathematical problems.

Miss Howard pays no heed, none whatsoever, to Grace Moore's deafening fragments of operatic performance, but continues to stand unmoved at the blackboard, grimly chalking up rows of figures on which we must manage somehow to concentrate, closing our ears resolutely to those gigantic bursts of siren song: 'One night of love, When two hearts were one . . .'

Ever since Mrs Oliver was replaced as our

266

instructress by Miss Howard we can't be sure, Pam and I, from morning to morning, what may be going to happen next. The Kiley children came to school yesterday carrying a bucket full of sea-water with the most peculiar sort of a jelly fish floating about in it. Rainbow-hued, and puffed up like a balloon, the strange creature, instead of being circular, as jellyfish are usually, was more the shape of a submarine. They had found it stranded on Crantock beach after a night of stormy weather, tangled in seaweed.

Miss Howard, peering into the bucket, as intrigued as we were, said that she thought it might possibly be a Portuguese Man o' War, which— apparently—is a species of jellyfish very seldom seen anywhere near the coast of Cornwall. She instructed Kathleen Kiley to look it up in one of the several big red encyclopedias kept on the topmost shelf of our schoolroom. And sure enough, Miss Howard, who knows such a lot about such a lot, was quite right. There, for proof, on a page of the great heavy volume, was a picture and the description of a Portuguese Man o'War: the Kileys' jellyfish. Instead of a geometry lesson, we were allowed to draw this rare visitor to our shores, and to colour our drawings, before the Kileys carried it back across the River Gannel and returned it to the sea off Crantock beach.

In another of Miss Howard's top shelf encyclopedias we have today looked up a plant called a sundew which catches and eats insects for nourishment, just as though it were an animal, and not—as, in fact, it is—a plant. Miss Howard knows the exact spot on Bodmin Moor where these incredible plants grow, and she has written a note to our various parents proposing—if they agree, and if the weather is fine—to take her group of pupils next weekend on a picnic outing, by bus, up to Bodmin Moor, to give us the chance of seeing a sundew growing, and catching insects, in its natural boggy habitat. Such outings are, in her view, educational. We think they are fun. Never in a million years could we envisage going with Mrs Oliver on an expedition up to Bodmin Moor so as to search out and make drawings of an insect-eating sundew—*never*!

Every morning at half-past ten o'clock precisely we have a five-minute interval between lessons in order to refresh our minds and our bodies with a glass of milk and a bun. It used to be Mrs Oliver, not us, who munched at currant buns and who spattered crumbs over our shoulders on to our open books. But Miss Howard is abstemious, providing buns for her pupils, but neither eating nor drinking in our company. Instead, she leaves us alone, and goes off to speak a word of consolation to Folly, who has to spend the hours when we are being educated imprisoned in his mistress's bedroom. And school-time is brought to a close each morning, unfailingly, with ten minutes of poetry.

Miss Howard sits in her chair, hands folded on her lap, not saying a word, but listening attentively while we take it in turns to read aloud to her from a book of poems, the lines we are to read having been marked for us in the margin: lines unforgettably haunting.

Stirred by an emotion we cannot wholly understand, we recite from Gray's 'Elegy written in a Country Churchyard': ' . . . *The lowing herd winds slowly o'er the lea, The ploughman homeward, plods his weary way, And leaves the world to darkness and to me . . .'* We are ravished by Keats's Arabian encounter: *'I met a traveller from an antique land . . .'* As to the comic tale of John Gilpin's misadventure, once committed to memory by my sister Pam and myself in our desperate endeavours to dissipate boredom, it can by no means compete with the bittersweet melancholy of Goldsmith's 'Deserted Village' and his portrait of the beloved schoolmaster: *'A man he was, to all the country dear And passing rich with forty pounds a year . . .'*

She is not a smiler, Miss Howard, and we have never heard her laugh, but she nonetheless understands the importance of treats. At the beginning of the Christmas holidays, the day after term ended, we five girls, her pupils, are invited to an afternoon tea party. It's a rather odd sensation for us to be climbing the dark little staircase on a Saturday afternoon, wearing our best going-out-to-tea dresses. We don't know what to expect, and feel awkward at first. But we needn't have worried. The blackboard has disappeared, and the encyclopedias on the top shelf are decorated with sprigs of holly. It doesn't seem like our schoolroom any more.

Miss Howard has prepared a feast for us: ham sandwiches, and a sponge-cake iced, and chocolate biscuits and lemonade. After tea, instead of lessons, we sit round the table playing games: memory games and guessing games and Chinese Whispers. We play Spillikins, and Up-Jenkins, and Consequences, and Happy Families, and the winners are given prizes of chocolate raisins. Unlike most other Christmas parties, there are no

269

balloons and no crackers (probably because she couldn't afford them), but we enjoy Miss Howard's Christmas party very much. She still doesn't laugh, but she sometimes—we see her—smiles. And so now we know that she can smile when she wants to, even if she doesn't want to very often.

Our new teacher prefers my sister Pam to me, and I understand why she does. When we came for our preliminary interview with her, the door between the sitting room and the schoolroom being slightly ajar, I overhead through the crack a few scraps of conversation that I wasn't intended to hear. Our parents were talking about us. Pam's name was mentioned, and Mummy said, apologetically, that she was a difficult child. Daddy said, in his cross voice,

'Difficult? I sometimes think she's not entirely right in the head, that girl—'

There was a murmur of dismay from our mother: 'Oh, Guthrie—no!'

'Your elder daughter,' I heard the new governess-person say, sharply, icily, 'struck *me*, Mr Hallsmith, as being a child of exceptional intelligence.' She was rebuking my father, ticking him off, almost as if she was *his* governess, and he was a naughty boy. How did she dare to?

Then one of them must have noticed that the door hadn't been completely shut; and shut it. Pam didn't hear what I heard, and I never told her. But I was upset. It was wrong of my parents to have said what they said. Pam isn't difficult with other people, only with them, and not always with them; and there's nothing at all the matter with her head—nothing *at all*.

I don't mind Miss Howard preferring Pam. In

fact, I'm glad that she likes my sister better than me: it makes things fairer. The reason why Mummy and Daddy prefer me to the Twins is because I am so afraid of getting into trouble that I will do anything—*anything*—to please them; and I am ashamed of myself for this. It means that, even though I don't tell downright lies (telling lies would be wicked), I'm not *behaving* truthfully. I pretend to have feelings I don't have, and they believe that what I'm pretending is what's real. Pretending is a way of hiding—my way—so as to be safe. I'm a deceiver.

Miss Howard sees through me; and I'm glad that she does. It's actually a relief. She has summed up the situation, and she doesn't care for little girls who play at being good in order to win their parents' approval. She isn't ever unkind, or unjust, but she has made it clear to me that although I may be a favourite with my mother and with my father, I am not a favourite with her.

But what she doesn't know is *why* I cultivate so assiduously the sycophantic role of goody-goody, for which I despise myself. She doesn't know I have, for years, been witness to the disastrous consequences my sister and my brother suffer by their failing to fulfil, either in character or in behaviour—or both—our parents' expectation of them.

*   *   *

Being my parents' pet may keep me out of danger, but it is not a security that can be taken for granted. It requires unremitting vigilance. There have been some narrow squeaks. The worst, which

271

occurred a few years ago, not long after we had moved from the Bungalow to Bay View Terrace, brought me so close to disaster that it made a deep and ineradicable impression on me. What sin I had committed I don't remember. My recollection is only that it resulted in the command we children dreaded above all else from our father: to go upstairs and wait for him in the bathroom.

I must have been four, or nearly four, at the time, and small for my age. In a state of blind panic I tried to conceal myself by squirming under the iron bath with its claw feet; but my head wouldn't follow my legs and body, and stuck out, unprotected. It was, I suppose, the extremity of my terror that saved me, causing Daddy, on arrival, to relent. In any case, I was not beaten by my father on that occasion, or, indeed, ever. The policy I adopted thereafter of unquestioning obedience has enabled me to evade the punishment I live still, perpetually, in fear of invoking.

For I have seen and heard what can happen—what does happen sometimes—to the Twins. That awful cut-throat razor-strop which hung once on the back of the bathroom door at Bay View Terrace has been transferred to the back of the bathroom door in Grosvenor House. The threat remains; although not carried out in practice nowadays as often as it used to be.

I used to sit on the stairs in Bay View Terrace hearing, horrified, in spite of hands clamped over ears, those blubbering, hiccuping howls from behind the closed door of the bathroom. Jim would be undergoing a beating: *a good thrashing*. For what? I don't recall. Perhaps I never knew; and neither, perhaps, did my poor brother Jim. Was it

272

for not getting his homework sums right? For not winning the high jump—or a sprinting prize—or winning any prize at all at the County School's annual Sports Day? (He, the son of a man with a whole row of silver cups on top of his desk for running and jumping). Was it for saying a swear word that Jim didn't know was a swear word? Or for having flat feet? A stammer? A double hernia? Or was it simply for being a boy? Boys have to expect a thrashing when they disappoint. *To thrash a boy will make a man of him*!

Ah! but what will it make—what has it made—of Jim's twin sister, Pam, who was always the taller, stronger of the two? A rebel, undoubtedly. She is not afraid, as I am, of our father. She stands up to Daddy; stands up against him. She does not, will not, ever beg him for mercy. She will—she does—defy him, fight him; hate him. Pam will never give in.

*   *   *

This year, we are confident, everything has changed for the better. Thrashings belong to the past. We have a new house now, a new car, a new teacher for me and Pam, the arrival of a new baby to look forward to. We are no longer impoverished. From now on all will be sunshine. Our hopes for a golden future soar to dizzy heights; too high, too dizzy.

When Jim comes home from school with a scraped knee and a sorry tale, we are dismayed. But worse is to follow. It transpires that he fell over in the playground, after being jeered at and then pushed and shoved by Dastubes, a French, or

273

possibly Belgian, fellow-pupil. Jim confesses, ashamedly, what he's not, until today, spoken of to anyone: that Dastubes has for weeks been making fun of him, tripping him up and calling him nasty names. Dastubes is a bully. He is also considerably bigger than Jim, and surrounded always by a gang of admiring supporters.

Our father, on hearing this woeful account, knows immediately what has to be done. Dastubes must be confronted. He must be given a taste of his own medicine. He must be challenged, and then defeated in open fight: *shown up*, in a properly constituted boxing match, for the despicable foreign coward he plainly is. That's how Englishmen—and Highland Scots too, of course— defend their honour, by slogging it out, and winning. We British won the Great War, didn't we?—no thanks to the French or the Belgians.

A boxing match? But Jim can't box. He is aghast. He knows nothing about the honourable Englishman's (or Scotsman's) tradition of boxing to assert his superiority.

Well, it's about time, says Daddy, that Jim did learn how to defend himself. Daddy will teach him. Daddy will arrange the whole matter, and will, in person, referee the match to make sure it's all square and above board. The note our father proceeds to write to his son's tormentor is on official Midland Bank paper, and signed with a flourish: G. Hallsmith, DSO, (Capt.) That'll fetch him!

Every evening for a week Jim is given instruction in the rules of the game—the science of boxing—on the patch of grass at the back of Grosvenor House. What counts, he's told, is

274

footwork, and being prepared, as soon as there's an opening, to dodge in fast with an uppercut, and then jab, jab, land a left and a right.

'You have to be springy—quick on your toes—keep moving—dance around him—' Daddy dances round Jim, who isn't quick on his toes. 'And don't drop your guard, boy—keep your fists up—up, *up*!—in front of your face, you little duffer, to protect it. Like this—look at me—' Besides the silver cups for jumping and sprinting, Daddy has a cup for boxing. Jim does as he is bidden, lifting his puny ungloved white-knuckled fists, up, *up*, to shield his frightened face. Much good will they do him as weapons of self-defence.

On Saturday afternoon Dastubes and his cohorts troop through the back gate. Dastubes is a big fleshy boy, with ruddy cheeks and very black hair. He is respectful to our father, and so are the friends who accompany him. Daddy explains to his audience the Queensbury rules of boxing: no hitting below the belt, and no grabbing hold of your adversary. The rounds will last for two minutes each, timed by his wristwatch.

'Shake hands before you start—that's the spirit; and may the best man win!'

Jim, stripped down to shorts and vest, is shivering in the sharp February wind. His teeth are chattering. He's terrified. I am sitting crouched on the concrete steps that connect the path encircling the house to the back garden, hands clamped, as in the bad old Bay View Terrace days, tight over my ears, but watching nevertheless, although sick with dread of the awful inevitable fate in store for my brother.

Daddy raises his arm. 'Are you ready?'

Dastubes' companions give a cheer for their hero, who, without the benefit of having been trained by our father, knows instinctively the vital importance of springy footwork, and the defensive posture, and of dodging in fast in order to land a left and a right with a quick jab-jab.

It's a massacre. Even before the second round is halfway through Jim's nose is bleeding, his lip has been split and one eye closed by a savage blow. Lucy, who was ironing in the kitchen, appears at the back door, pauses for a moment or so, and disappears. On her return she has our mother with her. Round 3. is about to begin.

'That will do, boys—that's quite enough,' says Mummy, loud and clear. 'You're to stop this fighting instantly—'

'They're not fighting, Janet,' our father calls across to her, peevishly, much annoyed by her intervention. 'Can't you see—we're holding a boxing match. It's a sporting event—a contest— and I'm in charge, I'm refereeing it, so as to make sure that everything's fair and square. There's nothing for you to worry about.'

I don't wait to hear another word. I get up and run, run—anywhere out of sight and sound of this unbearable scene of carnage. Whether Daddy makes his weeping bloodied son shake hands again with Dastubes, and whether or not he brings himself, as referee, to acknowledge and declare the big, hefty but foreign—and therefore inferior—boy the victor, I can't say. I never do know exactly how the boxing match ends, only that end it mercifully does, and that Jim, on Monday, takes a black eye to school with him, plus a number of other purpleish bruises disfiguring other parts of his anatomy.

Why, I wonder, just *why* did our father insist on what was bound to be a manifest humiliation for my wretchedly poorly equipped and unbelligerent brother? What alternative outcome could there have been? What else did Daddy expect? What was it he wanted, by that ill-matched match, to prove? And prove to whom?—himself or Jim?

My brother—Pam's twin—is so obviously not intended by nature to be a champion of the boxing ring. He doesn't aim to be any sort of a champion. Jim's aim is, as also is mine, simply to get by; to be, by hook or by crook, a survivor.

*   *   *

My father's affection for me, in such marked contrast to his uninhibited dislike of the Twins, is hard to understand or to explain. And because I can't either understand or explain why I should be thus favoured, it makes me deeply uneasy. It's as if the dragon who gobbles up children for breakfast had beckoned me into his den with the reassuring promise of: *I won't eat* YOU. But why not me? I feel my servile obedience is flimsy protection against the notoriously capricious temper of dragons. Why am I singled out to be the sole recipient of Daddy's confidences?

We have an affinity, my father has decided, in the sphere of literature, and as a consequence he gives me copies of books he remembers enjoying when he was a boy—*The Girl of the Limberlost*, *The Last of the Mohicans*, *The Virginian*—and wants to be told my considered opinion of them, as though I were a grown-up person.

277

He has also presented me with a hardbacked exercise-book in which to write my poems. I don't tell him that I am ashamed of the poetry I write. I know quite well how rubbishy it is, worse than third-rate—not to be compared with the mystical verses of Omar Khayyam or the splendour of 'Ozymandias'. Miss Howard has taught us, with 'The Deserted Village' and 'Elegy in a Country Churchyard', that poetry, to have any value, must be inspirational, arising from the soul of the poet. It has to ring true. My poems have no value. They don't ring true. They ring false. *I've got a little garden/All of my very own* . . . How ridiculous! I haven't got a little garden, all of my very own. It's what the people who come to tea with Mummy and Daddy expect me to recite for their amusement. I have to stand up in front of them—me, Elspeth—wearing my best dress, being shown off for my precocious talent and clapped for my performance. *Oh, how sweet*! I feel a fraud.

The poems I write are written to please my parents. And yet—and *yet* there is a thrill—I can't deny it—in possessing this book and filling its blank pages with my poetry. However soppy I know the poems are, I have myself composed them. One day I will write poetry that pleases me, and I won't repeat it aloud to anybody.

In early summer we sit side by side together, the two of us, Daddy and I. At our backs is the pebbledash house wall, overgrown by clusters of small pink rambler-roses, and before us, a yard or so off, the thick laurel hedge that blocks our view of Mount Wise's roadway. In this constricted area of privacy, perched on a wooden chair and a stool fetched out from the kitchen, my father reads to me the doggerel verse he has invented in the style, he says, of Edward Lear or Lewis Carroll—both famous names.

My father longs, obsessively, to be famous. *Fame* is what he craves. The writing of poetry he counts as being a useful second string to his bow. To acquire fame as a painter is, of course, Daddy's chief ambition, but pretty nearly anything will suffice, just so long as it earns him the public applause by which the famous are rewarded. Fame has the power of alchemy: it is able to transform the dull metal of daily drudgery into glittering gold. Fame is the most desirable of all prizes to strive after. This my father fervently believes. And if painting pictures doesn't win the prize for him, then how about poetry? Perhaps the humorous tale of a fox and a goose, and other satirical sagas manufactured by Daddy (who never makes jokes, and seldom laughs or smiles: his only discernible similarity to Miss Howard)—might not they do the trick and crown him with the glory of those coveted headlines? If Edward Lear and Lewis Carroll succeeded in becoming famous by writing such stuff, why not he also? What do I think?

I tell him that in my opinion his poems are good, and so are his illustrations of them: very good. And in this instance I don't have to fib. I do really think that, as doggerel verse, they are good. I especially admire his illustrations. There is nothing Daddy can't draw, and draw with the greatest facility, at lightning speed. He was born with this gift, an endowment I envy as well as admire. But it happens also to be the reason why our father is no longer as welcome as once he was at the Golf Club.

Daddy's pen-and-ink caricatures of the elderly

members who spend their time sitting inside the clubhouse at card-tables, playing bridge, have not gained him the delighted congratulations he had anticipated. He had mistakenly thought these fusty old fellows would be pleased, would be flattered to have their likenesses immortalised on cartridge paper (and by, what's more, a holder of the DSO), but to his astonishment, and anger, they weren't pleased, or flattered—not a bit. They were offended.

Instead of his clever, accurately observed and professionally executed caricatures leading on to commissions for serious portrait paintings as he had supposed would happen, the sketches have resulted in their perpetrator being cold-shouldered, looked on askance as a queer arty-crafty chap—not the sort of a chap anyone would choose to go round the links with, or invite to make up a foursome at bridge. *An odd fish, Hallsmith!* The advice of certain members— audibly murmured—is to steer clear of him. *Pity!— charming wife . . .*

Our father had pinned his latest hopes on the expectation of these carefully done drawings revealing him to Newquay's residents as a dedicated artist with a brilliant future, and not a mere lowly Bank employee. The response that his artwork provoked was both unforeseen and humiliating, reawakening Daddy's bitterness, always lurking just below the surface, at being forced to live in a world inhabited by blindly stupid philistines.

And so he has ceased, our father, to motor up on a Saturday afternoon, bachelor-free, to the Golf Club overlooking Fistral Bay. Well, he never did much care for golf. It was Mr Knight, that pushy Beachcroft Hotel owner, who had had the idiotic notion of sponsoring him for membership. Daddy's game was always, actually, tennis; never golf.

*　　　*　　　*

One morning I'm standing with my mother, who is talking to Mrs Mitchell, the doctor's wife, on the pavement outside the Great Western Railway Station, when they suddenly see, and, with nods and glances, recognise, the great man whose photograph has been reproduced in the local papers: Augustus John. He strides past them, and me, a tall figure with a beard and a wide-brimmed black felt hat and a brightly coloured silk scarf, close enough to be touched by us; past the stone horse-trough, the jingles, looking at no one.

Augustus John is a very famous artist indeed, and he is here today, in Newquay, because of tragedy. His son, Henry, has been drowned, bathing in Vugga Cove, a beauty spot with a reputation for having its dangerous currents disguised by a seductive appearance of tranquillity. We Hallsmiths have sometimes—not often— bathed there, without drowning.

Twice, last summer, we visited Vugga Cove for a Sunday picnic. Although it is well-known in Newquay as a deep-water swimming pool, created not by man but by the restless action of the waves, it isn't popular with swimmers. People seldom go there, partly on account of its inaccessibility, and partly because, being a considerable distance out to sea, Vugga Cove has no beach, no sand, and is neither more nor less than an indentation carved

281

by nature at the base of those cliffs which form the headland lying on the further side of Crantock. The tide out here is high at all hours of the day or night, and the captive water, slopping idly to and fro within an almost completely enclosed circle, has only a narrow passage of entrance or exit connecting it to the tempestuous outer ocean.

When Daddy drove his family there last August, he left the car on the grassy clifftop, and we scrambled down by easy stages to a wide flat sun-warmed shelf of rock, where we immediately made ourselves at home by spreading over it our baskets and towels and rugs, and as usual Daddy's old wartime paint-spattered trench-coat.

Before having lunch, we bathed. Mummy was anxious about the whole enterprise, but our father was adamant, insistent that his children must learn to take risks, and be—yes!—adventurous: no molly-coddling! Jim did manage to get excused by Mummy citing the disability of his double hernia, but Pam was all agog to cast herself recklessly into the water; and where Pam went, I could follow.

Daddy tied a rope round the waist of each of us in turn, and one by one we leapt into the sea's icy green embrace, swimming and splashing, fathoms out of our depth, until he hauled us up, like fish at the end of a line, dripping wet and exhilarated, on to the safety of the rocky plateau.

But Henry John didn't have a rope tied round his waist, and his famous father walks the streets of Newquay, wrapped in grief, oblivious to the whispers and the pointing fingers.

*   *   *

282

The shortest poem that my father has written is about me. In shame and acute discomfort, I listen to him reading it as we sit together, embowered by the pink rambler-roses:

> Little girl, I love you,
> And I'll tell you why—
> Something, something, sweet and true,
> I can put my trust in you
> Till I die.

His trust is, of course, wholly misplaced. I am far too frightened of him to be trustworthy. But the words he reads aloud to me scorch my brain, my conscience, as if they were tongues of fire. Daddy loves *me*: I know he does, because that's what the poem says. And because he is my father, I ought to love *him*. But I know too, secretly, that I don't, and that I can't. Not to love my father is wrong—it's worse than wrong: probably it's wicked, a sin. Daddy is telling me, here on the garden path, very privately, not just that he loves me, but that he trusts me to love him in return. This is what the poem means: he trusts me to love him—he thinks that I do; and I don't.

How can I bear the deceit, the guiltiness of not feeling what I ought to feel—what I pretend to feel; the guilt of knowing that I am devious, two-faced, a cowardly traitor, bent upon saving myself, at all costs, from being the object of my father's hatred and scorn, which appal me, from his anger, which terrifies me, as it terrifies my brother Jim.

I shan't be beaten with the strap that hangs on the back of the bathroom door as punishment for my sin, because nobody knows of it, except me. It is a dreadful burden, though, a weight like a stone inside me. I don't see how I can ever get rid of it. The best thing will be not to think about this badness of mine, buried out of sight. I shall try to forget it's there. Daddy won't guess—no one will guess—that I'm only pretending to love him. I'm good at pretending.

*   *   *

The sitting room of our new house has a low wide bay window on the side of Grosvenor Road, resulting in a slight extension of floor space which is annexed at weekends—if they are winter or spring, non-picnic weekends—by our father. Here, where daylight floods in unimpeded, he arranges his easel, lays out his brushes, opens his plain wooden box containing squidgy tubes of oily pigment, picks up his palette with the hole in it for his thumb to go through, props a canvas on the easel, positions his model, and sets to work on the portrait that he will dispatch, when finished, to compete and be judged amongst the hundreds of pictures sent in from all over the country as either worthy or not worthy of acceptance for the Summer Exhibition of the Royal Academy of London.

Every year, every single year, a picture painted by Daddy, expensively framed, and almost always a portrait—although occasionally, if no suitable portrait has been satisfactorily completed by the closing date, a landscape or seascape—is fitted with infinite care into a flat purpose-made packing-case, labelled, and borne away by British Rail to its ultimate destination in the distant

284

metropolis. Each year we see it off, believing that *this* time Daddy's masterpiece is bound to be accepted by those unknown power-wielding judges in London. And each year our father's painting, dispatched always in the glowing certainty of its undoubted success, is returned to him by British Rail in the same, but by now travel-scarred packing-case: rejected. *Rejected*!

Sometimes the model he uses is me, or it may be himself—a romanticised mirror-image. His attempts at painting our mother, inevitably begun in a mood of irritation, seldom progress beyond the first few sittings before being abandoned. He finds her features less rewarding, it would seem, than his own, or mine. This year it is my sister's turn to be the subject of Daddy's current entry in the Royal Academy stakes.

Pam resents extremely being obliged to wear, on an ordinary Sunday morning, her daffodil-yellow chiffon party dress—the dress that kind-hearted Mrs Brown has had made specially for her and included in the latest consignment of Felicity's outgrown clothes for me. She hates having to pose for Daddy, having to maintain her head at such-and-such an angle, to keep from fidgeting—to *stay still*! She obeys his instructions with the worst possible grace. And while, as her father's rebellious captive, she sits motionless, or nearly motionless before him in her charming yellow party frock, he tells her how disagreeable, how downright ugly— yes, *ugly*!—she is, with that unpleasantly sullen look on her face. Why can't she smile? She has the appearance, he informs her, of a white negress, with those thick lips of hers: blubber lips, he calls them.

What does Daddy mean by blubber lips? *Blubbing* is a word he frequently uses in exasperation to Jim: *Stop your blubbing, boy!* To blub means to cry. He is insulting Pam, taunting her now, because she won't smile for him. She won't cry for him—blub for him—either, whatever the rude and hurtful remarks he throws at her. She doesn't answer. She will sit there for as long as she must in front of him, fiercely silent.

Daddy paints my sister in her pretty dress, with her fair frizzy cloud of newly permed hair. He paints her mutinous expression and her angry blue eyes—eyes as angry as his own brown ones are so often. It is a good likeness. Daddy always does get a good likeness. What he finds worrisome is the actual handling of the paint itself—the tricks of the trade, as it were. He hasn't ever been taught how to deal with the medium, but he is convinced he has no need of teaching. Drawing was never a problem for our father: it came naturally. And as to painting, he can perfectly well learn, without a teacher, by trial and error, the secrets of working oil paint on to canvas. Why, of course he can! Wasn't he born an artist?

The Royal Academy doesn't exhibit his portrait of Pam in her yellow dress: like all of the others, they return it to Daddy, rejected.

Every year my father pores over the glossy pages of the Royal Academy's latest catalogue whereon are reproduced in miniature a number of those paintings lucky enough to have been selected for display in the most recent of its annual Summer Exhibitions. It is the only art-related publication to be found beneath our family roof. I too pore over the glossy pages, seeking enlightenment. What, I

286

wonder, is the reason for the success of this year's winning entries? Are they really better than the pictures painted by Daddy? Or is it a matter, simply, of luck?

I become familiar with the names that recur again and again, year after year: Augustus John, who likes to paint pictures of gipsies and their caravans; Dame Laura Knight, who goes in for circus performers; and Sir Alfred Munnings, who specialises in horses. Lamorna Birch, Someone-or-other Dugdale, Somebody Gunn—the names of Royal Academy exhibitors are the only names of painters, artists, I have ever heard of, past or present, in the entire history of the world, because they are the only ones that exist for, or are of any interest, to my father.

Apart from the yearly RA catalogue, my education in the field of art is limited to book illustrations and the boldly coloured posters advertising seaside resorts pasted up on hoardings outside the Great Western Railway Station. I know, of course, that they are not *real art*, these posters and book illustrations, even if they do stir my emotions, and often even thrill me, in a way the Royal Academy's catalogues never do. They just happen to be pictures which I love to gaze at: that's all. Royal Academy art—real art—is, I know, different. I don't say so aloud, but in my private estimation it's actually duller.

But I enjoy sitting for Daddy on Sunday mornings. I enjoy the smell of turpentine, and the sight of those little squiggly worms and blobs of paint—aquamarine, burnt sienna, carmine, ochre, white—that he squeezes out on to his palette. He has a collection of brushes to choose from, all of

287

them elegantly long and slender; much longer than the stubby watercolour brushes that Pam and I are accustomed to use. The brush-part of ours is floppy and soft, but his have short stiff bristly ends, like bits cut off his moustache.

Chiefly, though, I enjoy posing for Daddy as his model because it's a time of rare harmony, a peaceful unquarrelsome interlude, the rest of the family being absent. The two of us, Daddy and me, are alone in what counts, for a brief while, as his studio. He doesn't tick me off, or say nasty things about my face or my expression. We hardly speak. He screws up his eyes, as if it's not me at all he's looking at, but somebody quite else: the person who he will eventually cause to materialise on his canvas.

Sitting still doing nothing isn't a hardship for me; it's an easy unanxious way to pass the time. I don't fidget, as Pam does when she's modelling. Beyond the easel I can see the small upright oak desk where every weekday afternoon for an hour, regularly, our mother plants herself on the high square cross-stitch-embroidered stool, (its embroidery accomplished long ago by her Aunt Jessie in Anglesey), and where she covers, with her large firm clearly formed handwriting, sheet after sheet of paper. Letters flow from the broad unhesitating nib of Mummy's green fountain pen in a steady stream. So many letters! Who is it our mother directs all those letters to?

She writes to Georgina Chapman, resident in Canada, who was her best friend when they were VADs together during the Great War. She writes to Lilian Fisher, who lives in London, and also to the other Lilian, wife of Daddy's elder half-brother, our Uncle Malcolm, a doctor, (as is Uncle Ralph, the younger half-brother: doctors both). She writes to Biddy McNeile, to Elsie Walker, sisters of two of the men she had been going to, but never did marry: Basil, who died of TB; Geoffrey, who was killed in France.

What is it that Mummy, seated at the little old oak desk, writes every afternoon, unfailingly, compulsively, to her far-off circle of women friends? Is she creating a fantasy version of her life, her marriage, a fiction that, by avoiding the disappointing truth, manages to assure them, and herself, of a happiness not, alas, realised? Or is she having to unburden her woes in a daily catharsis of letters, letters, because this is the only way she can provide for herself the comfort so sadly lacking, and so sorely needed?

*   *   *

When you are told that something is going to happen, something wonderful, and then the weeks pass by and it doesn't happen, you think it never will. You give up expecting it to.

We had thought we should never move house; and then we did. It was the same with the baby. When our mother said we were going to have one, we imagined it would be soon; and it wasn't soon. Christmas came, and Christmas went, and we moved at last from Bay View Terrace into Grosvenor House. And then there were daffodils, and Easter, and still no baby appeared on the scene. We got used to it not arriving, to it not arriving *ever*, in spite of our mother growing gradually fatter and fatter. We had begun to feel

289

she would always be fat and have a big stomach, and we almost forgot it was the baby that she had told us was inside her which accounted for her stomach swelling up, and her skirts having to be altered and sewn on to elastic waistbands.

What puzzled me and Pam was how the baby inside Mummy would be able to get out. She hadn't told us how, and we didn't care to ask her, or Lucy, for an explanation. In fairy stories, when the King and the Queen—or when Mary in the Bible—had a baby, they simply had it, straight off: a wave of the wand, or angels announcing the birth, and there the baby was, either as a Princess in a palace or as Jesus in a stable: no fuss, no mention of big stomachs.

Pam and I did discuss the problem between ourselves, and reached the conclusion that our mother's belly button, by stretching wider and wider, would make an opening like a door for the baby to escape through. It seemed to be the only possible solution. And having decided that this was the answer to the difficulty, we put it out of our minds, preferring not to dwell on the slightly distasteful mental contemplation of our mother's body, which we had never seen, or wanted to see, unclothed.

In any case, our baby delayed being born for such an age we had very nearly ceased to believe in it by the beginning of May, when Jim's troublesome double hernia worsened all of a sudden. The truss he wore was no longer of any use, and something had to be done in a hurry. This time, instead of taking him to Truro, it was decided that the operation on my brother, which Dr Mitchell said was urgently necessary, should be performed in Purley Memorial Hospital, miles and miles away from Newquay but close to where Cousin Edith and Cousin Mildred live. Mummy could stay with them therefore, while Jim was having the operation, and he could stay with them after coming out of hospital. Then, when he was strong enough to travel on a railway, Daddy would fetch him home.

So off they went, the two of them, Jim white-faced, in pain and afraid, and our mother, in spite of an enormously big stomach, unafraid and determined to be cheerful. No amount of advice from her own mother, our Granny Laurie—who wrote from Oxford to say how most unwise it was of Janet to undertake an arduous and exhausting journey in her condition—nothing could persuade Mummy to change her mind. By *her condition* Granny Laurie meant that it's getting very near indeed to the date when this baby of ours is supposed to be born. Although Mummy chose to ignore the warnings, nevertheless she did agree to return home directly after Jim's operation, leaving it to the Martin cousins, as well as to Granny Hallsmith and our father's two sisters, Aunt Dorothy and Aunt Rosemary, who also live not far from Purley Memorial Hospital, to visit the invalid every afternoon.

And it's all happened without a hitch, confounding Granny Laurie's dark forebodings. Jim has had his operation, and Mummy is back again safely in Grosvenor House, having suffered no ill effects and with her tummy as big as ever.

Jim writes to us regularly. The postman delivers a letter from him practically every morning, and we reply almost as often. His handwriting is disgracefully bad, but perhaps it's difficult, writing in bed. We're very pleased to be sent so many letters, even if they are badly written. He tells us his news. The stitches have been taken out, he reports, and each day he's visited by different relations. It sounds as if the nurses are making a great fuss of him. In fact, we think Jim may actually be having a rather good time in hospital, and enjoying himself; and when he gets home he won't have to wear that disgusting truss any more.

I can't help wondering, silently, whether it's because my brother and sister are twins that they have had to have these operations, Pam for TB glands, and Jim for a double hernia? There doesn't seem to be anything the matter, I'm glad to say, with me, but I'm not a twin.

*   *   *

Summer is here. Already May has been and gone, and there still is no baby. We had just about given up all hope of it when, more than halfway through June, Nurse Rowe appears at the door of Grosvenor House with a suitcase in her hand, and our belief is instantly restored. She may not look much like a wand-waver or an angel-announcer, but as soon as this person, a stranger to us, materialises on the doorstep we are certain that a baby is really going to be born at last.

Not, though, immediately; not before a further week of waiting and having, meanwhile, to endure the unwelcome presence of a visitor we all of us, except for Mummy, detest. Nurse Rowe is called the Monthly Nurse, because a month is the length of time required, apparently, for a baby to get accustomed to being born, and for us to get accustomed to the managing of it.

From the first few moments of her arrival here Nurse Rowe has turned everything in the family topsy-turvy. Pam and I have been obliged to move into the spare bedroom so that she can have our bedroom, and Jim—only recently home again after staying for a luxurious ten days with Cousin Mildred in Sanderstead, Surrey, recovering from what was a serious operation—he has been turfed out of his bedroom too (we don't know exactly why), and allocated Lucy's now-and-again boxroom quarters.

Daddy says he can't abide Nurse Rowe, and we agree with him: we can't abide her either, and nor can Lucy. Nurse Rowe is quite old, and she's bossy and bad-tempered and extremely ugly; and she seems to think that she's in charge of the entire household, and can lay down the rules for how everyone has to behave. She doesn't like children, which is what me and the Twins are: not a bit. She only likes babies—and their mothers too, of course.

Our mother gets along swimmingly with awful Nurse Rowe; but Mummy always does enjoy anything to do with nursing and illness, because of her having looked after wounded soldiers in the Great War. So they joined forces immediately, Mummy and the Monthly Nurse, and were occupied for hours in each other's company, marking off lists of equipment and checking over piles of baby clothes together. There's been a cradle in Mummy's bedroom since the end of May, and downstairs by the porch entrance, ready and waiting, an empty pram with enormous wheels. As

293

to our father, for the past week he's hardly come home at all, spending every evening, and the whole of Saturday afternoon and Sunday at the Tennis Club.

Then, this morning, the 27th of June, Lucy woke us up—Pam and me first, and afterwards Jim—to break the news.

'You've got a lovely little baby brother,' she said.

And it's true: we have. He was born in the night, while we three were fast asleep. We knew nothing about it. Or at least, my sister Pam says that once, in the dark, she did think she heard Dr Mitchell's voice, and the sound of doors opening and shutting, but she had supposed it must be part of a dream. It wasn't a dream, though. Here he is—a real live new baby brother, with blue eyes and ginger hair; which means that now there are two boys as well as two girls in the Hallsmith family. What an amazing change!

*   *   *

I shall always remember this year, I'm certain I shall, as a golden year: the summer of *the baby*.

Ever since Nurse Rowe packed her bag and— thank goodness!—departed, he has been truly *our* baby. His full name is Guthrie Harvey, but we are to call him Harvey, which was the name of Daddy's father, and also of Daddy's younger brother. I rather wish he'd been given a different name—a name that would be quite his own, instead of belonging previously, twice, to people who are dead; especially as one person was an old man with a beard, and the other died young, and so sadly, in the 'flu epidemic. It isn't really fair to our baby, who ought to start off, I think, with a name as brand-new as himself. But it can't be altered. Harvey is what our parents have settled on, and that's that.

Me and Pam are allowed to hold him, and lift him in and out of his pram, and we can rock the pram gently, so as to send him to sleep, and we can sponge water over him when he's being bathed, and even sometimes feed him with his bottle of Nestlé's milk. I don't mind in the slightest, not now, that Rosie belongs to my sister. Having a baby is far, *far* more fun, as we had known it would be, than having a dolly.

Some mothers feed their babies with milk that comes out of their bosoms. That's actually what bosoms are for. Our mother stayed in bed for a fortnight after Harvey was born, resting, and one day I walked into her room when she was sitting up with her nightdress unbuttoned and her front showing all bare and bulgy. The baby was crammed against one of her bosoms. He was meant to be sucking milk out of it. The other bosom was hanging down, with a funny long red blob on the end. I had a dreadful shock, because it wasn't at all nice to look at. I wished I hadn't seen it. I went out of Mummy's room very quickly, and I tried to forget what I'd seen.

It didn't occur again, because Nurse Rowe said that Nestlé's Milk would be better for the baby than our mother's kind of milk. She bought a great many tins of Nestlé's Condensed Milk, and she mixed the milk from one little tin with warm water to make it runny, and then she gave it to our baby to drink out of a bottle. Instead of a cork, the bottle has a toffee-coloured rubber teat stretched over its opening, with a tiny hole, the size of a pin-prick, in the middle. If the hole was to be any bigger, the baby would choke, we were told. You learn such valuable information as this only when you have a real baby to take care of.

Babies don't have teeth, so they can't eat. A bottleful of milk is the same for them as a meal is for us. I'm glad the Monthly Nurse insisted on Harvey having Nestlé's Condensed Milk, and not the milk out of our mother's bosom, because now we can feed him ourselves when he's hungry. Also, the condensed milk that's left inside each tin before it's thrown away is absolutely delicious, very sweet, like a thick sort of sugary cream. We lick it off our fingers, and it's my belief Nurse Rowe liked the taste of it as much as we do. I caught her once eating it out of a tin with a teaspoon. Perhaps that was her reason for buying Nestlé's Condensed Milk in the first place.

The smell of a clean baby—which ours is, mostly—seems to linger everywhere, tingeing the atmosphere of the whole house. Our baby smells of scented soap, and talcum powder, and his gingery hair, which we love to sniff, is fragrant, like hay. When Pam and me go out for a walk with him, helping to push the pram, we keep having to stop, because almost everyone we meet wants to peep under the hood at Harvey. They all say how beautiful he is; which he is.

My sister and I are very proud of our baby; and Lucy and Mummy are proud of him too, of course. Jim doesn't take much notice. He hadn't wanted us to have a baby, and now that we've got one, he shows hardly any interest. Nor does our father. Daddy still spends all his spare time playing tennis up at the Club.

* * *

This is a summer of notable happenings, and the most notable, after the birth of Harvey, is a visit we have been expecting for some time from a tremendously famous man, known as T.E. Lawrence, or Lawrence of Arabia, but referred to by our mother simply as *Ned*, because her family and his family were neighbours long ago when Mummy was a little girl; and ever since then she and her brother Andrew and her four sisters had always been friends with the five Lawrence boys.

Will Lawrence, Ned's brother, was somebody our mother would have married if he hadn't been killed at the beginning of the Great War, flying an aeroplane over the trenches in France. Mrs Lawrence, *his* mother, blamed *our* mother for having encouraged Will to join the Royal Flying Corps, and she has refused to speak to Mummy ever since. But Ned Lawrence, who wasn't killed, became famous by living in Arabia, and riding about on a camel, and teaching Arab sheikhs how to fight. And now he's back in England, and has joined the Air Force—although not as a pilot—and his air station, or aerodrome, is conveniently near enough to Newquay for him to be able to pay a visit and have a picnic tea with us on the Great Western Beach. Mummy and he have been exchanging letters, to and fro, until it was all arranged, and a date fixed; and the date is today.

The tide being, luckily, right out, our father, who has got permission from Mr Oxley, the Bank Manager, to have this afternoon off, even though it isn't a Saturday, can walk across the sands to our corner, where we are waiting to welcome Mummy's famous friend.

Daddy has only seen T.E. Lawrence once before, and probably he hardly saw him that once. The occasion was when he married our mother-to-be, Janet Laurie, and she has told us that Ned Lawrence slipped into the church, and stood at the very back of it during the wedding ceremony, and left again immediately afterwards without saying a word to either of them.

Our father has pinned all his long-cherished hopes on this meeting. Today he will encounter, face to face, the world-renowned historic Lawrence of Arabia, on the sands of the Great Western Beach. Everything depends on Mummy's famous friend inviting Daddy to paint his portrait. With such a painting, exhibited in the Royal Academy, Daddy's reputation will be made, and his dream realised. He too will become famous—famous at last *as an artist*!

T.E. Lawrence—*Ned*—is late for his appointment, which had been set at three o'clock. We children hang about on the slipway, by the sweetie kiosk, ready to greet him and conduct him to where Mummy and Daddy are sitting, with Harvey, the baby, in the sheltered angle made by buttress and wall: *our* corner. But the famous visitor doesn't come, and doesn't come, until we grow tired of waiting for him. We scuffle around idly, bored, in the dry soft silvery sand that always accumulates above the high-tide mark, littered with empty cigarette packets and chocolate wrappers. Jim drifts away. And then, just when we've decided he isn't coming, ever, we see him on his motor-bicycle, weaving slowly, slowly down the hill. He brings the bike to a halt a few yards from Pam and me, switches off the engine, and dismounts. Here in front of us is the person, more celebrated even than Charlie Chaplin, about whom we have overheard our parents talking and talking in fevered anticipation: Lawrence of Arabia himself. We view his appearance with pity.

It is a gloriously warm summer's day. My sister and I are suntanned and barefooted—practically naked, indeed, in our skimpy bathing suits—whereas he is wearing a uniform of thick scratchy material, heavy clumpy boots, and knee-breeches. Our legs are bare, but his are bandaged from the ankles up, by what are called, we know, puttees. How horribly hot and uncomfortable he's bound to be, poor man, inside his layers of stuffy clothing! How he must wish, as we would wish if we were in his place, that he was dressed in no more than a bathing-costume, the same as us!

We approach him with caution, not certain how

299

to begin.

'Hullo!' we say, experimentally.

To our surprise, he doesn't say *Hullo*! in return. He removes his goggles. Perhaps he's deaf, and didn't hear what we said.

Pam introduces us. 'I'm Pam,' she announces, loud and clear, 'and this is Ellie—Elspeth.'

Mummy's friend, after glancing at each of us, briefly, unsmiling, gazes above our heads, and round about, with an air of impatience.

'I expect,' says Pam, politely, 'you're wondering where our father and mother are. That's why we've been waiting here, so as to show you where they are. I'm your godchild, actually,' she is brave enough to add.

At her last remark T.E. Lawrence glances again at my sister, without any increase of interest, but with some obvious annoyance. Her tiresome claim provokes him into the withering response that, for her information, he has more godchildren than he can count—*actually*.

'He might have been talking about having more spots of chickenpox than he could count, and not about children at all,' Pam, later on, declares to me, with indignation. For the fact is, T.E. Lawrence, the nation's hero, hurt my sister's feelings, her pride. He was rude to her, snubbed her unkindly, sneered; and she won't ever forgive him for it.

We thought that before following us on foot he would be sure to prop up his motor-bicycle, and leave it at the side of the road. But instead he lugs the huge bike along with him, grasping hold of the handlebars and being half-dragged down the slithery slope of the slipway by the weight of the massive machine he's trying to control. When its wheels reach the bottom of the slipway they sink into the loose heaps of powdery sand, and he has to struggle and strain to extricate them, frowning at the effort, and muttering under his breath, as if the final irritating straw of an irritating day is to have his motor-bike ignominiously stuck here, amongst the scattered rubbish of a Newquay beach.

We point him towards where our parents are sitting in deckchairs, with a rug spread, and baskets on the ground, and Harvey, the baby, in his pram. He sets off, Ned Lawrence, Mummy's friend, in their direction, and we stand and watch him go trudging laboriously across to our corner, a small man, made smaller, dwarfed, by the size of the motor-bike he's pushing.

'I didn't think he'd be so little,' says Pam, with a note of contempt in her voice.

'He didn't like us—did he?' I say.

'We don't care—we don't like *him*,' says my sister, furiously. 'Come on, Ellie, let's have a bathe. It isn't teatime yet—I'll race you to the sea—'.

The tide has turned, but is still far out when we espy our father striding rapidly away from us towards the harbour. But how very strange! He doesn't have to go back to work today—Mr Oxley gave Daddy a free afternoon.

We splash hurriedly out of the water and run as fast as we can up the beach to where Jim is engaged on digging a castle. We can see now that, except for the baby, Mummy is all alone in our corner.

'Jim! What's happened?'

Jim says he doesn't know what's happened.

'But where is he?—Mummy's friend?'

'He's gone,' says Jim, not bothering to pause in his digging activity.

'*Gone*?—but he's only just come—'

We rush, dripping wet and panting, to the slipway, and are in time to catch a glimpse of Ned Lawrence roaring away up the hill on his monster motor-bike, round the corner, and—yes—gone! His visit to the Hallsmith family on the Great Western Beach has lasted for less than half-an-hour.

What went wrong? Something must have done. Our brother Jim isn't able to throw any light on the matter. Busy at his digging, he wasn't within earshot; nor, anyway, paying much attention to the group. First, he says, they were standing up, talking, and then they were sitting down. And then, quite soon, the two men had jumped up again, and Jim thinks they might have been arguing; and then they suddenly, without any further warning signs, broke apart, and made off at top speed in opposite directions. That's all Jim can tell us about it.

Somebody must have said something that caused offence. Our father, as we are well aware, loses his temper very easily, and maybe Ned Lawrence also loses his temper easily. Besides which, we wonder whether possibly he was disappointed when he saw Mummy: they hadn't met for years. In the photographs of her, taken before she got married, Mummy is not merely tall and beautiful, but *exceedingly* slim, and this is probably how her friend expected her still to be. And she's not slim, of course, not any more—on the contrary. Her arms, in particular, are noticeably fat, and covered in freckles. Moreover,

Janet, our mother, has had four children since he last saw her, and he plainly doesn't at all care for children.

But if Ned Lawrence found the meeting a disappointment, how much more so has it been a disappointment for our father. The portrait that was to have made him famous will never now be painted. We don't know exactly *why* not. Our parents don't discuss it. The name of Mummy's famous friend will cease, from this day on, to be mentioned in our family.

*　　*　　*

The failure of Ned Lawrence's visit isn't this summer's only disappointment, although it is the worst. When a Royal Navy frigate anchors in the bay, quite close to land, the whole of Newquay buzzes with excitement. Nobody can recall such a visitation happening previously, and the general impression is that, simply by the vessel's stationary presence out at sea, Newquay is being done a singular honour, almost as if His Majesty, King George, had deigned to give us, in passing, a nod of recognition. How long it will remain, or what is its purpose in being there, nobody knows. Several days have gone by already, and every morning when we look out to sea, there it still is. Some Newquay residents have even had the good luck to observe members of the crew strolling about in the streets and shops like ordinary mortals.

The captain himself comes ashore, and our father tells us at lunchtime on Wednesday that not only has he, Daddy, chatted across the counter of the Midland Bank to this illustrious personage—

struck up an instant man-to-man friendship with him—but more, has had the temerity to invite him to tea with us in Grosvenor House on Saturday afternoon. According to Daddy, the Captain—a nice chap, who didn't put on any airs—was pleased as Punch at being asked, and said he'd bring a few of his officers along with him.

Goodness, what a thrilling prospect! The other customers in the Bank, respectfully listening to this exchange and in no hurry to be served, were green with envy, Daddy told us; and so was Mr Oxley.

At four o'clock on Saturday afternoon our dining-room table, covered by a beautiful lacy cloth, is spread with quantities of scrumptious food: a banquet. Unsure of exactly how many visitors will turn up, there are plates and plates of sandwiches, cakes and buns galore, dozens of buttered scones, and bowls of clotted cream and strawberry jam. The precious seldom-used wedding-present china has been produced, and likewise Mummy's Aunt Jessie's linen napkins, crotchet-edged. Mummy is wearing her frilly crêpe-de-chine blouse, and Lucy a fresh, newly starched apron. Ready for the influx of exotic strangers, a little nervous, but eagerly expectant, we wait.

We wait, and the minutes tick past, the half-hour, the hour. They don't arrive. They're late; they're very late. The sandwiches dry. They haven't come; they're not ever going to come. Lucy, in silence, clears the table.

No word of apology, nor yet of explanation, do we receive. Perhaps the affable Royal Naval captain forgot that he and his officers had been invited to tea by Captain (Retired) Hallsmith,

DSO; just forgot.

We stare seawards on Sunday, and the frigate is out there still, unconcernedly riding at anchor. But on Monday morning when we look, it has vanished.

*   *   *

The summer has had its disappointments for our father, but also its consolations, and even, indeed, its triumphs for him. Chief amongst them is Daddy's election to the post of Honorary Secretary of the Tennis Club. The position puts him, he considers, in undisputed charge of it; a charge he relishes to the extent that nowadays weekend picnic excursions with his family are of secondary importance. First and foremost, Daddy's free time from now on is to be allotted mainly to the business of running the Tennis Club. He is determined to make a success of it—a big success, big enough for those blithering old idiots at the Golf Club to sit up and be sorry. That'll show 'em what they've lost!

He and Wilton, the groundsman, indulge in long and mutually satisfying discussions. Wilton, despite his gloomy demeanour, is appreciative, rather than resentful of this collaboration. It indicates that the silent drudgery of his maintaining single-handed, year after year, five grass tennis courts is being officially, if belatedly recognised and registered. To please Mr Hallsmith, a fellow-survivor of the Great War, Wilton is prepared to take on additional work. Together they plan to increase the Club's amenity value by bringing back into use the two extra courts lying on a higher level at the far end of the Club's property which have been

allowed to revert to a state of wilderness through
the former apathy of Committee members.

But expansion and improvements come at a
price, and funds are low. Money is urgently
needed. Daddy, who knows all about money,
proposes various ways and means of raising it.
Instead of the somewhat lacklustre tournament
that took place once, and once only, during the
season, he now proceeds to organise a series of
tournaments that will be held at intervals
throughout the summer. Miss Veah and Miss
Isobel Clark-Ourry, assured by Daddy that their
participation in the scheme is absolutely essential,
promise him, fluttery with excitement, to return
from their Rose Café in Porth on every such
occasion so as to provide their famously delectable
cream teas. Handbills are displayed in the foyers of
Newquay's best hotels: visitors will be offered the
privilege of a special short-term membership, thus

306

enabling them either to compete in the tournaments or to enjoy the matches from the sidelines, as spectators.

The frequent, almost weekly meetings our father convenes in a room of the creosote-smelling pavilion are invariably well-attended, and his projects heartily supported. What an unexpected live wire Hallsmith is proving to be! Stirred out of its habitual drowsy torpor, Newquay Lawn Tennis Club becomes revitalised, a veritable honey pot, centre of healthy sporting activity and entertainment for persons of—naturally— acceptable social standing. And this astonishing regeneration is due entirely to the drive and energy of its recently appointed Secretary: namely, our father.

For Daddy, the rewards of his resounding Tennis Club success are many, not the least of them being that it demonstrates he can rival and even outshine Mummy in organisational ability, while also having the gratifying result of promoting him to a more equal footing with her in the eyes of the public. He and our mother are both of them, it's true, on the Cottage Hospital Committee, but they are there only because of her invaluable wartime nursing experience, and the fame attaching to Mummy once, years ago, driving ambulances about in London, and being Commandant of an Army convalescent hospital, and receiving a medal from King George for services rendered. Mr Hallsmith was invited to join the Cottage Hospital Committee purely and simply as Mrs Hallsmith's husband, and all too gallingly well he knows it.

When it comes to tennis and the Tennis Club,

however, their rôles are reversed. Mummy no longer plays tennis, although she did when she was younger. Today Daddy is the tennis player, and rather a good one. Rather good, but not—alas!— *quite* good enough.

He will reach the finals of the tournaments that he himself initiated, but he doesn't ever manage to win them. Whether the contests are singles or doubles, the outcome is the same: Daddy loses. If he is playing in a doubles match the failure might be blamed on his partner—Bo'sun Hooper, or Harry North perhaps, or dear sweetly smiling Mr Lodge. But if he is alone on his side of the net, who can he blame but himself? There is always, to be sure, the possibility of the umpire giving a wrong verdict: that ball wasn't *out*, it was *in*; it touched the line—didn't anyone else see how the chalk flew up? Or the trouble could be to do with his racquet, or the sun got in his eyes, or his opponent took a mean advantage, serving before he was ready. It's never fair, never his fault. He ought not to have been beaten; he deserves to have won.

The distressing fact of the matter is, our father, who wants always, passionately, to win the competitions he enters, never does win. And the bitterness of defeat is intensified by the silver cups on his rolltop desk: proof, proudly exhibited, that Daddy, when a schoolboy, was indeed a winner, champion of sprinting, jumping, hurdling, boxing. Why is it he can't succeed in repeating those glory days here, on Newquay's grass tennis courts, a couple of decades later?

We children suffer agonies during the last afternoon of pretty nearly every tournament. The finals, and sometimes the semi-finals, are played

308

on Court No. 1, in front of a pavilion crowded with eager spectators; and there our father will be, in his white flannels, facing across the net at perhaps Douglas Adey, six-foot-three inches tall, or perhaps Pig-faced Ralph with his permanently surly expression, or perhaps a holiday stranger, and we know we are going to have to watch Daddy being beaten again, in full view of all these watching people.

We sit in the first row of the audience, crouching, scrunched up, on the pavilion's long low plank step, the dry tarry smell of the baking-hot wood in our nostrils, flinching at every bloomer, every shot, misjudged, that will lead, as it must and does, to inevitable humiliating defeat.

Daddy is a bad loser. He is a very bad loser. He hates to lose. And we, his children, hate to have to witness him hating to lose. Everyone around us, behind us, is in such good spirits, laughing and talking, joking—not, of course, when the umpire, perched high on the top of his ladder, calls for silence, and the game begins. Then there is a deathly hush, broken only by the *ping*! of the ball being hit and the umpire's voice proclaiming the score. But between games, between matches, there is a party atmosphere. The sun shines, the sky is blue. All the people who have flocked up to the Tennis Club—players, spectators, visitors, residents—are happy, revelling in their day out, except for us. We can't enjoy the day. We are tense with the dread of how—we know—ineluctably, it will end. Oh Daddy, please win! Please, for our sakes, win! But he won't. He always loses the final match.

It is better, from our point of view, if Daddy is

knocked out earlier on in the tournament. Then there is a chance we children may be spared the ultimate shame of our father's uncontrollable ill-humour, his display of unsportsmanlike behaviour, exposed for all to see on Court No. 1.

*   *   *

Every year in August or September Sir Oliver Lodge pays a visit of several weeks to his holiday home, the house near the harbour built on top of Towan Beach's rocky little island, from which romantically inaccessible retreat he seldom emerges until the day of departure. It's widely reported in Newquay that the old man is busy writing a book, and shuts himself up out of sight so as not to be distracted or disturbed in his work.

Sir Oliver Lodge is extremely famous on account of the scientific interest he takes in something called spiritualism, which Pam and I think, although we aren't quite sure, is about what happens to people when they die. Our parents either can't or don't want to explain to us children what exactly spiritualism is. Mummy finds it an uncomfortable topic because she is religious, and our father finds it uncomfortable because he isn't religious. She thinks it may very probably be wrong to delve into such matters, and he thinks it's a load of stuff and nonsense.

But whatever they think, there is no denying the subject of spiritualism is nowadays immensely popular with a great many readers of daily newspapers. There is also no denying that Sir Oliver Lodge has a title, and lots of money, and is an internationally famous figure. When, therefore, our parents are invited to venture over that airy footbridge to have dinner with him on his island, their worrisome uncertainties cease all at once to be worrisome, and without hesitating for a moment, they accept.

The invitation, rarely given to outsiders and consequently implying exceptional favour, is issued to them through the agency of the older of his two sons, known to the Hallsmith family as *our Mr Lodge*. We call him this partly because, unlike his brother Noel and his two sisters, he visits Newquay with the utmost regularity every summer, and holds a permanent membership card for the Tennis Club, a privilege accorded usually only to residents. Middle-aged and shy, he plays tennis moderately well, is polite and amiable to everyone, but seems to feel especially drawn to our parents, rather as a frail craft might seek shelter in the lee of sturdier vessels, and they being—naturally— flattered by his diffident admiration and overtures of friendship, are more than ready to respond; which is why, above all else, he's known to us as *our Mr Lodge*.

The two Misses Lodge, his sisters, wear skirts that reach down almost to their ankles when they play tennis, and frilly cotton old-fashioned sun-bonnets, one pink and one blue, which make them look, even though they are by no means young, like the illustrations of milkmaids in a book of nursery rhymes. They, and the younger Mr Lodge—who is not at all shy—are infrequent visitors to Newquay, never staying for long, and while here spending much less time up at the Tennis Club than *our Mr Lodge* does.

Today has been the day of the summer season's culminating tournament, and it has now ended: the lavish teas provided by Miss Veah and Miss Isobel Clark-Ourry eaten, the last match played. Now comes the prize-giving, an event unprecedented in our Tennis Club's history, and considered sufficiently newsworthy to attract the attention of reporters and photographers from the local press.

Egged on no doubt by his elder son, Sir Oliver Lodge has graciously contributed a very handsome silver cup which will be awarded annually hereafter to the winner of the Men's Singles. It stands, glittering in the evening sunshine, at the centre of the green baize cloth that covers a trestle table fetched out from the committee room and set up in front of the crowded pavilion. On either side of this, the main trophy, are a number of smaller cups donated by certain hoteliers, and by a few of the grander and more ambitious shop-keepers.

Sir Oliver Lodge himself has been persuaded to leave his island fortress in order to present the prizes. Never before have the winners of the Men's Singles, the Men's Doubles, the Mixed Doubles, as well as the Ladies' Singles *and* the Ladies'

Doubles, been rewarded with silver cups! And the runners-up, too, will have consolation prizes: not cups, to be sure, but boxes of chocolates, and tickets for a Cosy Nook concert-party performance; and, in the case of Harry North and our father, defeated finalists in the Men's Doubles, a bottle of sherry apiece. Harry North, mopping away at his shiny bald head with a silk handkerchief, smiles with pleasure all over his chubby round face, but his partner in defeat is not able to raise a similar smile. It could have been worse: Daddy isn't actually scowling, and he does manage a muttered, but just audible *Thank you, thank you*, when receiving his bottle, the prize that can bring, for him, no consolation.

Speeches are made. There is much clapping and laughter. Cameras click. And our Mr Lodge, dear kind understanding friend that he is, proposes a vote of thanks to Mr Hallsmith, who, as Secretary, has this year wrought such a miracle in the fortunes of Newquay's Lawn Tennis Club. Surely the applause, the clapping, the cries of *Hear, hear*! must be of more value to Daddy than a silver cup and have the effect of sweetening the dryness of the unwanted sherry?

And yes, he is pleased; he is nodding, nodding, almost embarrassed, almost on the verge of a smile, gratified—yes! But he would still rather be holding instead of a bottle, what Douglas Adey so moodily, carelessly dangles: the silver goblet of the Singles' winner. Douglas Adey owes his success, as is obvious, to his towering height, to being inches taller than anyone else, an unbeatable advantage when serving. *It isn't fair*!

His duty done, Sir Oliver Lodge is on the point

313

of departure. Before he leaves, however, my mother propels me towards the long white Father Christmassy beard of the great man. I have been instructed to ask him to sign my autograph book. I hold it up, open at the first page, but am dumb, so that she, pretending amusement to disguise her vexation with Elspeth, has to utter the request on my behalf. This autograph book of mine is new, a birthday present from Lilian Fisher, my godmother, (although I happen to be aware of the shop in Newquay, a stationer's, where Mummy bought it). Autograph books, I've been told, are what people get other people to write their names in. But why? Why should a person's name, written on a blank page—a signature—be a particularly interesting thing to have? I don't know why.

Sir Oliver Lodge does obligingly write his name in my autograph book, and then he stoops over— he is nearly as tall as Douglas Adey—and plants a kiss on the top of my head. A signature *and* a kiss from Sir Oliver Lodge—goodness, everyone declares, how lucky I am, how honoured!

I should think myself much luckier if I had been taken to tea in the secretive red-roofed house on Towan Beach island, as was my sister Pam the day after our parents dined there. Apparently one of the Miss Lodges, in a burst of impulsive sociability, invited Mummy to come to tea the following afternoon and to bring a daughter with her. Miss Rosaleen Lodge had spoken of *a* daughter, not of two little girls, and so Pam alone was selected for the treat—the wonderful treat.

I had yearned to walk across that fairy-tale bridge. Did it bounce underfoot and sway with every step? Did she feel dizzy, so high above the chasm it spans? How were the rooms in that mysterious house furnished? What sort of food, what cakes were Pam and Mummy offered for tea?

My sister wouldn't answer any of my questions. She won't speak a word to me about her enthralling experience, from which I was excluded. Usually our experiences are shared, but not in this instance. Pam, for reasons also unshared, refuses to satisfy my curiosity. Why does she remain, I wonder, inflexibly uncommunicative? Did my sister do or say something disgraceful in that august company?—something to shame the Hallsmith family? Was it something, perhaps, about spiritualism? Our mother's lips are sealed as tightly shut as are Pam's lips. I shall never know what occurred that afternoon. But to have had a kiss bestowed on my head by Sir Oliver Lodge today, and his name written in my autograph book, is no compensation for being deprived of a visit to his fabulous island, any more than Daddy's bottle of sherry compensates him for failing to win the sparkling silver cup of a champion. For me too, it isn't *fair*!

Mrs Cardell and her daughter Betty have carried off all four of the Ladies' cups, to the extreme chagrin of Mrs Davis and *her* daughter. Once again the athletic, self-confident Cardells have demonstrated that they are easily the better players, able between them, as always, to sweep the board, leaving the Davis pair, dumpy, dark and dour, to fume unavailingly, as always, in the background.

Betty Cardell is nineteen, and she has the longest brownest legs and the loudest laugh of anyone up at the Club. She serves aces like a man,

315

with a smashing overarm, and she wears, not a dress, but the shortest shorts imaginable. The length of those legs, and the shortness of her shorts (scandalously short, say some) are bound to shock the older staider Club visitors, which is, possibly, her intention: to shock is to be modern.

Although they are diplomatically careful not to express such an opinion in public, our parents don't approve of Betty Cardell; and for that matter, nor do their children. She is too loud and too pleased with herself: a swanky show-off! But there is another Betty belonging to the Club of whom we do approve wholeheartedly.

Betty Spooner doesn't wear shorts. Her tennis dress, a regulation, if imperfect, white, is habitually crumpled and in need of an iron, while one of her canvas tennis shoes will, as often as not, be missing a lace and tied up with string. She also is constantly laughing, but her laughter is never strident, and it seems for this Betty to be of equal unimportance whether she wins or whether she loses her matches. Generally, since her playing is at best haphazard and, at worst, wildly erratic, she loses them. And yet, despite her being a server of double faults and a wearer of shabby dresses, Betty Spooner is more in demand as a partner by the men at the Club than brilliant Betty Cardell.

Towards the Twins and me, Betty Spooner and Lewarne Hosking behave in exactly the same way as they behave towards our parents, with just the same unconsidered friendliness; which is how we know that they really are fond of children. People who aren't fond of children ignore us: they appear not to notice that we're there. Betty Spooner and Bo'sun Hooper and the elder of the two

316

Mr Lodges, and Lewarne Hosking whenever he's on holiday from Liverpool and staying in his bungalow at Porth—these are the grown-ups at the Club who count as being our friends as well as friends of our parents, year after year.

Today's tournament brings to a close for another year the season at Newquay's Lawn Tennis Club. The crowd of players and spectators begin to disperse. The green baize cloth lies wrinkled and bare, its prizes all distributed. Below, in the field where cars were parked—our cowslip field in springtime—engines are heard being revved up, doors are slamming. The day, the tournament, the season itself, is over.

With the light now fading, darkening, Wilton can be seen in the distance, far off, a solitary figure going about his business, winding the nets down, stacking the chairs. Nobody thought of proposing a vote of thanks to Wilton, the groundsman.

*　　　*　　　*

It's winter again. No more bathing or picnics on the beach until next year, and next year is so very remote it might as well be never. Meanwhile, we have to invent other weekend amusements.

If it's raining I sometimes play marbles with my brother Jim, both of us kneeling on the floor of the entrance hall, which is cold and hard but the right place for marbles because of being tiled instead of carpeted. Jim says marbles is the game everyone's playing at his school this term. He has taught me the rules and how to flick a marble with my thumb so that it hits the other marbles and scatters them—or some of them, anyway—clean out of the

317

ring which he's chalked on the tiles. An extra-large marble is called an alley, and an alley is very beautiful, I think, with spirals of different colours twisting up inside the glass. Jim says that if he manages to win a second alley at school he'll give it to me.

One Saturday afternoon in November I'm allowed to go with my brother and Bradford Johns and Peter Mitchell and Luke, the son of Dr Gadstone, to the roller-skating Palais which has been opened this autumn near to the centre of town. The sixpence it costs each of us to buy a ticket pays for hiring roller-skates as well. None of the boys has ever roller skated before, and nor have I, but it isn't half as difficult as I had imagined it would be. Quite soon, in fact, I'm quicker than they are, and I can race on past them—past Peter Mitchell and Luke Gadstone and Jim and Bradford Johns—tearing round and round and *round* the skating rink, faster and faster. At first it's a terrific thrill, better even than when I learnt to bicycle on Jim's fairy cycle (a present from Lewarne Hosking which later disappeared: a thief stole it). I feel almost as if I'm flying.

By the third Saturday, though, it's beginning to get a bit boring, simply speeding round and round in a circle, and I'm tired of the noisy echoing clatter, and the stuffy atmosphere. The boys, too, are fed up with roller-skating. They've had enough, and don't want to do it any more. They would rather climb trees in Oliver Jenkins' garden. And Jim says that in future he'd prefer to stay at home and stick stamps into the stamp album that Uncle Malcolm gave him for his birthday on the 16th of October. Instead of buying a sixpenny Palais ticket on Saturdays he can spend his pocket money in the shop beyond the harbour where a man sells packets of assorted foreign stamps from countries all over the world. Jim looks the countries up, and islands and rivers and capital cities, in the atlas that Uncle Malcolm—who hasn't got any children of his own—also gave him. Geography was always my brother's favourite subject.

As for Pam, she never did want to join our roller-skating gang. What she wants is to be left alone to draw and paint pictures. Daddy's two sisters, our Aunt Dorothy and Aunt Rosemary, sent her a big new watercolour paintbox, and five little pots of poster paint, and a considerable supply of paper and pencils, for her birthday; which is, of course, on the 16th of October, the same date as Jim's birthday. It was the best present that Pam had. Aunt Dorothy and Aunt Rosemary run a small school for very young children in the house in a village near London where they live with our Granny Hallsmith. I don't know why it is that, while Aunt Margaret and Aunt Molly and Aunt Nancy—three of Mummy's four sisters— occasionally visit us, Aunt Dorothy and Aunt Rosemary never come to Newquay. But Granny Hallsmith comes every summer, and she probably reported that what Pam enjoys doing more than anything else, and what Pam's especially good at doing, is drawing and painting.

So I'm the one who goes out each afternoon, if the weather is fine, with Lucy Coles, helping her to push Harvey, our baby, in his pram. Babies must be taken for a regular afternoon walk in the fresh air to keep them healthy: it's essential. And Mummy always lies down when lunch is over, because

319

having a baby was very exhausting for her, and she needs to rest a lot, in order to recover her strength.

Lucy clears away the dishes and washes up, and then we set off, me and her and Harvey, either along Mount Wise towards Pentire Head, or else— my choice—in the other direction. At the bottom of Eastcliffe Avenue we branch left, on to a recently constructed concrete road that loops round, and uphill, and emerges finally opposite the far end of Barrowfields. Concrete is a perfect surface for roller-skating, and Jim has let me borrow the roller-skates our mother spent his birthday money from aunts and from Granny Laurie on buying for him, thinking he would be pleased; but he wasn't pleased at all. What Jim would have liked Mummy to buy with his birthday money, if she had only thought of consulting him beforehand, was a globe of the world.

Because they haven't quite finished building the houses, or the pavements, there is no traffic as yet on this wide concrete road, so it's entirely safe. I can whizz ahead of Lucy, and swoop round and come gliding back to her, without any danger of getting knocked over by a car. Afternoon walks are sometimes dreadfully dull, but I look forward now to going out with Lucy Coles and the pram. These walks have become a daily treat for me. Roller-skating on an empty concrete roadway is much more fun than being confined inside a crowded stuffy old Palais, and I don't even have to pay for the pleasure with a sixpenny ticket—it's free!

This is the Hallsmith family's first Christmas at our new address. A year ago we were still cooped up at No. 9 Bay View Terrace. What a lot has changed since then. For me and my sister the crowning marvel of a year of marvels is when a carrier-van delivers to our door a surprise crate from Lewarne Hosking in Liverpool. The crate contains—wonder of wonders!—a truly miraculous doll's house. Never before have we seen or dreamed of such a doll's house. Its whole front section swings open to reveal an interior of fully furnished rooms, including a bathroom and a kitchen. There is a staircase leading from the ground floor to the floor above, and a family is already in residence, complete with the baby in its cradle. There are rugs, and chandeliers, and pictures on the walls, framed, and various patterns of wallpaper—yes, actually wallpaper!—and fireplaces and a geranium in a pot, and, most astonishing of all, a table reading-lamp that really lights up.

Our brother Jim, who isn't usually interested in anything to do with dolls, is nevertheless impelled irresistibly to inspect every fascinating detail of this doll's house, and it's he who discovers that the lamp is connected to a battery hidden behind the miniature sofa.

Surely no children have ever been given a more entrancing Christmas present than this, by a kinder or more generous friend than Lewarne Hosking?

*   *   *

It's night-time, and Lucy is sitting beside my bed, close by my pillow, reading aloud to me an extremely exciting adventure story. *Treasure Island* was Jim's Christmas present from Granny Hallsmith. She always now gives us books for presents. Jim himself is, at this very minute, in the

Mount Wise Nursing Home having his appendix cut out by Dr Mitchell. He had to be fetched away early from Joan Wallace's party because of him being suddenly, violently sick, and doubled-up with an agonising stomach ache. Jim blamed it on the meringue he had just eaten. The pain was so bad, and he was crying so hard, that Mrs Wallace telephoned for Dr Mitchell; and Dr Mitchell drove up to the Headland Hotel at once in his car, and pronounced it to be a case of acute appendicitis, requiring Jim to have an immediate operation. It was an emergency, he said, and he sent for an ambulance to transport our brother, without a moment's delay, to the Mount Wise Nursing Home. The nearest proper hospital is in Truro— miles too far off when it's an emergency.

We don't have a telephone in Grosvenor House, and so Mrs Wallace volunteered to drive Pam and Elspeth home in her motor car, thinking it only right that she should be the one to break the news of Jim's misfortune to Mrs Hallsmith, his mother.

I don't see why me and Pam couldn't have stayed on till the end of the party: it wouldn't have made any difference to Jim, and it felt funny and upsetting, us being bundled out of the Headland Hotel's ballroom like that, in a hurry, when all the other children were playing Musical Chairs, and shouting and laughing, not having the least idea of what was happening to our brother.

Lucy and me and Harvey, the baby, are alone in the house. Pam insisted on going with Mummy and Daddy to the Nursing Home. She said that she had to go because of being Jim's twin. They've been there for hours and hours. It's very late. I should think it's probably the middle of the night, but I

322

don't feel sleepy, which is why I asked Lucy to read to me. I like Lucy's reading voice. Mummy calls it a dreary drone, but *I* find it soothing. If Lucy read with more pauses, and more of an up-and-down expression, the story might be *too* exciting for me.

The blind man is coming tap-tap-tapping along the road with his stick. He's on his way to deliver the Black Spot to the old sea captain, which is dreadful. The Black Spot is a sign that the old sea captain, who drinks too much rum and sings about sixteen men on a dead man's chest, will die.

'Lucy,' I say, interrupting her, 'do you think it was the meringue that gave Jim his emergency?'

'No—never!' says Lucy. 'It wouldn't be a meringue give it him.'

'Jim said it was.'

'Well, he's wrong, Jim is. It couldn't have been for eating a meringue he got his appendicitis.'

'Mrs Wallace told Mummy that Dr Mitchell said it's an *acute* appendicitis. What exactly *is* an acute appendicitis, Lucy?' I ask her.

'Oh well,' says Lucy, '—well, it's bad. It's very bad, is that,' she says.

'Will he die, Lucy?' I say.

'Jim?—die?—goodness gracious me, no! What a question! Dr Mitchell won't let your brother die. He'll have Jim operated on, and as right as rain by morning—you see if he don't. Your Lucy's telling you, and you can take your Lucy's word for it—there's no call for you to be a-feared of anybody dying—'

She lays the book down; tucks me in tighter, smoothes my forehead.

'Now then, Elspeth,' she says, '—do you want me to keep on with reading this tale to you, or not?'

Contented, I tell her to keep on, and when she does I allow myself to slip into a cosy state of half-dozing, half-listening. Sticks tap-tapping, and blind men, and sea shanties, *Ho ho ho and a bottle of rum*, meringues and emergencies, all drift together in a Lucy's reading-voice muddle. The bedside light is yellowish and low, the curtains are drawn, shutting out the darkness. Everything in the morning will be as right as rain, because Lucy has said so. Lucy is with me, droning on. I'm safe, and my brother Jim isn't going to be given the Black Spot. There is nothing to fear.

*   *   *

Committee meetings occupy a great many of our parents' winter and spring evenings, and a great deal of their conversation after they've come home, which is excrutiatingly boring for us children. One of the things I'm determined I'll never do when I grow up is to go to a committee meeting. Some of them, to be sure, are duller than others. The most boring are in connection with the building of the Cottage Hospital, and the least boring are deciding on which play to choose for the Amateur Dramatic Society to perform in the Pavilion Theatre after next Easter.

Newquay's Amateur Dramatic Society had almost ceased to exist before our parents joined it last year. Both Mummy and Daddy have always nursed a belief that they are gifted with a talent for acting, and have hankered to exchange anonymous seats in the audience of a theatre for the blaze of its footlights, and here is a splendid opportunity to do so. According to Mrs Mitchell, the revival of the Society's popularity is wholly due to the energy and enthusiasm of Mr and Mrs Hallsmith in organising discussion groups and sending off to a publishing firm for copies of plays to be read and voted upon.

Blue paperback copies of *The Sport of Kings*, and *Ambrose Applejohn's Adventure*, and *Tilly of Bloomsbury* duly arrive through the post from Samuel French Ltd, and are pounced on by me whenever they happen to be lying around, available. Reading a play, I've discovered, isn't like reading a book. Mostly it's printed in dialogue, which means that the characters have non-stop conversations with each other; but there are instructions as well, in brackets, telling them what to do and how to behave while they are chatting together.

Ambrose Applejohn's Adventure is a very strange and surprising play, with real robbers at the beginning of it, and then a dream scene about pirates and buried treasure. When Ambrose Applejohn wakes up he knows he can use the same kind of trickery that foiled the wicked pirates in his dream to overpower the real-life robbers holding him a prisoner in his house. I think it's a brilliant idea for a plot, but Jim—who also read the play—says that he doesn't understand the point of its dramatic ending: *'Aces—all aces!'* Why should a clever trick in a dream help to defeat the real robbers by a completely different clever trick when Ambrose wakes up?

Before I'm able to explain this to him, our father, who is unluckily in the room and listening to us talking, loses his temper with Jim (as he so often does), and angrily declares that only a brainless blithering idiot of a boy could fail to grasp the similarity of the two clever wheezes. I can grasp the similarity, but I don't say that I can; I don't say a word. Jim, though, isn't an idiot, or brainless: not at all. Daddy may be good at painting pictures and at arithmetic, but Jim could beat him at geography any day of the week.

Daddy is keen to act the chief rôle in *The Sport of Kings*, but Mummy is against this play being chosen because it's all about horse racing and gambling, which is immoral. Finally the Amateur Dramatic Society settles on *Tilly of Bloomsbury*, with Mrs Mitchell as the heroine and our father acting opposite her. My sister Pam is given a walk-on part as the Tweenie. When I ask Pam what a Tweenie is, she asks Mummy, and Mummy says it means a Between-Maid. Between what and what? I don't know, and nor does Pam.

Rehearsals take place in various members' houses throughout the winter, and a short while after Easter the play is performed in the Pavilion Theatre on the Towan Beach esplanade for three consecutive nights. I am allowed to go to the dress rehearsal and to watch it from the front row of the stalls. The theatre is almost empty. It's a shock to see Pam, my sister, walking on to the stage, carrying a coal scuttle. She's wearing one of Lucy's aprons, and her hair is screwed into a tight little bun and fastened at the back of her neck with some of Mummy's hairpins. She knows where I'm sitting, but she doesn't look at me. Afterwards I ask her what it felt like for her to walk across a real stage, pretending to be a Tweenie, but she shrugs her shoulders and won't say much about it, except that acting is easy.

Tilly of Bloomsbury receives absolutely rave reviews in the local papers. Mummy is mentioned, but the specially glowing words of praise are for Mr Hallsmith, and for pretty Mrs Mitchell. So our father has become famous, which is what he always longs to be. But his fame is only in Newquay, and it won't last for very long. What he really wants is to be world-famous, and for *ever*.

On Mummy's dressing table in our parents' bedroom is a green cardboard box with gold writing on it, full of chunky greasy sticks of theatrical make-up. When we know Mummy and Daddy are safely out for the evening at a committee meeting, or a bridge party, Pam and I experiment with the scarlet lipstick, and the powder and rouge. We don't dare to do it very often because the make-up is more difficult to get off than to put on, and we are afraid of leaving telltale smears on our hankies or on the sponge that we try to wash our mouths and cheeks clean with. Actresses on a stage *have* to wear make-up, so it's all right for them. It's only when a girl who's not acting on the stage wears lipstick that it's a sign of her being *fast*, and particularly *fast* if the lipstick is a lovely bright scarlet colour.

*   *   *

Our father at home is inclined to be silent and of a generally morose disposition. This being so, the wonder is how he manages, as he not infrequently does, to strike up an acquaintance, or even a brief passing friendship, with the Midland Bank's more glamorous temporary customers who visit Newquay, like tropical migrant birds, for the summer season. Lacking our mother's ease as a conversationalist, how on earth does he contrive the necessary sociable intercourse?

What is it about our taciturn father that causes, for instance, the tall strong handsome tiger-trainer in Bertram Mills' Travelling Circus to entertain Daddy with descriptions of his life—a life begun in some savage northern province of India—while nonchalantly writing out a cheque; and to offer him, moreover, as evidence of friendliness, free tickets for a Saturday afternoon performance?

We can observe the immediate consequence of this delightful chance encounter in Daddy's altered demeanour; in how he squares his shoulders, and steps out more boldly, and swings his stick more carelessly, implying that something of the heroic character of an Indian tiger-trainer has, by mere association, rubbed off on Captain G. Hallsmith, DSO, himself a hero of the Great War. For there can be no doubt that a man who has the nerve to train tigers is a god-like figure, transcending our father's otherwise inflexible belief in the inferiority of all foreigners to the British, and in darkie-foreigners being absolutely the lowest of the low.

Or again, what is the quality possessed by our intimidating parent, but unperceived by us, that encourages the mother of two lovely young girls, dancers in the Cosy Nook's concert-party, to confide in him the details of her straitened financial circumstances as a war-widow, difficulties which oblige her to have recourse to the unladylike expedient of allowing her well-educated girls to appear on the programme of a touring seaside company? She is indeed, our father assures Mummy, a lady, and therefore to be pitied for her plight, and invited to have tea with us.

Here is another puzzle. We have been taught by Daddy that a woman should be called a woman, and not a lady. It is for Lucy to speak of a woman as a lady, but not us. This woman, though, the struggling brave war-widow, is declared by our father to be a lady—meaning what? That she deserves to be treated with a certain degree of deference, as someone who was born grander than, for example, Lucy Coles, or Lucy's sister Lily? Me and Pam try to untangle the confusion. We mustn't say: *Look at that lady over there*; but we can say: *That woman over there is a lady*. Try as we may to sort the matter out, it remains a muddle.

They do come to tea with us, quite as if they were ordinary people, and we children are taken, as a very special treat, to an evening show in the ramshackle Cosy Nook Theatre, a building close to the sand on the far side of Tolcarne Beach, where we watch the Balloon Dance performed by the two charming sisters. We are entranced by their balloons, which are *gigantic*, the biggest balloons we have ever seen, but we don't think much of their dancing. We think the nice lady-woman's daughters don't actually know how to dance; they are simply moving around with elegant slow-motion steps, in beautiful gauzy dresses, patting the huge balloons about in the air, and pretending they're dancing.

The tiger-trainer doesn't come to tea with us, but we go to the circus. An enormous tent has been erected on the opposite side of the road to Barrowfields. Inside, it smells of hay and horses, and is packed with excited spectators, tier upon tier of an audience rising up and up in a great big semi-circle. We sit on hard plank-benches high above the arena, and more thrilling for us to see than the elephants and the acrobats, and the bareback riders and the clowns, is Daddy's friend, wearing a magnificent Indian costume and a jewelled headdress, surrounded by terrifying tigers that do whatever he tells them to do, obeying his commands as meekly as if they were pet animals, dogs or cats.

A totally different sort of a circus is also visiting Newquay for the summer season, advertised in advance by posters and handbills, and by a little toy of an aeroplane buzzing to and fro above the crowded beaches, trailing in its wake a long and very narrow pennant like a fluttering ribbon. On the ribbon was printed, in giant capital letters: SIR ALAN COBHAM'S FLYING CIRCUS—with the dates announcing when the circus would be here.

And here it is, a circus such as we never could have imagined. For a while each morning, and again each afternoon, all holiday activity on the Great Western Beach comes to a halt, and we children stand, in company with hundreds of sightseers, rooted to the spot, spellbound and speechless, craning our necks and shading our eyes to follow the death-defying aerobatics being enacted in the blue summer sky above our heads.

Sir Alan Cobham's flying-machines, which rather resemble box-kites, and are almost, it would seem, as fragile as kites, twist and turn, dive and soar, zooming sometimes low enough for us to see quite clearly the leather helmet and goggles of the pilot in his open cockpit; see him smiling, laughing, waving to us, before he swerves up and away, climbing steeply into the vast empty expanse above. When an engine cuts out and the biplane appears to fall, powerless, turning, turning, as helpless as a dry leaf, our breath cuts out with it. And then, at the very last second of safety before plunging into the sea, the engine roars back into life, the wings lift, and we breathe again.

Dodging, frolicking, these little biplanes chase one another like puppies at play, miraculously scrawling messages in streamers of white smoke issuing from their tails for the hordes of spectators beneath them, gaping skywards, to read: words written on thin air which, as soon as written, blur, and evolve into fluffy puffs of cloud, and drift off lazily, slowly evaporating.

At the cost of half-a-crown a passenger can be strapped into the vacant seat behind the pilot and be taken up for a five-minute spin. Betty Spooner went up for a flip the first day the circus arrived, and her pilot looped the loop with her, not once but twice. We saw them doing it. And she went up the day after, and looped the loop again. If Betty weren't, as it's well-known she invariably is, short of money we think she would go up for a flip every single day of this fortnight when the Flying Circus is visiting Newquay; but five bob is probably as much, or more, than Betty Spooner can really afford to spend on having fun.

We are disappointed to learn that there is no possibility of our father inviting Sir Alan—or better still, one of his pilots—to tea with us in Grosvenor House, because he is unfortunately not a customer of the Midland Bank, but entrusts his money instead to Paul Hewish's father's rival establishment, Barclay's Bank, on the other side of the street. We would so love to have a pilot to tea.

On the whole we consider, my sister and I, that it might be even more thrilling to make friends with a pilot than with a tiger-trainer.

Flying is all the rage nowadays. I've been told about Colonel Lindberg, who flew by himself across the Atlantic Ocean from America—a very long way indeed—when I was three years old. And since then all sorts of people are flying about the world, and breaking records, and becoming famous, and having their photographs printed in the newspapers. It's a pity, we think, that Amy Johnson, a celebrated flyer, isn't pretty, not in the least, although the *Daily Mail* and the *Daily Herald* pretend, for some reason, that she is.

The *Daily Herald* is the newspaper Lucy buys. It's a newish and, in our parents' opinion, a low-class paper. They call it *a rag*, and are a bit uneasy for fear it may have an inflaming effect on the views of our placid Lucy Coles. Whenever she has any free time, which isn't very often, Lucy sits in her chair in the kitchen and reads it.

The chair in the kitchen that counts as Lucy's can be folded up like a deckchair, only unlike a deckchair it has wooden armrests, and there is a strip of red-patterned carpeting slung between the top and bottom bars instead of canvas. Consequently it's much more comfortable than a deckchair on the beach, as I happen to know, because now and then, while she's busy working, Lucy lets me sit in it. That's the best time, sitting in the kitchen in the red-carpety chair, for reading Lucy the stories I've written; or it might be a poem, perhaps. I enjoy reading aloud to Lucy almost as much as I enjoy her reading aloud to me.

Recently I read Lucy the account in her *Daily*

Herald of Jim Mollison—another record-breaker, who last year flew an aeroplane from Australia to England in nine days—getting married to Amy Johnson. The *Daily Herald* says that he is in love with her, but I don't believe it, because Jim Mollison is a handsome man and Amy Johnson is extremely ugly. Lucy agrees with me. She thinks that Amy Johnson is very ugly too.

*   *   *

Tomorrow is my birthday. I shall be nine years old. There will be presents for me and a birthday cake. Next year I shall be ten. I wish I didn't have to get older. Awful things occur when you get older; when you're growing up.

My sister Pam is growing up. She was always taller than Jim, her Twin, but now she's *inches* taller. I feel as though she's leaving me behind, going on ahead of me. We've separated. She's different from what she once was in all sorts of ways; different from me. She's changing.

And it isn't only that my sister's growing taller. There are worse things happening to Pam than growing taller. She's beginning to have hair in places where she never used to have hair: in her armpits, as well as *down below*. And there is something that's happening to her worse even than having hair in the wrong places and growing taller—something really *really* dreadful.

Every few weeks now my sister Pam isn't able to bathe, or to put on a bathing-dress: she can't. She has blood coming out of her, and it's not because she's cut herself: the blood comes from somewhere right inside her stomach. It doesn't happen to boys, only to girls, and it happens to all girls—Mummy's explained to me—when they reach a certain age; and so it's bound to happen to me too, eventually. It's called the Curse, and that's a good name for it. You mustn't talk about the Curse to anyone, not to anyone at all, especially not to boys. It's a secret from Jim. It's a sort of girls' horrible disgusting secret. Pam doesn't talk about it even to me, and we used to talk about everything together.

When I get the Curse, as I surely must one day, my life won't be worth living. And even that isn't all. As well as hair in the wrong places, and the Curse, Pam's chest has begun to swell into the kind of blobs that will end up by being what women have in front of themselves: bosoms. I don't want to have beastly bosoms, or those patches of nasty hair, or the Curse—I don't want to, I *don't* want to!

I'm sitting alone after picnic tea on the step of our beach hut, and I'm thinking that today is the last day I shall ever be eight; and that it's very nearly tomorrow already. I'll never be eight again. So I've clenched my fists and I'm hammering at my chest, which is flat still and not lumpy, as Pam's is beginning to be. When I get bosoms it won't be possible for me to thump on my chest as I'm doing at this moment, because bosoms are soft and squashy, and you have to be careful in case of hurting them. Bosoms, I know, are tender, like bruises, and—like bruises—not thumpable.

The fact is, there's nothing I can do to prevent myself getting older and older, year by year. It's bound to happen. Today I'm eight, and tomorrow I shall be nine.

Well, nine is all right. I quite like the idea of being nine, but that's where I would choose to

334

stop, if I was allowed to choose: at nine. I don't
want to go on any further than that, though. I
don't want to have to grow up, but the trouble is, I
don't see how it can be avoided; which means that
I'm doomed.

And there isn't anyone I can talk to about these
worries of mine. Even if I could put them into
words, and then make myself speak the words out
loud—which would be very difficult—there's
nobody who would understand. I should probably
be scolded, and laughed at, and told I mustn't be
silly. Not even Lucy Coles would understand;
although Lucy would never scold me, or scoff at
me for being silly.

* * *

Since our mother inherited the money that her
Uncle Stuart left her in his will, there have been all
sorts of changes and improvements in how we live.
The main differences are a new car, a new house, a
wireless, new furniture. But there are also a
number of smaller extravagances—treats that we
would never previously have had. For instance,
very often now when we're picnicing in our corner
of the Great Western Beach and the tide is far
enough out, Pam and me are allowed to walk
across the sands to the Stevens Café on the road a
short distance up beyond the harbour, returning as
fast as we can with a hot Cornish pasty for each of
us (not counting Harvey, of course).

Mummy always used to bring our picnic lunch
down to the beach, with the fish pie or pasties that
she had cooked at home wrapped in wads of
newspaper to keep them warm, and packed into a

basket. But now our pasties can be collected straight from the Stevens Café's oven, ready-cooked, and it isn't a question any more of whether we can afford them, but only whether the tide is in or out. And nowadays, when I go shopping with her, she may add strawberries to her list, or even *peaches*, and hardly bother to ask the greengrocer what price they are.

The best of the new treats, though, is our daily vanilla ice-cream cornet which Mummy buys for us—the larger of the two sizes—from a shop called the Quoit Dairy in a turning up beside the railway station on our way home at the end of a long day spent on the beach. Our mother declares that since they are made in a dairy they are sure to be wholesome, unlike—according to Daddy—what the Italian Stafferis manufacture in their dubious back-street quarters.

Stopping on the homeward journey for Quoit Dairy cornets has become a regular habit, an inducement to prevent us flagging as we toil up the steep Great Western hill, tousle-haired and weary after hours of bathing and sunshine, sand in our shoes, and the skin of our faces burning with the dry saltiness of sea water: an ice-cream habit that, no matter how regular, never ceases to be a treat.

On my birthday Mummy escorted us three children to the much grander Ice-Cream Parlour that has just been opened on the slope leading down to Towan Beach, and when we were sitting at a table she ordered Knickerbocker Glories from the waitress. Knickerbocker Glories are ice-creams which the Americans have invented, and they are served in a tall glass vase, and are so big it took us ages to eat them. This was a treat that wouldn't and couldn't have happened before our mother got the inheritance from her dear dead Uncle Stuart. We were far too poor then (although we weren't supposed to say so) for delicious daily Quoit Dairy ice-cream cornets, and certainly too poor for Knickerbocker Glories on my birthday.

I think it really pleases Mummy to be extravagant, and not always obliged, as she once was, to pinch and scrape, and economise on food, and never have new clothes but only ones that she'd made herself, or old ones altered and refurbished, or garments handed on to her from Cousin Edith. Her evening dress of black lace came from Cousin Edith, and so did her best summer hat, a black Leghorn straw.

She was wearing the black-lace-Cousin-Edith-dress the first time my sister Pam and I went with our parents to a Beachcroft Hotel dance. Mr and Mrs Knight, who own the Beachcroft Hotel, have a dance in their ballroom every Saturday evening throughout the season for the entertainment of the hotel guests, and on some such evenings our mother and father are invited, as friends of the Knights, to drive down after supper and join in the dancing. It was Mrs Knight who suggested that the two little Hallsmith girls might find it amusing to be brought along as well one evening, when they could observe the fashionable scene discreetly from the shelter of an alcove.

She intended it, we knew, as a kindness, but to stay awake after our normal bedtime so as to watch grown-ups enjoying themselves wasn't actually very enjoyable for us. *Actually*, having to sit apart in a corner, quiet and still and unobtrusive, and not be allowed to dance around on the ballroom floor to the music being played by the orchestra, as all the grown-ups were doing, got more and more boring. We didn't say so, because to say so would have been rude, but Knickerbocker Glories are a much better treat.

This evening, however—another Saturday—me and Pam are going again to the Beachcroft Hotel with our parents, and the reason why we won't be bored, and why we want to go this time, is that our mother will be wearing her new dance-frock, bought a few days ago from Madame Hawke's very expensive shop, and which is bound, we are sure, to create a sensation in the ballroom. Only us two have so far had a glimpse of the new dress, and we think it is spectacular! Made of yards and yards of lettuce-green taffeta ribbon, the cascade of overlapping frills will rustle, as if they were leaves on a tree rustling in the wind, whenever she moves a step.

Mummy was planning to give our father a surprise, and she succeeds: surprised he undoubtedly is. The moment she appears in the doorway, the row breaks out. He takes just one horrified look, and orders her to go upstairs *at once*, and remove the monstrosity. Nothing will induce him, he says, to be seen in public with his wife rigged out in that absurd costume, making a guy of herself. She is to change into her decent black-lace-Cousin-Edith-dress, and be sharp about it, too—we're running late.

'Oh, but what nonsense, Guth!' says Mummy, gaily. 'Change out of my new frock?—of course I shan't! You like it, children, don't you?' she says, giving a twirl as she speaks.

We nod, speechless. We think it's a Cinderella-going-to-the-ball dress: absolutely fabulous.

'Oh Mum, you look a picture,' says Lucy, clasping her hands together, rapt with admiration. 'It's beautiful, it is.'

'You see?' says Mummy, defying her husband's command.

Rustle, rustle, off we go, with Daddy a thunder-cloud at the wheel.

But this evening's Beachcroft Hotel outing, so wretchedly begun, is a disaster, and we depart early, Mummy offering the excuse of a headache. As soon as we reach home the row bursts out afresh. Me and my sister creep away to bed, but we can hear the dispute, angry and miserable, continuing. It keeps us from falling asleep.

The fact is, our father doesn't approve of *any* of the clothes that Mummy chooses for herself. He simply detests the brown crêpe-de-chine day-dress bought by her recently, not from Madame Hawke, but from another equally expensive shop next to the Dorothy Café. He said, when she first put it on, that it made her look a regular frump. To be honest, I don't much care for it either, but then, I always have considered brown to be a very dull colour.

He is even more insulting about the frilly green dance-frock. It is a ridiculous dress, he says woundingly, for a woman of our mother's age to wear, and she reminds him in it of the idiotic doll-thing the Vidal-Rowes hide their telephone underneath. Her deplorable purchase must be returned, he informs his wife by way of clinching the argument, to Madame Hawke on Monday morning—and *that's final*!

But the dress has been worn, says Mummy,

339

shocked: she has worn it to the Beachcroft Hotel dance. How can she possibly return a dress that is no longer new?

Madame Hawke won't know that it's been worn, declares our father, and if Janet, his wife, refuses to take the ghastly item of clothing back, he'll take it back himself.

And so he does. On Monday morning he starts out for work with the cardboard box irretrievably clamped beneath an arm. We shall see no more of the lettuce-green frilly ribbon Cinderella dance-frock.

It has been one of the loudest and the very worst of their quarrels, and Mummy cried a lot, because she really truly loved that dress.

The brown crêpe-de-chine still hangs in her wardrobe. Although she hasn't tried to return this unfortunate choice of hers to the shop it came from, she never wears it.

*   *   *

Does our father possess, I wonder, what is known as an appreciation of music? To a limited degree, perhaps he does. When in a good mood, he will sing in the bathroom while shaving, loudly and tunefully, songs from popular operettas. He is also keenly, even obsessively aware of line and colour. His wife, on the contrary, besides having—he maintains—no ear for, or knowledge of, music, has no artistic taste whatever: is blind, as well as deaf! To these criticisms levelled at her our mother remains impervious, being unshakeably convinced that there isn't a shred of truth in them.

But is there?—and if so, how much truth? With

regard to art and music, he may be right, although brutally harsh in his judgement. What about literature?

Mummy never reads poetry, and seldom opens a book, whereas our father, in addition to his fondness for the *Rubaiyat of Omar Khayyam*, can and does declaim with gusto Kipling's 'If' and can and often does recite, word-perfect and with genuine emotion, Masefield's 'Sea-Fever'. His imagination is fired still by the adventure stories of his youth—by tales of prospecting for gold, of cowboys and Red Indians, of pirates buccaneering on the high seas, of coral islands. Where is the kindred soul with whom he could share, should he wish to, these half-remembered, half-forgotten fragments of fictional romance? He couldn't ever share them with our mother. It has to be me; there isn't anyone else.

Guthrie—Daddy—was the second child of the second marriage of his dour old Scottish father, sandwiched closely in between his older brother, the handsome laughing extrovert Martin, and his sister Dorothy, tall, equally handsome, deep-voiced and bossy. They overwhelmed him, those two, rendering the silent unassertive sensitive boy, so unlike either of them, insignificant.

Then there was Guthrie's younger brother, Harvey, handsome also, and self-confident as well, in spite of a lame leg. And last of all Rosemary, the baby, the pretty family darling, petted and spoilt by everyone.

In this domestic circle Guthrie was the odd one out, not favoured by his charming sunny-tempered mother, who, mistaking reserve for chilliness, found him an awkward unlovable child, and handed him over to be raised by his elderly Old Testament-addicted Presbyterian father, a disciplinarian and a strong believer in original sin; a believer likewise in severely quelling, as a Christian duty, any signs his docile son displayed of original joy.

And when, at the end of 1918, Guthrie returned from his German prisoner-of-war camp, alive, while so many, including both his brothers, were dead, what did he almost immediately do? Before a year was out, who did he marry? A woman older than himself by eight years; a woman taller than him, as tall as his sister Dorothy. A beautiful woman, much courted, universally admired; a capable courageous heroine with a flair for organising, decorated by King George for services to her country. Moreover—and who could blame her?—a woman determined that she wasn't going to suffer, not if she could help it, the sorry fate of her three older sisters, and of countless other pitiable females deprived of men and marriage and the comfort of children by the Great War's indiscriminate slaughter.

And what of Janet, our mother? What of *her* childhood and upbringing?

What must it have meant to be the red-haired tomboyish favourite daughter of a father lost to her at the age of twelve when he, a non-swimmer sailing in Southampton Water, was drowned? Janet also had a mother of whose children she, like Guthrie, was the least beloved or understood: Mrs Laurie, an impoverished widow burdened with five daughters and a son.

For Janet the years that followed on her father's accidental death were unremittingly dismal. But at seventeen she was enabled, as by a miracle, to fly free of the mournful maternal nest. When still practically a schoolgirl. (and shortly after being expelled from Oxford High School for Girls after imprudently permitting a drapery-shop assistant to slip a note into her hand while she was out walking with her classmates in prim crocodile formation), Janet Laurie had the good fortune to meet and become engaged to Basil McNeile, a Divinity undergraduate. His large tennis-playing vicarage family welcomed her warmly into their midst, and the prospect that she saw stretching serenely ahead was one of idyllic happiness. To be happily, enviably married, an adored and successful wife, was all she wanted in the future that she then believed awaited her. But again and again, and yet *again*, most cruelly, the envisaged happiness

343

vanished from in front of her eyes. By the time she had reached her early thirties the chances of it, in a devastated post-war world, were slim indeed.

Nevertheless, before the end of September, 1919, she had captured her young ex-officer and acquired the status of a married woman. And furthermore, their union, which might have been regarded by some cynical onlookers with pessimism, seemed at the start of it, to Janet and to Guthrie, full of optimistic promise.

Reality destroyed the dream. Their wedding-day hopes, founded on innocence and a total unworldly ignorance of the person each of them was marrying, were soon extinguished. Apart from a mutual passion for being out-of-doors, they were as temperamentally ill-matched a pair as it is possible to imagine.

Guthrie, with his yearning to be the centre of attention, found himself sidelined, the husband merely of a woman who, while she lacked any vestige—he considered—of his artistic brilliance, was yet, in their small Newquay firmament, a star that always, effortlessly outshone him: *not fair*!

The unfulfilment of that early hopeful promise, and the resulting bitterness of disappointment, cast a shadow over all our lives, and year by year the despair of a situation that they—and to a lesser extent, we children—were trapped inside, with no apparent avenue of escape, increased. The episode of the lettuce-green frilly dance-frock was a milestone along an ever steepening decline.

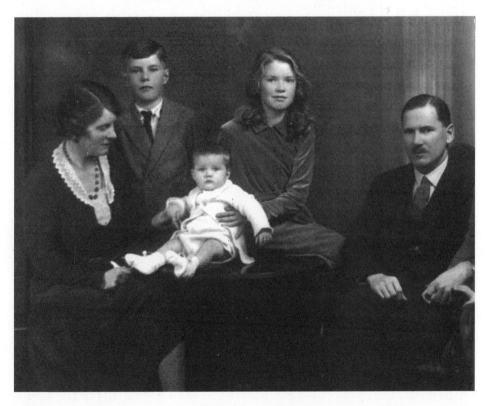

The studio camera has here recorded the aftermath of a colossal family row. I am missing from the group, having later cut myself out of the picture, leaving only, as evidence of my presence, the hand my father is gripping in his.

*   *   *

Autumn brings more changes—a change for me anyway, and an even bigger change for my brother Jim.

I've started having dancing lessons with a Miss Taylor, who is young and pretty and has just moved into one of the bungalows built at the far end of the new concrete road where last winter I was roller-skating on my afternoon walks with Lucy and our baby in his pram.

These lessons are the result of Mummy and me happening to bump into a group of St Kilda's pupils out on Pentire Head with their teacher last April. The teacher, who stopped to talk to Mummy, said how greatly it was regretted by the school that Mrs Hallsmith's two delightful daughters no longer attended St Kilda's dancing classes in the Victoria Hotel. Elspeth in particular, she said, had shown a quite remarkable talent for the medium of dance. She didn't mention Pam by name.

'Goodness!' exclaimed my mother, sounding more amused than impressed by this piece of information. 'I didn't realise we had such a gifted little dancer in the family!'

Some while afterwards Mummy asked me if I would like to have dancing lessons with Miss Wendy Taylor, a recent arrival in Newquay who had spoken to our father in the Bank regarding the dance classes that she proposed holding as soon as the builders had finished building her bungalow.

I told Mummy that yes, I would like it very much indeed: because I do *love* dancing. But I shouldn't

346

have answered *yes* if she had suggested me sharing classes again with the St Kilda's pupils in the Victoria Hotel. We always used to feel that by not being pupils of the school ourselves we weren't properly included. We didn't fit in, and it wasn't at all a nice feeling.

My sister doesn't have the same longing, a secret passion for dancing, that I have, and so I set off without Pam, every Friday afternoon. Lucy Coles is in charge of me, and in charge also of Harvey, just as she used to be when we went on our roller-skating walks last winter and spring. Only Harvey now, having grown too big to ride in his bouncy baby-pram, is buckled instead into a pushchair for the indispensable daily airing. We part company at Miss Taylor's gate, and they fetch me away an hour later.

I enjoy everything to do with my present dancing lessons in the newly built bungalow of Miss Wendy Taylor. Besides me, she teaches three other girls of approximately the same age as I am. Miss Taylor is always welcoming and smiling, and she never gets cross. Her dress is white, and very short and skimpy, sleeveless, with a pleated skirt. She teaches us free-expression dancing, which means we have to pretend to be a shower of rain, or daffodils in a breeze, or the dawn, or something of that sort, and we can use our imaginations to invent any movements or steps we think will freely express whatever it is we are pretending to be.

Her front room, where we dance, is like a miniature ballroom: that is to say, it has a bare shiny floor and big bay windows, and is entirely empty except for the piano, and a gramophone on a table, and a bar along one wall which we hold on

347

to while we do slow stretching exercises. We also learn the precise five ballet positions for our arms and legs and feet, but the ballet shoes we wear don't have block toes, and so we aren't able to stand right up on our pointes, which I should think might be difficult, as well as probably painful.

My ballet shoes are what I like almost more than anything else about my Friday afternoon lessons. They are made of very soft pale-blue kid leather, with pale-blue satin ribbons to tie round my ankles, and I *adore* them!

The change that takes place in my brother Jim's life is altogether different. I had expected he would be pleased when he heard he was to be sent away to a boarding school, but he wasn't pleased: he was very upset. Bradford Johns and Peter Mitchell are also going away to school, but their school, called Blundells, is near Tiverton, whereas Jim's boarding school is in Exeter, Devon. When Jim is told that he's to be sent off by himself to Exeter School, miles and miles away from the family, he does a lot of blubbing, which infuriates our father. He calls Jim a snivelling little milksop.

Mummy has a list of all the clothes that are required to be bought for my brother to take to school with him. She prints his name with black marking-ink on white cotton tape, and every single garment has his name sewn into it. She has bought as well from John Julian's emporium a big new green canvas-type trunk, reinforced by strips of wood, apparently known as a cabin trunk.

'It sounds as if you're going to sea in a boat,' I say to Jim, hoping he'll think it's funny, and laugh. But he doesn't laugh at this joke of mine. He isn't in a laughing mood.

I help Mummy to pack the cabin trunk with the piles of new clothes, and she ticks them off on the list as they're packed, item by item. My brother Jim has also to be provided with something called a tuck-box. *Tuck* means extra food: special treats. This additional article of regulation equipment is a smallish heavy square wooden box, fastened with a padlock and key. Mummy fills it with several pots of homemade jam—blackberry-and-apple jam and marrow-and-ginger jam—and a home-made cake, some scones, a bag of toffees, and a tin of biscuits. The tuck-box has metal corners, and a handle on either side to carry it by. It looks rather like a pirate's treasure chest: exciting! Jim isn't excited, though. He blubs and snivels inconsolably, tormented by fear of the unknown boarding school that is about to swallow him up.

Because of an untimely bout of tonsillitis my brother Jim will be a week late arriving at Ackland House for the beginning of the winter term. Ackland House, the junior branch of Exeter School, is for boys under fourteen. Reprieved!— but only for a week. The next Saturday afternoon our parents load their son Jim and his trunk and his tuck-box into the car, ready for the long cross-country drive to Exeter. The dreaded ineluctable moment of departure is here. Pam will stay in Newquay with Lucy and Harvey, but I am being allowed to sit on the back seat next to my unhappy brother, where I do the best I can to cheer him up.

'It'll be fun!' I say to him, bracingly. And I do truly think that going to a boarding school might— possibly—turn out to be fun. Jim doesn't answer. He doesn't speak a word to me during the whole of the journey. He sits like a stone.

We reach our destination of Exeter; thread a way through the narrow streets to Exeter School; deposit Jim and his luggage. Wasting no time in hanging about, our father climbs up behind the wheel again, switches on the engine, reverses the car. The housemaster and his wife stand on the front step of Ackland House to wave off the parents of their new boy. They had asked us kindly if we would care to come inside for a cup of tea, but our father refuses the invitation. We can't stop, he says; we have to get home.

Jim stands on the step between them. He doesn't wave, as they do. When I look back over my shoulder, although the housemaster and his wife have disappeared, Jim is still standing there, on his own, still not waving, just watching us drive away in the car, leaving him.

I start to cry then, but very quietly, so that Daddy won't notice my blubbing and tell me not to be a snivelling milksop.

*   *   *

Our mother has been invited to sit at the head of the table as the principal guest at the Midland Bank's official dinner-party, held annually in Truro for important people, and to make a speech on behalf of the ladies present. The invitation is a tremendous honour for Mummy, and no doubt it is intended and believed that Captain (Retd.) G. Hallsmith, DSO—cashier of the Bank's Newquay branch—will, as her husband, feel himself to be equally honoured. But this is not how Daddy sees it. Once again Janet, his wife, has been singled out to play an admired central role, and he

350

left skulking in her shadow.

Mummy, aglow with excitement, is quite undaunted by the prospect of having all eyes fastened upon her when she stands up to give her speech at the end of the dinner. For this momentous occasion she will wear the loose bridge jacket that Cousin Edith has handed on to her, made of softest finest black silk chiffon, embossed with a cut-out design in beige velvet: a garment that has the desired appearance of being—as it surely was—very expensive.

She tries it on for us over the long black-lace-Cousin-Edith-evening-dress, and we applaud. But our father, critical as ever, declares that the colour combination of black and beige doesn't at all suit Mummy's complexion, and she, for once, agrees with him. Encouraged by Lucy, she takes the risk of immersing the delicate fabric in a cold-water dye, and to her infinite relief the chiffon remains black and the creamy velvet turns a shade of deep rich burnt-orange. So that's all right!

Having satisfactorily settled the details of her wardrobe, she has then to write the speech. This entails many hours of scribbling away at her desk, and many more hours of reciting her scribbles aloud as she walks about the house; for she means to learn it by heart and deliver it as an actress would, without the help of a script or even of any notes. She wants it to sound as spontaneous as if she were making it up as she goes along, and the jokes as though she's inventing them on the spur of the moment. For there will be jokes in her speech; and it is these jokes, more than anything else, that cause my father, silent but dangerously attentive, to watch her with that look I've caught on his face before: the look of hate.

Mummy describes how once Her Majesty, Queen Mary, visiting the hospital wards in London during the Great War, stooped over the bed of a wounded soldier to ask him graciously at what battle he received his wound? Whenever, in their conversation, the man told her it was at *Wipers*, Queen Mary repeated the name, but each time with the correct pronunciation: *Ypres*. As soon as Her Majesty had moved on, ' "Pore lidy," ' said the soldier, (and here Mummy, the actress, assumes a comically Cockney accent), ' "she didn't 'alf 'ave a 'orrible fit of the 'iccups!" '

They will laugh in Truro at this and other humourous wartime tales, and clap and cheer our mother, perhaps, for her lively rendering of them. But our father has no memories of the Great War that he can bring himself to laugh at; no memories, none, about which jokes can be made. And so, as he listens to his wife blithely rehearsing what she is proud to have written by herself, unaided, he hates her—I see his hate—for failing utterly to understand the horror that war in France, in the trenches, truly was.

On the evening of the Midland Bank dinner, off they drive together to Truro, sitting side by side in our big Austin tourer, Mummy wrapped up to the eyes in the luxurious full-length red-squirrel fur coat that had been Mrs Bazin's wedding present to her; the present for a wedding that never happened.

And when they return from Truro late that night, we children tumble out of bed, half-asleep and late though it is, to hear from our mother how the speech was indeed a triumph, as she, and we,

352

had known it would be. How she was—yes!—clapped and cheered, and afterwards congratulated, again and again.

From Daddy we hear not a word, either regarding the dinner or the speech. He doesn't refer to the evening and the part that his wife so triumphantly played in it, ever; not by a single word. But I remember how he looked at her before they went, when she was practising her jokey stories, and I know, I *know* what he was feeling: hatred.

*   *   *

It is the summer term, and our foreign friend, Ada Møeller, has joined me and Pam and the two Kiley girls and Mollie Purchase for lessons with Miss Howard. This isn't the first time Ada has joined us for lessons. Apparently Miss Howard is willing to take her on as an extra temporary pupil whenever Ada's mother's health deteriorates and she is sent over from Denmark on a visit to Mrs Miller in Trenance House to be out of the way until matters at home improve.

Ada has grown inches taller since the original visit to her Aunt Astrid, and she can speak and understand English very well now. We like her quite as much as we did at the beginning. She continues to be wonderfully good-tempered, laughing and smiling, and still bobbing a curtsey to grown-ups, and still as pretty as ever; or even prettier. We wonder whether it's usual for Danish girls to have curly golden hair and cornflower-blue eyes, and to wear the picturesque frilly pinafore smocks worn by Ada Møeller, and if that's why she

isn't vain or showy-off about her prettiness—
because she isn't, not in the very slightest. We
rejoice in her company. To find ourselves a trio
with Ada, instead of the mere pair we are without
her, greatly increases the daily pleasure of walking
down through Newquay's main shopping quarter in
the fresh emptiness of the summery mornings to
Miss Howard's apartment near the harbour, and
back together through the busy jostling crowds
when lessons are over.

On several occasions, as we are homeward
bound, we have our picture taken by the street
photographer who plants his big camera on its
wooden tripod a few yards beyond the
greengrocer, where the pavement widens enough
for him to be able to snap the pedestrians without
inconveniencing them. We don't have to stop, or

pose for him, or even slow our steps. He photographs us just as we're naturally walking towards him—snap, snap, snap—three times, and holds out a card for us to take as we go past.

If we want to have copies of the photographs they can be bought at his shop, and as they aren't expensive Mummy sometimes does give Pam the money, or Mrs Miller gives her niece Ada the money, and then we collect the prints and share them between us. We have copies of the snapshots he took a couple or so years ago of me and my sister with Granny Hallsmith, when Granny was staying for a week and had come to meet us one morning on our way back from lessons.

There is another photographer who positions himself at the top of the Great Western Beach's hill, and later during the summer, in July, after the school term finishes and Ada Møeller has returned to her mother in Denmark, Cousin Mildred Martin arrives by train for her regular Newquay visit, and we are all snap-snapped more than once by this other street photographer; all of us except, of course, for Daddy, he being hard at work alone on the further side of town (alone, that is to say, not counting Mr Oxley, his despised Manager) shut up within the imprisoning walls of the Midland Bank. But here, free as air, are the rest of us recorded on top of the hill looking windswept and happy, Mummy wheeling Harvey in his pushchair, at the end of a long day spent with our generous jolly Cousin Mildred down on the sands.

In these photographs my brother Jim also appears. Because of school having broken up he is home for the summer holidays. Jim is the only one in the group who doesn't look particularly happy.

355

He has been at Exeter School for a whole year now, and although he would far rather not have to be sent away from Newquay and his family when term starts again in September, he's getting used to it; or at least, I think he is. Jim doesn't actually enjoy boarding school; but then, he doesn't enjoy anything much.

*   *   *

Mrs Miller has rented Trenance House to the YMCA for the month of August, and gone off on a cruise of the Norweigan fjords in a luxury liner with her two elderly companions, Dr Hankin and Mr Rainsforth. We know that Trenance House has only been abandoned for a month, but it feels funny to us, having the place we are so familiar with overrun by strangers. The young men and women of this Christian Association are extremely friendly and energetic, and hand out leaflets, and organise games and sporting events and sessions of Bible-reading and hymn-singing on Tolcarne Beach with a gathering that consists of, mostly, us and a few of the visitor-children, standing about in our bathing costumes.

We've always thought that hymns are meant to be sung in a church. *Carols* are sung in the street, says Pam, reminding me. But carols at Christmas, I say, aren't proper hymns: they're different. It does feel, we agree, exceedingly odd, and not quite *right* for us to be singing 'Onward Christian Soldiers' outside in blazing sunshine, while wearing hardly any clothes at all—practically naked; and, what's more, on Tolcarne Beach, which is the smart hotel beach where Pam and I seldom dare to venture.

356

But we do splash round from our Great Western Beach once or twice, drawn there by curiosity, and Pam wins a sandcastle competition, because she had the clever idea of building a square house instead of a castle, and writing in pebbles: THE HOUSE BUILT ON SAND; which was something they had read aloud to us out of the Bible.

They advertised a treasure hunt for children, too, in the Trenance House garden, and Mummy allows us to go to that as well; suitably dressed, this time. It should have been fun—a treasure hunt!— but somehow we still don't feel entirely comfortable. Partly we are dazzled by the personalities and appearance of these young grown-ups, who seem to us to be, all of them, astonishingly glamorous, like real live film stars; but who also seem, like film stars, as if they aren't quite real; which makes us uneasy. So after the treasure-hunt afternoon, and the sandcastle competition, we haven't been back to Trenance House or to Tolcarne Beach, and we shan't go, we've decided, for as long as Mrs Miller is abroad and her property let.

Shrimping is more in our line than singing hymns on Tolcarne Beach. Rex and Eve Dyer have been spending a fortnight with Mrs Mulroney, their grandmother accompanied by their Aunt Audrey, and it's Audrey who has introduced us Hallsmith children, and her nephew and niece, to the sport of shrimping.

Every outgoing tide leaves behind, at the base of the Great Western Beach's cliffs, and surrounding the various isolated newly revealed rocks as well, shallow pools of clear sea water populated by darting shrimps and by tiny sandy-coloured speckled flatfish perfectly camouflaged beneath a thin layer of sand. It amuses us to disturb these lurking flatfish with our bare toes in order to observe how swiftly, when dug up, they re-bury themselves, wriggling out of sight again in a moment.

The shrimps we catch are small and transparent; so small they aren't worth—as we soon realise— the trouble of lugging them home in a bucket for Lucy to cook. Boiled, they become pink and opaque, a transformation fascinating at first, but by the time their heads and tails, and their legs and their shells have been laboriously removed, a mere fragment of rubbery pink flesh remains for us to eat. Consequently, after one or two such experiments, we cease regarding them as a source of nourishment. It's enough of a game for us to count how many shrimps we manage to catch, keeping a daily score; and then, when the day's over, we can tip them back, alive, out of the pail to be reunited with the incoming tide.

Never before have we beheld a shrimping net equal to the one possessed by Audrey Mulroney. It isn't a toy, but a serious piece of fishing equipment, bearing no resemblance to the cheap and flimsy nets made of wire and bamboo and muslin, tied in bundles and on sale at the entrance to Timothy White's, the ironmongers, which we have long scorned for being babyish, fit only for London tourists and charabanc trippers to buy. This net is fastened to a pole like a broom handle. It hangs from a semi-circular strong metal frame. The twelve-inch, or wider, wooden bar, shaped into a wedge and fixed across the front of the frame, acts as a sturdy scooping device. Daddy, who admires Audrey Mulroney, says that her shrimping net is *the real thing*! And now it's ours. At the end of her fortnight's holiday with Rex and Eve Dyer, she has given it, most kindly, as a parting present to the Hallsmith family.

Of us three it's Jim who chiefly benefits from Audrey Mulroney's generosity. Jim has developed, rather unexpectedly, a passion for shrimping; and we are pleased, my sister and I, that he has. He doesn't care for bathing, as we do, because the coldness of the water makes his teeth chatter and turns him blue and shivery almost immediately. Surfing helps to keep a person warm, but Jim doesn't surf. Having had operations for a double-hernia and for appendicitis, he's afraid of being jabbed in his stomach and injured by the edge of the surfboard; and in fact, if the waves were very rough, it might easily happen. So we're glad to think our brother, Pam's non-identical Twin, has discovered something at last that, besides being safe, he really does enjoy doing on the beach.

We ourselves like to paddle in the pools, and to inspect at close range the activity of their miniature inhabitants, but as to shrimping, we aren't as interested in it now as once we were. The novelty has worn off. On the whole we prefer to fill the hours down on the Great Western Beach with swimming and surfing, reading books and picking up shells and sunbathing. Jim, as far as we are concerned, is welcome to take over ownership of the shrimping net and carry on shrimping by himself to his heart's content. We see him in the distance, a solitary figure, bending double, absorbed, with a concentration usually reserved for his hobby of stamp-collecting, in the pursuit and capture of little tantalising inedible shrimps.

*　　　*　　　*

It was thought we should have to forego our Sunday excursions to Holywell Bay until Harvey can manage to walk on his own legs the considerable distance from where we park the car to where we traditionally picnic at the further side of the vast expanse of sand. Last year our mother could still carry him, but Harvey's not a baby any more; he's a little boy. Too heavy, as he now is, for Mummy to carry, the wheels of his pushchair would get stuck in the dunes, and in the soft surface of the shoreline stretching beyond the dunes.

Our father resolves the dilemma of how to convey Harvey across Holywell Bay by inventing what he describes as a litter. White men, heroic explorers of tropical Africa, are jog-trotted through the jungle, he informs us, on just such

litters, borne aloft by teams of darkie servants.

It is the Twins who are obliged to perform the necessary function of darkie servants, Pam at the front and Jim at the back—unwilling slaves *indeed*—each grasping hold of two poles, between which is slung a sheet whereon their younger brother sits, he acting his part, quite as unwillingly, of jungle explorer. While for Harvey the jolting bumpy trek may seem boringly endless, for the Twins, with every stumbling step they take (jogtrotting is plainly out of the question) the weight of their burden increases. Our father, the slave-driver, shows them no mercy. If he had a whip he would assuredly crack it, urging the sullen team on to greater endeavour. Why can't they go faster? Daddy is mightily proud of his invention. For the rest of us, though, Holywell Bay picnics this year are Sunday outings to be dreaded.

The summer of 1933, the summer when I have

my tenth birthday, we shall remember for its acrimonious Holywell Bay picnics; and for shrimping on the Great Western Beach; and for the religious exploits of Mrs Miller's Trenance House tenants. But more than anything else that has happened, the holidays will be remembered by us for our promotion at the Tennis Club from the lowly rank of passive spectators, which we always were, to becoming active participants ourselves in the sport of lawn tennis: enthusiastic students of a game we have, until now, understood—enviously— to be reserved for privileged adults, never for children, to play. The veto was lifted by unanimous agreement at the Club's annual Easter meeting, on purpose to benefit the Secretary's children—us!— in recognition of our faithful attendance, year after year, crouched on the step of the pavilion, watching.

Oh joy!

*   *   *

The two top courts, which were once no better than an area of weedy wilderness, are now, due to Wilton's hard work, reclaimed and fit for use during the Club's frequent and increasingly popular tournaments when every court in needed.

It's up here on this higher level that we Hallsmith children are allowed to play tennis at any time we want; or allowed, rather, to try to teach ourselves *how* to play tennis. Being, as we are, at a considerable distance from the pavilion where members, wandering in on weekday evenings, congregate, it could feel a bit cut off and lonely if it weren't for the presence of Wilton, who

362

is bound to be somewhere in the vicinity, going silently about his groundsman's business. He doesn't engage in conversation, or speak a word, or even appear to notice us, but we have the definite impression that Wilton is nevertheless a friend of ours, and that with him about we aren't on our own.

The few balls with which we have been provided have had all the fluff rubbed off them, and our racquets are unwanted or forgotten relics, dug out from the back of a pavilion cupboard. My racquet is the worst of the lot. It's prehistoric, and the strings—those that aren't broken—instead of being tight, are soft and spongy. But it's better than nothing, says Daddy; good enough, he says, for a complete beginner—which I am—to start on. To make my racquet lighter, he sawed through the unwieldy wooden handle, shortening it by three or four inches.

I'm learning to serve underarm. This is on account of me being so small. Men don't ever serve underarm, but some grown-up women do, such as, for instance, the two Misses Lodge; not, in their case, because they're small—they aren't—but because they're women, and underarm serving is considered to be more ladylike. My sister Pam, who is nearly as tall, at twelve, as a grown-up, serves overarm. She has declared to me that she means to learn to serve as well as Betty Cardell does; and I expect, if Pam means to, she will.

Every evening now, after having tea on the Great Western Beach, we troop up to the Club's grounds on the summit of Trenance Hill and practise playing tennis. Daddy, the Club Secretary, by paying the specially reduced subscription fee for

363

children, has officially registered the Twins and me as junior members.

Sometimes Betty Spooner joins us on the top courts, and then it's much more fun, and we can have a proper doubles match, with two players on each side of the net. We try to copy her strokes, and she calls out, *Oh, good shot*! running around and laughing, quite as though it's fun for her too, and she isn't just being kind.

Occasionally, when Betty is with us, our father strolls up as well, and we are given instruction on how a back-hander ought to be swiped. We have to stand sideways on to the ball, with our feet planted like *this*, and we must hit it like *that*; and even when we muff it, as we often do, he doesn't get cross. Owing to so much practice, and to help from Betty and advice from Daddy, our tennis playing has improved by leaps and bounds. Of course, we've watched grown-ups playing tennis for ages and ages, and have learnt from the sidelines how it should be done, and the rules of the game, and how to score deuce and 'vantage points, and so on.

Non-playing members, if they want only to watch, also pay a reduced subscription rate. Dr Bell and his daughter, Miss Molly Bell, have recently come to live in Newquay, and they are non-playing Tennis Club members. At first it was difficult, for two reasons, not to stare at them. In spite of him being old and a man, and her being a woman and his daughter, they do look most curiously alike. They wear precisely the same thick horn-rimmed spectacles, and walk and talk very slowly, and poke their heads forward in exactly the same way, reminding us of the Misses Clark-Ourry's tortoises emerging from winter hibernation.

The second reason for not staring rudely, and the main difference between them, is that Miss Molly Bell wears pancake make-up on her face. We have never seen anyone wearing pancake make-up before. It's as if her skin has been coated with a type of muddy mask. She wears lipstick too, scarlet lipstick, but no one could possibly imagine Miss Molly Bell is intending to be *fast* by wearing bright red lipstick. They are very friendly to us children, and to all the other members, and as a result have become generally accepted. Dr and Miss Molly Bell turn up at the Club so regularly it might be thought they haven't got anything else to do; and perhaps they haven't.

It was Betty Spooner who told us the mud stuff on Miss Molly Bell's face is called pancake make-up. We can ask Betty these sort of questions. Betty doesn't wear any make-up herself. If it were not for her spotty complexion, she would be extremely pretty, we think. And our parents think so too. They are both very fond of her—Daddy in particular—because (or at least, we suppose it's because) Betty Spooner, we have heard them say, is so *refreshingly natural*. They mean, by *refreshingly natural*, that she doesn't put on any grand airs, or wear make-up, or show off: all of which is true. When Betty Spooner looped the loop in one of Sir Alan Cobham's aeroplanes it wasn't for the sake of showing off, but for the sheer excitement of flying: for fun!

Another non-playing and very regular member of our Tennis Club is a youngish tallish man, a summer visitor, with wavy fair hair and a limp and a spaniel dog. He leans on a stick when he walks,

365

or when he stands. He doesn't say how he got his limp, and we don't enquire, but it's what prevents him playing tennis and makes him into simply a spectator, like the Bells. His name is Mr John Anderson. Oddly enough, the person he seems to want to talk to most, and to gaze at, is my sister Pam, which, considering her age and the horrid insulting remarks of our father when he's painting her portrait, is really very strange.

'If you were a few years older, Pam,' he said to her once, 'I should ask you to marry me.'

Fancy Mr John Anderson, a grown-up, saying that! He was joking, of course, but Pam was, I knew, secretly pleased. We haven't repeated what he said to our parents in case they didn't realise it was a joke, and were shocked. You can't always be certain in advance, when you're a child, what would be right and what would be wrong—what would be shocking—to repeat.

I made a mistake today; an awful mistake. Mr John Anderson arrived at the Club without his dog, his beautiful golden spaniel. We asked him where it was.

'Oh,' says he, in a loud and cheerful voice—not whispering—'I've sent her off to kennels to be mated.'

Confident of having an interesting item of news to pass on, I repeat this information—loudly, as well—to our parents; who are scandalised.

'Hush, Elspeth—hush!' says my mother, looking over her shoulder to see if anyone has overheard me. 'That's not the kind of thing for a little girl to talk about—'

It isn't nice, they say, in polite society to speak of animals being—being—well, mated—not nice at

366

all: disgusting, in fact.

'Dirty—filthy talk!—and to a child!' exclaims my father, shooting angry glances across the pavilion at Mr John Anderson, who remains unaware, apparently, of the anguish he is causing me.

I have gone hot all over with shame, with acute embarrassment. My parents are shocked, and so I'm shocked as well. Obviously, I've blundered. But how have I blundered? *Mating*, I have always thought, is another word for *marrying*, which grown-ups do, so why shouldn't animals? Why is the topic unmentionable in polite society? Doesn't Mr John Anderson count as polite society? *Dirty talk*, my father called it. Why? What's dirty about it? I have no idea what is.

*   *   *

Betty Spooner has a car!

That she has it is due entirely to our father. The man in the garage from whom we bought our big expensive maroon Austin tourer happened to tell Daddy that he had been landed in part-exchange with a little old two-seater Ford, which, not having the extra space on his premises to keep it, he was anxious to get rid of in a hurry, and was therefore prepared to sell very cheaply. Could Mr Hallsmith put him in touch, perhaps, with a possible buyer?

Daddy at once thought of Betty Spooner. The trouble was, Betty never has any money, not more than just enough for her daily bus fares in and out of Newquay to the Tennis Club. She and her mother, it is believed, subsist on the tiny pension that continues to trickle in following the death (if he is dead) of Colonel Spooner, Betty's father; or perhaps on a remittance allowed them by his family. We know nothing about Betty's missing father, or his family, or indeed about Betty and her mother, except that they live alone together some miles outside Newquay, and are as poor as church mice.

The garageman, Osborne, stated that the vehicle he had on offer was in perfect mechanical order and going for a song only because of having taken a few knocks in its time and needing to be smartened up a bit. If Mr Hallsmith's young friend found herself short of ready cash, said the accommodating garageman—a good customer of Daddy's at the Midland Bank, even as our father is a good and valued customer at his garage, where we always get our petrol—she could pay for the Ford by easy stages, in monthly instalments.

Betty Spooner, when told by Daddy of this chance to become a motor-car owner herself, was ecstatic. A car!—but how wonderful! It's what she had always dreamed of having. As to the money required for the purchase price, not a huge amount of money—fifteen pounds—Betty was positive that she could raise it somehow. Yes, oh *yes*! And so the deal was duly signed and sealed, with our father, as financial adviser and agent of the transaction, crowning his sponsorship by the uncommonly liberal gesture of lending her, from his personal pocket, the initial five pounds deposit. And this very day Betty Spooner's motor car is to be delivered to the front door of Grosvenor House, so that we may have the pleasure of seeing her take possession of it.

The morning and afternoon we spend on the Great Western Beach; and then we play tennis up at the Club; and now it's evening and the whole Hallsmith family, and Lucy too, and Betty Spooner, are crammed into the porch, waiting for the arrival of the little second-hand open two-seater Ford.

And here, drawing up by the pavement outside, here it is: battered certainly, its grey paintwork scratched and dented, its upholstery worn, the lid of its dickey-seat discreetly closed, its canvas hood folded flat, no doubt concealing holes in the fabric, but in the sight of Betty, and in our sight as well, a wondrous object to behold.

Osborne, the garageman, has no sooner extricated himself from behind the steering wheel than Betty slips into his place. He bends over to point out to her the various pedals, the gears, the instruments on the dashboard, but she shakes her head, brushing him off impatiently. She doesn't need him, she says, to explain to her. She *knows* how to drive a car! She is laughing, laughing, wildly excited.

'Hop in!' she commands him, laughing still. 'Come on—hop in! We pass your garage—I'll drop you off there.'

He doesn't argue. He climbs into the passenger seat. The engine starts immediately, conks out, starts again. With a jerk and a wobble, and another jerk, they are off. One of Betty's hands on the steering wheel, the other dangerously waving to us, the little grey motor car swerves away and vanishes down Bury Road.

The next day, Sunday, Daddy suggests that after picnicking at Porth we might drive some few miles further along the coast and drop in on Betty Spooner and her mother for a cup of tea. It would set our minds at rest, he says, to be sure she got home safely, and we can hear if the car is behaving itself, and also make the acquaintance of Mrs Spooner.

So this is what we do: a disastrous decision.

Our friendship with Betty is, and has always been, a Newquay Lawn Tennis Club friendship. It is at the Club, and only at the Club, that we meet. We have never visited Betty Spooner in her home. Daddy says he knows the name of the village where she lives, but no more than that, and when we get to what should be the village, it doesn't exist. There is a windy crossroads, a finger-post indicating the whereabouts of an invisible farm, a bank of milk churns, a letter box deep-set into dry stone walling, a sign that marks the stopping place for a bus, and a row of wayside cottages. Is it in one of these cottages they live? Where else? Mummy leans from the car to attract the attention of an elderly man smoking a pipe, propped on his gate. Can he please tell us where we might find Mrs Spooner and her daughter? He removes his pipe to answer Mummy.

'You looking for them Spooners, eh?' he says, referring to them not quite as our parents would deem to be respectful. 'Keep goin',' he says, motioning ahead with his pipe. 'T'aint far. Down on the flat, their house is. Stands alone—you can't miss it.'

We have missed it, though, a good many times in the past. The coastal road runs behind and above the wide featureless inlet where we have never previously paused, there being no inducement to pause unless you were friends with the inhabitants of the single square modern ugly slate-roofed house, built in error, surely: the error made once but not repeated. It stands, as the man Mummy asked had said it did, alone, and plumb in the centre of a marshy desert of coarse grass and scrubby stunted bushes, practically on a level with the pebbly dreary shore.

This is where Betty Spooner lives. We know that it's bound to be here, on this bleak patch of no-man's-land, because, parked beside the desolate building's low surrounding concrete wall—a hopelessly flimsy defence against invading winter tides—is the jaunty little grey two-seater, which here, in such a dismal setting, seems, to have lost its jauntiness.

Daddy drives down off the road, following a sandy potholed grass-grown track, and brakes our big shiny Austin alongside the little Ford. Mummy knocks at the front door. Betty opens it. She must have been standing at a window, watching us approach. There is no surprise on her face; no welcome either. She wishes we weren't here, and *we* wish we weren't here.

'Hullo!' says Betty Spooner, brusquely; not the Betty Spooner we are familiar with. She doesn't smile, she doesn't laugh. 'I'll put the kettle on.'

We stay for tea, because we have to stay half-an-hour at least, now that we *are* here, and Betty produces some slices of stale cake and a tin of crumbling biscuits, also stale. She introduces us to her mother, Mrs Spooner, who shambles in from another room and says nothing, but eyes her daughter's visitors suspiciously. Can this fat old woman, blowsy, red-faced, with wild greying uncombed hair, really be Betty Spooner's mother?

In the room where we are sitting the wallpaper

is blotched by damp and peeling off the walls, and such is the condition of the scanty pieces of furniture, an unsteady table and a few disintegrating chairs, they could almost have been retrieved from a rubbish dump. Not wanting to look as though we're looking, what we see is noted furtively, out of the corners of our eyes.

We don't stay long. When we leave Betty Spooner comes outside with us. Mummy, on saying goodbye to Betty, unexpectedly kisses her. Mummy doesn't often kiss people; she's not a great kisser—she hardly ever kisses us, her own children, except for a goodnight peck on the cheek. So it is remarkable, her parting embrace of Betty Spooner.

Later I question my sister Pam as to the meaning of a word our parents uttered in their low-toned exchange when we were driving away, and which was caught by my straining ear.

'What is a—a alick-holic, Pam?' I ask her.

'*Alcoholic*,' she corrects me. 'It's a person', she says, after a moment's reflection, 'who drinks too much—too many cocktails, and—and glasses of sherry, and whisky; a person who gets drunk a lot.'

I am apalled. 'Betty Spooner drinks too much *whisky*?'

'No, not Betty, silly. It's her mother they were talking about—Mrs Spooner. She's an al-co-holic,' says my knowledgeable sister, pronouncing the difficult word with care, slowly.

The forlorn circumstances regarding Mrs Spooner and her daughter, and where and how they live, of which we are now aware, has made, for some reason, a difference to our friendship with Betty Spooner. Instead of her being cheerful and carefree in our company, as before, she is awkward and inclined to avoid us up at the Tennis Club; and we feel awkward, likewise. Something special was spoiled, somehow, by that visit, and we are sorry we went.

*   *   *

This coming August I shall have my eleventh birthday. It seems to be a year when everybody is getting married. Not everybody *really*, but when we bump into Enid Hosking by chance one morning she tells us that her brother, Lewarne, is going to be married at Easter, in Liverpool, the town where he and his family live and carry on their business as a firm of solicitors. Shortly after the wedding, Enid says, Lewarne intends to bring Nancy, his wife—as she will be by then—to stay in their Porth bungalow. So that's when we shall meet her, and when Lewarne will be able to show her off to all his Newquay friends.

Enid says that Nancy is very pretty, but she doesn't, it seems, play tennis or anyway not much, and rather badly. Lewarne has declared that he means to give her lessons when they are staying at Porth. He himself likes to play tennis as often as possible on holiday, and since the Hoskings have their own private grass tennis court conveniently situated right in front of the bungalow, it will be a perfect opportunity.

Bo'sun Hooper, another one of our grown-up tennis-playing great friends, has also decided to get married this year. We didn't know about his wedding in advance. It was a bolt from the blue (which means a total surprise) for all of us. He drove his new young receptionist over to Truro one weekend, and when he drove her back she had become his new young wife. He's been married before, of course. Sheila Hooper's mother died when she was a baby, so this is a second wife for him. Pig-faced Ralph said, when he heard the news—and everybody up at the Tennis Club was talking about it, with astonishment—he said that the new Mrs Hooper was young enough to be Bo'sun Hooper's daughter.

I think Pig-faced Ralph was exaggerating a bit, because Sheila Hooper, the real daughter, is younger than me by three years at least, if not more. But certainly Bo'sun Hooper's new wife, who was the Great Western Hotel's receptionist until quite recently, is very young indeed. She doesn't look much older than my sister Pam. As a matter of fact they've made friends with each other, she and Pam, down on the beach, and sometimes they sit for hours, the two of them, side by side on the sand, laughing and talking together as though they were the same age; which is by no means the case. It's just that my sister looks older than she actually is, and the new Mrs Hooper looks a good deal younger than I suppose she must be.

She's what is known as a platinum blonde. Jean Harlow, the Hollywood film star, is a platinum blonde, but that's because Jean Harlow dyes her hair. The pale silvery shade of the new Mrs Bo'sun Hooper's hair is natural. It is extremely unusual— remarkable, even—to be a natural platinum blonde. I don't know what she and my sister talk about. Pam doesn't tell me.

Towards the end of this year another wedding is due to take place: not a marriage similar to Lewarne Hosking's and Bo'sun Hooper's, which

374

are of interest merely to us local residents, but a Royal wedding, an event of national significance. The papers have been filled with photographs of people in high society, and titbits of gossipy information, ever since the announcement made from Buckingham Palace by the King and Queen of the engagement of their son, Prince George, Duke of Kent.

He it was who long ago promised to open—once it had finished being built—Newquay's Cottage Hospital; and the building of it is at last on the verge of completion. Prince George, we read, is to marry—but only *after* he's kept his promise and officially opened our Cottage Hospital—Princess Marina of Greece, a foreigner. Princes and Princesses are obliged to marry foreigners, in spite of Daddy's low opinion of them, on account of there never being enough royal personages available at home to choose from. Lucy's *Daily Herald* has explained all this to her, and she explains it to me.

As if by common consent, every single Newquay shop window is now decorated in variations of greeny-blue, the Greek Princess's favourite colour; which happens also to be (as well as pink) my favourite colour. Pam says you can't have more than one favourite of anything, but I say if I want to have two favourites, pink *and* blue, *both*, I can, so there. This beautiful greeny-blue colour has been given a special name in honour of the foreign Princess: Marina blue.

When they get married, next November, by way of celebration the whole of the British public is to be granted a holiday from work. I wonder why they decided, Prince George and his bride, to have their wedding in November. Except for Guy Fawkes Day on the fifth, it is, I think, the most awful dismal month of the entire year. If ever I marry anyone I shall do it in the summer, probably on my birthday, when the weather's fine and hot, and the sky's blue: bathing weather.

*   *   *

We bathe, and have always bathed, in the sea. Nor have we ever, until now, imagined ourselves bathing anywhere *but* in the sea. So far as we are concerned, that's what the sea is for. Film stars in Hollywood have swimming pools. With one notable exception, there are no swimming pools in Newquay.

Then one evening at the supper table our father informs us of a highly complimentary invitation issued to him across the counter that morning by Mrs Winant, a rich, and therefore valued, although temporary customer of the Midland Bank. She has three little girls of about the same age as us and she has asked if Mr Hallsmith would be so very kind (this is how she phrased it) as to let his children have tea with hers the following afternoon. They are over here from the United States of America on a flying visit to Mrs Winant's mother, old Mrs Baker. Because of the demanding nature of Mr Winant's job, he was unable to accompany his family on the trip, and has had to be left behind in America. Mr Winant is a diplomat—whatever that means. We think, but are not sure, that he might be an Ambassador. We don't know what that means either, only that it is extremely important; almost as important, we think, as

376

Royalty.

The arrival of Mrs Winant and her daughters from the further shores of the Atlantic Ocean has broken a spell, although old Mrs Baker, the Winant girls' widowed grandmother, is not by any means a Sleeping Beauty. Nowadays, however, practically nobody calls, apart from tradespeople, at the huge and extraordinary house tucked away out of sight where old Mrs Baker lives as a semi-invalid recluse, ministered to by a number of servants, but otherwise alone. The famously bizarre edifice she lives in was built some considerable while ago by Mrs Baker's husband when he retired from the world of business. He has been dead now for many years, but when alive Mr Baker amassed—we don't know how—an immense fortune, much of which he then proceeded to lavish on the creation of a fabulous mansion: the realisation, no doubt, of a dream long-held. But the mystery is why he chose to locate his dream house where he did locate it. How could he have remained oblivious to the obvious fact of the site he selected being so wildly incongruous? Mr Baker named his architectural marvel *Lewinnick*. In Newquay, though, it is always referred to, rudely, as *Baker's Folly*.

The palatial sprawling rose-red construction, built on the north side—the sunless side—of Pentire Head, clings to wave-battered windswept granite-grey cliffs like some exotic bird of paradise that has lost its compass bearings and been forced to find a precarious ledge to roost on far from its native habitat. In grown-up discussions we children have heard, without being any the wiser for hearing it, the word *Florentine*.

Is that what Baker's Folly is?—Florentine? It has, naturally, no garden. In such a position, how could it have a garden? The tessellated marble floors, the pillars, arches, patios, terraces, flights of steps adorned with terracotta urns, drop down and down, steeply, to a wide open paved space at the bottom, an arena, with a platform, or stage perhaps, over to the right; and on the last and lowest level of all, close to the deep green restless sea, behold: a swimming pool!

All this we discover, as we might discover the fantasy palace of Kubla Khan, when Mummy motors us out to Pentire Head for our teatime appointment (we could easily have walked the distance, but arriving by car is thought to be more appropriate to such an occasion); a visit that from its very beginning astonishes us.

The Lewinnick driveway winds down off the headland in between banks overhung by curtains of a luscious dangling plant, its greenery studded with bright pink flowers, and comes to an end at the house's front entrance which, unlike any front entrance we have ever previously known, is at the top and the back of the house. Facing towards and close to the cliff, there is here no view, or sound even, of the nearby sea. How peculiar!

Once inside, we are met and greeted by Hilary, Ursula and Valerie Winant, and after having been presented to their grandmother, a hugely fat old lady wrapped in shawls and barely visible in the stuffy dark heavily curtained drawing-room cluttered with what seem to be vaguely foreign objects, they lead us off on an outside tour of Baker's Folly.

Stepping clear of the dim interior, we are

378

dumbfounded by what confronts us: the incredible cliff-hanging domain of an *Arabian Nights* illustration. That such a wonder could exist in reality we had not supposed to be possible.

The three little girls, our guides, are real enough. They wear dresses, identical except in size, with puff-sleeves and smocking and white collars. Hilary, the eldest, has the watchful serious air of a junior substitute mother, responsible for the behaviour of the other two. Ursula, the middle sister, rather overweight and with sticking-out teeth but a constant good-natured smile, seldom speaks. The youngest, Valerie, besides being the prettiest and the liveliest of the trio, is a chatterer. Although they are nice to us, we feel awkward and we can't help responding stiffly. Pam and me would have preferred to explore the terraces on our own, instead of them conducting us politely around. We find their American accents hard to get used to, and they are so *very* well-behaved. Their manners are perfect.

At every high tide the swimming pool is replenished by the sea, and the tide is high now. We lean on a stone balustrade, gazing at the spectacle of spray, flung up by waves breaking on the rocks beneath, cascading over the marble pavement which surrounds the pool. How thrilling! We wish we had brought our bathing costumes along, but Hilary says that we shouldn't have been allowed to bathe if we had. No one is allowed to bathe, or even descend the last flight of steps to the lowest level, when the tide is high: it's considered to be too dangerous.

'And anyway, the water's terribly cold,' says Hilary.

'It's *freezing*!' says Valerie.

We Hallsmiths are accustomed (or me and Pam are; not Jim) to the iciness of the north Cornish sea, but we don't say so: it might give an impression of showing-off.

'Our pool back home is heated,' Ursula tells us.

Wishing to return their hospitality, we invite them to tea the following afternoon on the Great Western Beach; and they come. They decline—politely—to bathe, or to remove, despite the scorchingly hot sunshine, any article of clothing, apart from their shoes and their socks when we play, first, French cricket, and then later, after tea, rounders with Damian and the Wilson boys, and Eve and Rex Dyer and the Wichelows. Rounders, they say, is much the same as American baseball. And they absolutely adore our antiquated beach hut. It's just the cutest thing, they declare, that they ever laid eyes on!

Mrs Winant is elegant, but without being *grand*, which is what we had expected and rather feared she would be. She's friendly, and likes to joke with us children. Tall and slim, she has dark hair and is surprisingly pretty and young-looking. You would never guess that old Mrs Baker was her mother. Perhaps she is so entirely different because of living in America. Or perhaps it's because of being married to a diplomat (or to an Ambassador, it may be). As we watch Mrs Winant and her three well-behaved girls being driven away up the hill from the Great Western Beach in Mrs Baker's big expensive Bentley by Mrs Baker's uniformed chauffeur, Mummy says, with decided approval, but also with a sigh:

'She is a very charming woman, Mrs Winant.'

380

They had got on well together. Sitting in deckchairs in front of our beach hut, their conversation was as animated as if they had been acquainted for years. I wonder why Mummy sighed.

We were meant to go again to Lewinnick. It was arranged that we should walk out to Pentire Head one morning when the tide would be low and it would therefore be safe to bathe in that adventurously unique swimming pool down on the rocks. But we have been disappointed.

The Winants' visit to old Mrs Baker was cut short by a cable from Mr Winant in Washington. According to the cabled message, his wife and their three daughters must *immediately* get aboard an aeroplane and fly to Paris, the capital city of France, where he will meet them. In twenty-four hours they are gone.

'Well,' says Mummy, 'that's what you have to be prepared for—sudden changes of plan—when you move in diplomatic circles'.

'Here today and gone tomorrow,' Pam remarks, airily.

I wish I'd thought of saying that. *Here today and gone tomorrow*: I repeat the phrase to myself, in private, practising the careless throwaway tone of my sister's voice, while with one hand I hold an imaginary cocktail, and with the other an imaginary cigarette. How sophisticated it sounds!

We didn't after all experience the thrill of bathing in a sea-filled swimming pool, but we have, unforgettably, stood and walked, as hardly any Newquay residents can claim to have done, on the fabulous terraces of Baker's Folly.

*   *   *

I've begun to realise that growing up might not be—doesn't *have* to be—so bad. Not all grown-ups waste whole afternoons of their time 'sitting indoors at bridge tables, or talk on and *on* (unless they're squabbling) about the boring committee meeting they've just attended. You *could* grow up to be like the Wichelows, who enjoy playing rounders on the beach with us children; or like Mrs Winant, who laughs, and flies off to Paris in an aeroplane at the drop of a hat. You could be a Hollywood film star. There are heaps of possibilities for *not* getting stuck in a dull job, and being dull yourself, and miserable and cross.

I shan't get stuck when I grow up. I mean to escape and be free to do whatever I want to do. It will have to be an out-of-doors occupation, because I love the weather—every sort of weather: wind and rain and storms and sunshine—and if I was one of those people who work in an office or shut inside a bank, I should miss the weather entirely, which would be awful; not much better than going to prison. I might decide to become an explorer. Or I might marry a diplomat. But whatever it is I do, I've begun to think that being grown up could actually—with a bit of luck—be fun.

We've had a good deal of fun in the summer holidays this year. At the end of nearly every day, after getting home from the beach, we spend a further couple of hours or so up at the Tennis Club. For my eleventh birthday I've been given a proper racquet. It isn't second-hand; it's a racquet my parents bought for me new, from a shop. We've heard that when the lawn-tennis season comes round again there is to be a Junior Tournament organised for any person under the age of eighteen to enter, and this is the main reason why we are practising so hard.

But also, with practice, we are, of course, improving at the game, and the more we improve, the more we enjoy playing it. Besides, we relish a sense we now have, as official subscription-paying members, of *belonging* to the Club; and of belonging, we feel, on an equal footing with its grown up members. Recently our Tennis Club has assumed a central position in the widening horizons of Pam and Jim and me.

On a certain September evening, a casual remark regarding the exceptionally high tide that happens to be due this very day, uttered in the Tennis Club pavilion during the usual inconsequential parting chit-chat between visitors and residents, at once inspires a group of boisterous young men and girls to pile hilariously into their motorcars with the stated intention of racing one another, helter-skelter, honking their horns, down to the bottom of the Great Western hill for an invigorating dip before supper.

To our joy, we children, instead of being left out, are invited to join the bathing party, and urged to squeeze ourselves in amongst a bunch of cheerful adults. And our father not only gives us permission to go, but consents to come with us. In this all-too-rare indulgent mood of his we catch a surprising—almost a shocking—glimpse of somebody we have never ever met, a complete stranger, who lets himself be swept up in the stampede; somebody younger than Daddy, somebody eager and boyish.

383

Our *father*?—boyish? How *can* he be? We suppose (talking about it afterwards) that the jolly camaraderie of the moment must have infected him; it being, perhaps, a reminder of other carefree summery moments in a distant, unimaginably youthful past.

Jack the Beachman and Stevens and the horses have dragged their army of bathing huts well out of reach of the high tide; a tide so rough and high it invades the slipway and even rushes, like a hungry monster, yards up the tarmacked road where it has no business to venture. Not a trace of beach remains exposed to view. The region of dry powdery much-trampled-over soft sand that lies, littered with sweet-wrappings and empty ginger-pop bottles, above what is the normal high-watermark, has been inundated, swamped and washed clean, purified by waves that hurl themselves again and again against an inflexible stone wall. These waves, flung back, defeated, and travelling violently in a reverse direction, collide, as they must, with the next advancing line of breakers: a collision that results always in glittering fountains of spray and foam.

It requires an extra high tide, and an onshore wind, for an audience to be presented with such a mesmerising free-of-charge performance, and the holiday-makers who, lingering too long, have had to grab hold of rugs and baskets and bags, abandoning in frantic haste their picnic encampments and beating a disorderly retreat to the protection of the sea wall, now cluster together behind it, gazing in fascination at the Atlantic Ocean's wild antics.

Their entertainment is greatly enhanced by our

late arrival, a gang of lunatics plunging with whoops and yells and apparent recklessness into the stormy sea; which, although tremendously exciting, is neither deep nor dangerous, only rather dirty, with the flotsam and jetsam of orange peel and similar discarded rubbish slopping around on the surface of the agitated water. In any different circumstances we children would have been disgusted by the orange peel and the blobs of floating scummy filth, but today it seems to make the whole impromptu enterprise more thrillingly adult. This is not what bathing is generally like!

*   *   *

I don't really know what exactly we are meant to be doing here, on Fistral Beach, after dark, except that there's a curious kind of hide-and-seek being played. I've no idea who is the person hiding; or where, or why; or who is looking for who; or what happens when someone is found. The rules of the game haven't been properly explained to me. But I don't mind; they told me the name of the game: it's *Jack o'Lantern*. And I think that Jack o'Lantern may very well be an Australian version of hide-and-seek. It was the Wilsons chiefly, with Damian Eastman and the Kileys and the Christies, who organised this evening's beach party, and the Wilsons, of course, are Australian.

I'm not sure that I myself, actually, was invited, but the Twins were, and often when Pam and Jim get invitations I'm allowed to tag along with them. I wanted so extremely much not to be left behind that Mummy said if I wore my thick jersey, because the evenings are growing chilly now, and if I

385

promised her to stay close to Pam, I could go too. This after-dark Fistral Bay party isn't intended to be for children; it's for young grown-ups. Damian Eastman and Jack Wilson, and Wilfred and David, the Wilcox brothers, and Celia Cox and her brother David, and Duncan Christie, count as young grown-ups, and they are all here. But I've bumped into Miriam Kiley several times, and she's two years younger than me; she's the youngest of the Kileys, the large family of boys and girls who live in Crantock.

We were instructed to bring torches with us, or better still, a lantern, but we Hallsmiths don't have either torches or a lantern. It doesn't seem to matter, though. Heaps of people do have torches, and some have metal-and-glass lanterns with candles inside, the sort that carol singers, when it's Christmas, carry from house to house, dangling at the end of a stick. I can see lights bobbing up and down, and flashing on and off, all over the place; and I can hear, faintly, the sound of whistles, and laughter and shrieks, and voices calling. Fistral Beach is huge, and the distant shouts and cries, blown on the wind, are partly drowned by the nearer, louder noise of waves crashing ashore. These massive white billows come looming out of nowhere. They are like the ghosts of the waves of the day that's gone: thunderous phantom breakers. Above me the night sky is crowded with stars, while here on the beach, up by the dunes, there's a big bonfire burning, with silhouetted figures flitting backwards and forwards in front of the flames. Everything is extraordinary, and quite unreal. I feel as if I'm in a dream.

The three of us, me and Pam and Jim, walked

through the town, past the harbour, and on to Fistral Bay, with our new friend Robert Langley, while it was afternoon still. Then, almost at once—as soon as the sun disappeared and the light began to fade—my sister and I were somehow separated; but I don't care. It isn't frightening. Even if I can't see the faces of the people who are chasing to and fro and hollering at each other, and even if most of them are a good deal older than me, I know who they are; or at least, I know practically everyone. And I know that Mummy is going to drive up with Mrs Mitchell fairly late—at ten o'clock, she said—and that she'll fetch us home safely; so I'm not worried about getting lost, even if, just for now, I am on my own, in the dark. It's exhilarating.

This is the last of the summer holiday season's memorable events. A week more, and school will begin again: it will be the start of the winter term. Tomorrow we shall have to say goodbye to Robert, who isn't really so much *our* new friend as Pam's new friend. He is the grandson of Sir Oliver Lodge. His father was killed in the Great War. Robert is nearly seventeen, and he is Mrs Langley's only son; her only child.

Robert is in love with Pam. I can tell it by the way he looks at her. I wish he was in love with me, but I'm too small for him to notice. Next summer Robert Langley will be returning to Newquay with his mother, and by next summer I'm sure to have grown a bit; but I don't think it will make any difference.

*   *   *

Since it's now October and has become too cold

for bathing, our father has ruled that each day after lunch my sister and I must, *without fail*, go for an invigorating walk, accompanied by Lucy Coles, who will be trundling Harvey in his pushchair. Argument is useless, and no excuses are tolerated: a rule is a rule. Our father has an inflexible conviction that regular exercise and fresh air are as vitally important for the health of growing children as it is for them to ward off the scurvy by swallowing every soggy leaf in their daily ration of *greens*, (beastly cabbage!) whether slug-infested or not.

Luckily, Pam and I both like fresh air, the fresher the better, but these dutiful afternoon walks are on the whole a rather dullish form of activity. In order, therefore, to lessen the boredom, we have invented a system of, day by day, varying the chosen routes. For instance, if we traipse up Mount Wise to Pentire Head on a Monday, on Tuesday we'll set forth in an opposite direction, one that leads us, perhaps, beyond the railings above Tolcarne Beach to Barrowfields, the grassy cliff-top area owned by Newquay Council and freely available to the public.

Whatever our final destination, when we reach it Harvey is unbuckled from his pushchair, and we proceed to play football with him, strenuously, or pig-in-the-middle, or catch-me-if-you-can, racing around in circles until we are all three healthily hot and out of breath. Lucy isn't a growing child, and so she doesn't have to run about and get exhausted, as we are obliged to do. She sits and watches us, placidly.

Our favourite walk takes us down on to the Great Western Beach at low tide. Almost always we are the only people to be seen down there. It's hard to believe this empty beach in October is the same beach that swarms with hundreds and hundreds of holiday-makers during the summer. Usually, when we first arrive here, before we've scuffed it up ourselves, the only markings visible on an immense, newly washed, uninhabited stretch of sand are the tiny prints left by the feet of seagulls landing in flocks to search for food.

But this afternoon we find the sand has been disturbed by more than seagulls. There is a double churned-up trail of horses' hooves galloping in a straight line across from the slipway to the harbour. We can see the riders, two specks in the distance. Then they turn, and come cantering towards us along the edge of the water, kicking up showers of spray, and as they draw near we realise that the leading rider is young Mrs Bo'sun Hooper. We don't recognise the man who is with her, on the other horse. We wave at them, and call out, but I don't think Mrs Bo'sun Hooper sees or hears us. She doesn't, in any case, wave back.

When we later describe what for us was a strikingly beautiful sight, like something out of a film, Daddy says Bo'sun Hooper told him weeks ago that his young platinum-haired wife had expressed a desire to have riding lessons. The purpose of her learning how to ride herself, he explained to our father, is because she wants to be able to teach her little stepdaughter, Sheila, so as they can eventually go riding together. The man on the second horse must have been Mrs Bo'sun Hooper's riding-master.

The following Thursday afternoon our chosen walk, as it happens, is down by the River Gannel, where we are pleased and surprised to see her and her riding-master again. This time they are so close to us we have to stand aside to let them pass. Pam, who made friends with Mrs Bo'sun Hooper on the beach last summer, says *Hullo!* to her, and Mrs Bo'sun Hooper says *Hullo!* to Pam in reply, but that's all. She and her teacher don't stop, even though they are going quite slowly, not even trotting: just ambling along. I expect it's difficult to stop and have a conversation when you're on a horse.

*   *   *

Our parents are away for the weekend. They have gone up to London to stay in the Cumberland Hotel, taking advantage of the national holiday granted to everybody in honour of Prince George and Princess Marina getting married. We are glad they've gone. It's not just, for the rest of us, a relief to have a respite, however brief it may be, from the daily domestic disagreements—from Daddy's moodiness and Mummy's tears—but what my sister Pam and I are secretly hoping is that the shared enjoyment by our parents of the city's festive extravaganzas may possibly result in a more harmonious atmosphere after their return to Grosvenor House. They've bought tickets, we know, for the theatre, a popular musical comedy, and if later on our father gives voice while in the bathroom, shaving, to the songs of Nelson Eddy, we shall be fairly certain their London gallivanting was a success. Ah!—but will it last, his good humour?—last for how long? We hope against hope an armistice will have been established and

390

will endure, at least until Christmas, so we may all reap the benefit of it.

We are not nearly so glad that in their absence our Aunt Nancy has come to take charge of the household. Aunt Nancy is the third of Mummy's three older unmarried sisters, and we would much rather she hadn't come to stay with us. It simply isn't necessary: Pam and Lucy between them are perfectly capable of looking after Harvey for two nights and two days, and Aunt Nancy doesn't know the first thing about children, or how to deal with them. We love our dear Aunt Molly; but our Aunt Nancy is a very different sort of person. It's not that we dislike her, exactly (as we do our Aunt Margaret), but we aren't quite comfortable with Aunt Nancy. She does have some really peculiar ideas, we think.

On the actual day of the Royal Wedding she decides that we will mark its historical importance by catching a bus to Porth and having a picnic down on the estuary sands, unaware, apparently, that it's November now, and the wrong weather for picnics: much too cold. We *never* have picnics in the winter. But Aunt Nancy has made her mind up: this is what we will do.

Lucy, tight-lipped and disapproving, insists on keeping Harvey at home. And as for Pam, she refuses point-blank to go picnicking anywhere in November. Which leaves me and my brother Jim, who has travelled back on a train from Exeter School for the weekend, to catch a coastal bus out of Newquay in company with our eccentric aunt. Both of us fervently wish we could manage, as Pam has done, to dig our heels in and refuse to go; but we feel if we did it might be too disappointing for

Aunt Nancy, who has already cut the sandwiches and filled a thermos flask with tea. The fact is, we can't help being rather sorry for her, because she is so very odd.

As soon as we step off the bus at Porth, it starts to rain. We have to find a cave where we can shelter while we eat our picnic. The cave is on the side of Porth we never go to: the shady side. The big house that commands the headland above belongs to the Tangye family, and there are notices planted all over the place with PRIVATE PROPERTY painted on them. The roof of the cave drips, and the rocks we huddle on are damp and chilly. I don't suppose anyone else in the whole of the British Isles has chosen to celebrate the London wedding of Prince George and his bride, Princess Marina, by sitting shivering in a wet cave, with the rain pouring down outside, and the tide coming in, eating potted-meat sandwiches and soggy biscuits.

*   *   *

Another winter has gone past. It will soon be summer again. This is the year of the Silver Jubilee, a commemoration of when King George and Queen Mary were crowned, a quarter of a century ago. They have been on the throne for twenty-five years, which sounds to us like a very long time indeed; but we are informed by Miss Howard that the reign of Queen Victoria was even longer. Nevertheless, the present monarchy has lasted sufficiently long for the nation once more to rejoice, and to be granted a further public holiday for its rejoicing.

Newquay shopkeepers, who so recently made sure the goods they displayed were all in shades of the Princess's favourite colour, aquamarine, have now, as a demonstration of loyalty, decorated their windows entirely with the red, white and blue of the Union Jack, our British flag. *Everything*, it seems, in this early summer of 1935, has to be red and white and blue, to the exclusion of any other colours.

My sister Pam and I have been invited to stay for the week of the Silver Jubilee, *by ourselves*, with Cousin Mildred and Cousin Edith Martin. The village of Sanderstead, Surrey, where the Martins live, is fairly near to London, and therefore to Buckingham Palace: the royal residence (as we are very well aware) of their majesties, the King and Queen. Buckingham Palace is where our mother had to go at the end of the Great War to receive her Red Cross Medal; and where King George pinned the DSO, awarded for an act of extreme heroism, on to our father's chest, after his return from a German prisoner-of-war camp in December, 1918.

Mummy has impressed on Pam and me how lucky we are to have been invited by Daddy's rich stockbroking relations to witness, as we shall do, from a first-floor balcony in the City of London, a glittering procession of carriages packed with kings and queens, and dukes and duchesses, Indian rajahs and foreign ambassadors, and goodness *knows* who else besides, driving up to the steps of St Paul's Cathedral for a solemn service of thanksgiving on what will undoubtedly be a grand historical occasion. And she sets to work immediately, kneeling on the floor to cut out from

393

yards of seersucker—which is the name of a newly invented nubbly-bubbly cotton material, chosen by Mummy as being especially appropriate—the two frocks that she then proceeds to run up like lightning on her Singer sewing machine. We call them our Jubilee dresses, because of the fashionable red and blue lines woven in a pattern of checks on a white background. For this memorable visit my sister and I will be patriotically decked out, like the Newquay shop-windows, in red, white and blue.

Our father has insisted that it's quite in order and as safe as houses for me and Pam to be put on a train to London with no grown-up in charge. It's normal practice nowadays, he declares, for children to travel on trains unaccompanied. The ticket-collector, if given a tip (a small one) will promise to keep an eye on us. Increasingly annoyed, he tells our worried mother that she is not to worry: there is absolutely nothing to worry about.

'For heaven's sake, Janet,' says he, 'stop fussing. They aren't a couple of babies any more—they're growing up, and a good thing too.' He reminds her, irritably, that our brother Jim now travels to and from his Exeter School on a train by himself. 'And you don't make a fuss over that.'

'But they're girls, Guth—Pam and Elspeth—not boys,' our mother pleads. What she wants is for him to agree to her coming with us on the journey.

It's of no use: her entreaties fall on deaf ears. He simply won't hear of it. Boys have to get used to standing on their own feet, and so do girls—the sooner the better. And when she persists in arguing that boys and girls are different, he refuses to listen to her nonsense. Boys and girls, he says,—they all have to learn. Children, whether male or female, ought not to be—*mustn't* be—mollycoddled. And for once, we think he's right.

We *are* growing up: it's true. And to be considered old enough now to embark on a journey by train adventurously alone is a cause of considerable pride for my sister Pam and me. Our father has said that girls have to learn, and—yes!—we are ready and eager to do so. But learn what, exactly? Of this we are uncertain.

Early one morning, having kissed our anxious-eyed mother goodbye on the platform, we climb aboard the Cornish Express in the Great Western Railway Station, each of us carrying a miniature suitcase, and a packet of sandwiches provided by Lucy. We have been instructed *not* to wave out of the train at Mummy, but to sit down straight away, and other than to go—and only *if absolutely necessary*—to the WC, *not* to stir from our seats until we arrive at the terminus, Paddington Station, where Cousin Mildred will be meeting us.

To our surprise we discover, settled into a corner opposite and calmly reading a book, Miss Costello, a member of the Tennis Club, who is also, as it happens, travelling up to London today for the Silver Jubilee festivities. Afterwards, instead of returning directly to Newquay, which we shall be doing, she intends to stay on for the world-famous championship tennis matches that take place annually at Wimbledon, a region of London: *as a spectator*, she explains to us, correcting our mistaken assumption that it was to be as a competitor. Apart from this piece of information with regard to Wimbledon, Miss Costello utters hardly a word for the rest of the six-hour journey, making it plain that she prefers reading to conversation.

When she plays tennis herself, Miss Costello always wears a stripey silk bandeau round her forehead, just above her eyebrows, and a skirt unmodishly long but elegant, and she serves underarm, like me and the Miss Lodges. She isn't the slightest bit interested in children, and never bothers to chat to us in the Club's pavilion, as Betty Spooner does. Even so, it is rather a relief (not that we would ever dream of admitting it) to find that we have for company, no matter how uncommunicative our companion may be, a familiar Newquay resident, actually a member of the Tennis Club. And I can't help wondering: is she here simply by chance, by a fortunate coincidence, or did Mummy—while managing to prevent our father knowing of it—somehow arrange for Miss Costello to be travelling up to London on the very same day, and in the very same compartment as us, her two unprotected (except, that's to say, for the ticket-collector's promised eye) little daughters?

*   *   *

Cousin Mildred Martin is our most regular visitor, coming to spend a fortnight at the seaside every summer, unfailingly, with her Hallsmith relations, usually in August. This year, however, she has planned to have her visit earlier than usual so that my sister Pam and I are spared the dangers—real or imaginary—of travelling on the Great Western Railway from London to Newquay by ourselves.

Because Cousin Mildred, a dedicated Girl Guider, is as different as it's possible to be from Miss Costello, our return journey is much more enjoyable and lively than was our journey up to London. We rattle homewards in high spirits, looking forward to being greeted by our family as conquering heroes, and to entertaining an enthralled audience with boastful descriptions of gilded carriages crammed full of royal and other aristocratic personages. The gorgeous parade of sparkling diamond tiaras and golden-braided uniforms and ostrich feathers galore was a spectacle dazzling to behold—and we beheld it!

But we are sadly mistaken in supposing that this unique experience of ours guarantees us making a triumphant entrance at home. On the contrary, far from being bombarded with questions, the welcome we receive on arrival is disappointingly flat and unenthusiastic: oddly muted. Nobody asks us what we have done, or what wonderful sights we have seen. The prevailing atmosphere of the household is one of unmitigated gloom, with no hint of left-over Silver Jubilee jubilation. Crestfallen, we are at a loss to account for our unexpectedly lacklustre reception. There must be a reason. What can have happened in the few days— a mere week—while we were absent? And soon enough the reason does become apparent—or anyway, the first half of it does, for all Newquay society is talking about the local scandal.

Bluntly, shockingly put, young Mrs Bo'sun Hooper of the Great Western Hotel, one fine May morning ran off with her handsome riding-master.

Ran off is what I catch again and again, murmured in undertones. The picture I have in my mind though, vividly, is not of two people *running off*, hand-in-hand, on foot, as the expression seems to suggest, but of two riders galloping into the distance, with spray splashing up from their horses' hooves, away and away, getting smaller and smaller, disappearing.

The second part of the scandal, being worse, far worse, is successfully concealed from my attentive ears. But Pam ferrets out the awful truth, and at night, in the dark, in a whisper, I hear it from her: when pretty young platinum-haired Mrs Bo'sun Hooper ran away—or galloped off—she broke Bo'sun Hooper's heart, and he shot himself.

I am disbelieving, horrified. 'With a gun?'

'Well, of course with a gun, stupid,' says my sister, impatient at such idiocy.

Bo'sun Hooper, our nice kind happy jokey friend, who for years past, for as long as I can remember anything, has admired our mother and played tennis with our father, is dead: gone. He has vanished out of our lives as finally, irretrievably, as his runaway wife. It is a dreadful, dreadful thing to have occurred, and no wonder Daddy's mood is black and angry, and Mummy's eyes are red with weeping behind her closed bedroom door.

*   *   *

I have been practising every evening for the Junior Tennis Tournament which is to take place in the school holidays, when the big hotels are sure to be full of visitors' children. As it's an experiment the Club's committee has decided this year's Junior Tournament will consist of only mixed doubles, no singles matches. The Twins mean to enter their names for the under-eighteen section, and I shall put my name down for the under-fourteens. I don't suppose there will be many under-fourteen competitors.

I wish I could solve the bothersome problem of why it is I sometimes play tennis brilliantly, surprising myself, and at other times very badly indeed. *Erratic*, I'm told is the term that describes my performance on the tennis court. When I serve aces, or hit a ball amazingly fast across, and not into the net, it's a pure fluke. Since I don't know how I did it, I have no notion of how it can be repeated, and have simply to hope for another lucky shot. This means I make an undependable partner; and *this* means that the Junior Tennis Tournament, although an exciting, is also an anxious prospect.

More important than anything else about any game, our father believes, is to win it. Winning, for him, is of paramount importance. Occasionally, therefore, he will spare us a few minutes to demonstrate the correct method of dealing with backhands and forehands, lobs and volleys, but on the whole we are left to learn as best we may by trial and error how the strokes ought to be played. He seems to think that because we are Hallsmith children, *his* children, we will automatically excel at the game of tennis, taking to it as a matter of course like ducks to water.

Instruction, our father maintains, is largely a waste of time, and he applies the same dubious principle to his painting. Being a naturally gifted artist, he, Guthrie Hallsmith (DSO), knows perfectly well, thank you very much, how to paint, and there is nobody who can teach him anything at all about what he already instinctively knows: nobody! Artists are not made by slavish imitation; they are created at birth, and to study the techniques employed by other artists (or, for that matter, other tennis players) in order to derive benefit from their achievements would be an utterly pointless exercise.

In spite of Daddy almost never winning his tennis matches, and having the pictures he sends off regularly, each year, to the Royal Academy, each year rejected, it continues nonetheless to be his unshakeable conviction that the light of nature is more illuminating than any amount of teaching or example. He does allow himself to buy the Royal Academy's Summer Exhibition annual catalogue, and casts a bitter eye over the glossy reproductions of its successful entries (why isn't his latest portrait included amongst them?), but this is as far as he goes in taking note of the work of rival painters, whether they are alive or dead, famous or not.

*   *   *

One of the contradictions of our life that I can't manage to make sense of—and the older I get, the more it perplexes me—is that we are presented to local society as a remarkable family, quite out of the ordinary and a cut above all other Newquay families, yet when at home, inside, and the door firmly shut on the world, then the theatrical glue that sticks us together dissolves. Behind the scenes—the spotlight, as it were, switched off—we children are shown that each of us is, as an individual, in no way remarkable, but wretchedly inadequate, with nothing of which to be proud; the reverse, in fact: much of which to be ashamed.

If I am the family member least affected by the inevitable confusion arising from being obliged continually to adjust the image we have of ourselves from public to private, superior to inferior, it is mainly because Daddy assumes that we have in common, he and I, an appreciation of English literature. This assumption I cravenly foster, since it acts as a sheltering bulwark, protecting me against what I most of all dread: becoming a focus for my father's crippling contempt, so frighteningly observable elsewhere.

And yet my willingness to play the part he from time to time assigns me as his little pet companion, although expedient, isn't entirely ignoble; I do truly love the books Daddy gives me and the poetry that he reads aloud to me.

Unforgettable are the lines of John Masefield's poem, 'Sea-Fever'. My heart expands with the thrill of hearing them spoken by my father: *For the call of the running tide/Is a wild call and a clear call that may not be denied.*

Oh, wonderful!

When he is declaiming the poem written by Thomas Hood, beginning, *I remember, I remember/The house where I was born/The little window where the sun/Came peeping in at morn*, he sits, gripping my hand, not looking at my face, but staring straight ahead at sights visible only to him. And from the intensity of his gaze, and the tightness of his grip, and a certain alteration in the tone of his voice, it seems to me the poet—years ago dead—must be expressing for Daddy the deeply hidden anguished feelings that my father isn't himself able to express. *He never came a wink too soon/Nor brought too long a day/But now I often wish the night/Had borne my breath away!*

By chance my mother overhears a rendering of this particular poem, and she stops beside us to scold Guthrie, her husband, severely, regardless of the consequences, for the unsuitability of what he is reciting to me. The sad haunting wistful cadences, and the sentiments they convey, are declared by Mummy, her cheeks flushing pink with indignation, to be morbid, unhealthily depressing, degenerate even, and wholly unfit for Elspeth, aged eleven—or indeed, for any child—to listen to.

She delivered the same verdict of *degenerate, unhealthy—immoral!*—on Omar Khayyam's incomparably beautiful verses that I secretly hoard as treasure by committing them to memory: *Awake! for Morning in the Bowl of Night/Has flung the Stone that puts the Stars to Flight . . .*

My father's brow darkens. 'You know nothing about it, Janet—nothing!' He gets up and walks away, furious. And I am bound, unhappily, to agree with him. About poetry, the intoxicating power of words—marvellous words—Mummy knows nothing.

For the Twins there is no such poetic oasis, no meeting place, no reconciliation with our father. Jim he has always regarded as a dull-witted clumsy boy, and both have to be reminded frequently, and sometimes forcefully, not merely how tiresome they are, unworthy material for any son or daughter of his, but also—Pam in particular—how excessively unattractive is the personality and the appearance of each of them. Their only saving grace is that they belong to the Hallsmith family, and they had better thank their lucky stars they do!

Our mother, to be sure, loves her Twins, and worries for them. Obviously, she does. But that is because she is by nature a good and a loving mother, not because—or seldom because—they are children who deserve whatever indulgences may be meted out to them.

For Pam and Jim, my defiant sister and my bewildered brother, life is an unremittingly rocky uphill climb, a pathway strewn with obstacles.

*   *   *

It will soon be my birthday. On the 21st of August I shall be twelve. And it isn't just that I'm changing as I get older: everything else is changing as well. Instead of what I've been from the very beginning, one half of a pair of sisters, Pam has gone on ahead of me, and left me behind on my own, abandoned me to sink or swim without her. She's growing up a lot quicker than I am, and although we have lessons every day as usual with Miss Howard there's a gap between us, and it's a gap that widens daily. My sister is nearly as tall now as our mother, besides which, in spite of Daddy's rudeness to her, I can see she really is very pretty. Everybody, except our father, thinks that she is. The man with the spaniel-dog up at the Tennis Club is in love with her, and so is Robert Langley.

Jim, because he's a boy (and still shorter by a couple of inches than Pam), has always been the odd excluded one of the three, trailing along separately in the wake of us girls, wanting and struggling to draw level, but almost always outdistanced. He and I will never count as a pair in the way Pam and I did, but from time to time we do join forces, team up, and those early attempts at roller-skating, and Jim teaching me how to play marbles, and his hobby of stamp-collecting that he occasionally allows me to share, and other similar activities, have resulted in us forging a special kind of bond. And this bond of ours is the reason I shan't ever abandon *him* to his fate, come what may. How could I? For the truth of the matter is, I am Jim's only certain supporter in stormy weather, and even if I don't dare to say or do much—or, to be honest, anything at all—to show my support openly, at least he knows that I'm on the same side as him. I daresay an extra brother would provide the necessary backing in a crisis, but Harvey's no help of course, being, as yet, more of a baby than a brother.

Every day the outgoing tide on the Great Western Beach reveals, as it ebbs, the rock which, when we were younger, we used to run races round; a small solitary seaweedy rock isolated in the middle of acres of sand. That's how I feel nowadays: isolated.

But the curious fact I'm starting to realise is that I'm not exactly on my own after all. There's me, and then there's another me. The second me lives inside my head and we hold conversations in secret about what we notice, and when we disagree with my parents' views. I have recently found myself more and more doubtful regarding a good many of my father's opinions—and sometimes, indeed, of my mother's opinions also. And I wonder: am I obliged to accept, unquestioningly, all that my parents believe? Is it wicked for a daughter, which is what I am, to be critical of their beliefs?—to remain unconvinced? Even when, as so frequently happens, they differ, he and she, is one of them bound—if not my father, then my mother—to be right in every instance? Could they not sometimes both be wrong?

Actually, it does seem to me quite often as if they *are* both completely wrong. Since Pam has ceased to be available for the sort of confidential discussions that once the two of us were accustomed to having together, these are unspoken doubts of mine, anxieties not uttered aloud. Instead of talking things over with my sister, I talk them over silently now with this other, newly discovered Ellie.

'Whatever is going on in that funny little head of yours, Elspeth?' my mother says to me.

And I say to her: 'Nothing, Mummy—nothing

special.'

I don't *have* to tell her, or anyone, my thoughts, and it may be better—safer—not to tell anyone else; better to keep quiet.

*   *   *

It's a breezy sunshiny afternoon in July, and we are setting off on foot up Mount Wise towards Pentire Head, the Twins and me, with Robert Langley, seventeen years old, as the leader of our adventurous expedition. For to us Hallsmith children it does seem to be adventurous: an excitingly new experience. Even Jim is in boisterous high spirits. We are on our way to see William Shakespeare's drama, *The Taming of the Shrew*, a performance of which is to be given out-of-doors at Baker's Folly by a company of travelling Shakespearean actors.

It was last year when Hilary and Ursula and Valerie Winant conducted me and Pam down and down, from one of their grandmother's terraces to the next, and we remember well the stone stage built at the far end of the bottom terrace, with a flight of steps leading up on either side of it, and the rough craggy tussocky cliff rising sheer behind, and the wild ocean waves close by. A more dramatic setting for the presentation of a drama it is impossible to imagine.

Although we three have never yet seen a play of William Shakespeare's being enacted, Robert has. He tells us that when they put on *Julius Caesar* at his boarding school he was Brutus, and had to pretend to stab his best friend who was taking the part of Caesar, Emperor of Rome, dressed in a toga and wearing a crown of laurel leaves. He doesn't have to explain the plot to us, actually, because we've read the stories of these famous plays—or some of them, anyway, including *The Taming of the Shrew*—in a little red book entitled *Lamb's Tales from Shakespeare* which Granny once gave us.

It was Robert who suggested our outing today. Handbills advertising the event have been stuck up all over the place. I think he probably meant it to be an outing for just him and my sister Pam, but when Jim and I asked if we could come too he didn't object, or appear to mind in the least. He's very good-tempered, Robert, always laughing. His mother, Mrs Langley, used to be a Miss Lodge until she married Robert's father (who was unfortunately killed in the Great War), and she has been friends with Mrs Winant, the daughter of old Mrs Baker, since the days when they were both young, which is why Robert Langley is always welcome at Lewinnick (he doesn't call it Baker's Folly, and we don't either, not if we're talking to him). Robert can go there any time he wants to, without having to wait for an invitation, and can bathe whenever he likes in the spectacularly twice-daily sea-replenished swimming pool down on the rocks; providing only, that's to say, the tide is far enough out for the pool to be safe.

Today, though, is different. We aren't going to Lewinnick today as friends of the Baker family, but instead as anonymous members of the public, to buy tickets and sit in the audience watching a theatrical performance. On Mount Wise we join an increasing number of walkers, all marching with an air of purpose towards Pentire. We guess their destination to be the same as ours, and when the headland is reached it's clear we've guessed right. The few cars that steer slowly past us, driving cautiously across the bumpy springy turf undermined by hordes of burrowing rabbits, are likewise aiming for Baker's Folly and the same afternoon's entertainment.

So here we are on the exposed heights of Pentire Head, Robert and me and the Twins, amongst a multiplying throng of our fellow merry-makers. In the shared atmosphere of carefree carnival gaiety we smile at total strangers, as though we were acquainted. Sunshine burns the skin of our faces, and we have to balance ourselves against the buffeting of the warm strong Atlantic wind by leaning forwards into it. Robert offers me one of his arms to hang on to, and I hop and skip along beside him, blissfully happy. Above, in the blue sky, seagulls wheel and swoop, while here below, in front of my bare legs, butterflies, flitting indecisively over the tops of nodding fragile harebells, are blown apart and scattered by the breezes that taste of salt, and smell of honey wafted in gusts from golden-yellow gorse bushes.

I feel exultant. I feel full to the brim and overflowing with enjoyment; and I wish the sensation that I have now of being burstingly alive could go on and on for ever. Life ought always, I think, to be like this: always as wonderful as it is *now*!

Yet it isn't entirely surprising to me, the wonderfulness of the moment. For some inexplicable reason I had expected the whole of 1935, the year when I shall become twelve, to be glorious: delights unfolding, non-stop, one after another. The Jubilee trip to London for me and my sister Pam was to have been simply the start of it. Our usual Great Western Beach picnics would this year be far better than usual, I was positive, and the games of cricket and rounders with Robert Langley and Jack and Pat Wilson and Damian Eastman, and other regular holiday visitors, such as the Wichelows, and Rex and Eve Dyer, more than ever fun for everybody.

Later on in the season we children will be competing in the Tennis Club's experimental Junior Tournament. And my brother Jim has let me into the secret of the present I'll be getting on the 21st of August from Daddy and Mummy: they've decided to buy me, he heard them saying, what I've been longing for, one of the newly manufactured lightweight curved balsa wood surfboards to replace the old heavy clumsy two-plank board I've had for ages.

And sometime also during August, in some person's garden, the pupils of Miss Wendy Taylor's Dance Academy are to give a display for charity. I forget whether the proceeds will go to the Cottage Hospital Fund or to the Red Cross, but it doesn't matter—both of them are charities. The best of it is I shall be dancing a solo item personifying *Mist*, barefooted on the person's lawn, waving veils of gauzy grey chiffon. Miss Wendy Taylor says it's called Isadora Duncan freestyle dancing, and it's my favourite kind. I prefer it to ballet, because, as the steps and the movements are my own invention, I can't ever really make a mistake.

This is how I *had* envisaged the summer of 1935. It was going to be perfect, a succession of weeks packed with interesting and enthralling events, without a single flaw. But in reality, I have realised, what you may with confidence plan, often doesn't turn out the way you anticipated. Sad and dreadful things do occur, quite unexpectedly; have, in fact, occurred.

First, there was the shocking death of Bo'sun Hooper, directly followed by the fatal accident of Mummy's childhood friend, the man she refers to as Ned, but everyone else calls Lawrence of Arabia, killed when riding his motor-bike in a narrow country lane; the same huge motor-bike we watched him struggling to push across the soft sand of the Great Western Beach that day he came to have tea with us, and quarrelled with our father, and left almost immediately in a huff. As well as an account of his accident, all that he once did to make himself so terrifically famous in Arabia has been reported again and again in the newspapers.

Mummy was, and still is, extremely upset; which I can understand. For anyone to be bowled over by a second awful tragedy before having had a chance to recover from the first, is very bad luck indeed, and I am truly sorry for my poor mother.

Nevertheless, I intend, if possible, to stay clear of all this unhappiness at home, my mother's weeping and my father's black moods. I don't want to be sad myself. I want to be happy; and today I am. Today, therefore, is a day I mean to remember, to hang on to as tightly as I'm hanging on to Robert's arm, so that it will last, and the memory be like an illustration, a picture in a book, of what happiness feels like; what it *is*.

At the entrance to Baker's Folly driveway, seated at a table and attired in garments that we suppose must be Elizabethan, is a young woman selling tickets. Our mother has given Pam enough money to pay for Robert as well as for us three. Robert tries to argue, but he has to stop protesting because we're holding up the queue behind us.

The drive dips down, very sudden and steep, and at once the wind is cut off, and so is the sunshine. It's as if we've said goodbye to the everyday world and are venturing into a nether region, as Persephone did in the ancient Greek legend we read about years ago with Mrs Oliver. We descend between high banks completely covered by the plant that has brilliantly carmine-pink starry flowers and a dense mass of trailing foliage, its triangular leaves more like succulent green spears than leaves. We don't know the name of this plant, but we've been told it's Mediterranean. There's a considerable amount of it in Newquay, especially above the harbour, and also dangling from the walls of Sir Oliver Lodge's garden perched on the summit of the Towan Beach island. When Pam and I were small it used to amuse us to pick one of the triangular spears and snap it in half, bending the halves backwards to form the shape of a juicy diamond.

The drive turns a corner and here, close before us, is the house. Notices, hand-written, and arrows painted boldly on cardboard, direct us away from the front door to a path leading round the side of the building, thus ensuring that old Mrs Baker's privacy isn't invaded or disturbed by a mob of disorderly pleasure-seekers. Though indeed we ticket-bearing members of the public behave ourselves with the utmost discretion, tramping as quietly as it is possible to tread on gravel past the house's discouragingly tight-shut façade, and even hushing our voices in conversation. But having wound our way down successive flights of steps, no sooner do we reach the lowest level and discover row upon row of chairs placed ready to welcome us than the unwarranted and faintly uncomfortable fear of trespassing on private property evaporates.

Far from the gloomy underworld of our imagination we find ourselves once again in sunshine, for the sun has crept round the tip of Pentire Head and its beams illuminate a scene of joyous fantasy. Surely, though, these are not actors and actresses wearing fancy-dress, but real live inhabitants of a foreign city, Verona, in a bygone century, strolling about, or running busily on errands, calling gaily to each other, and all perfectly at ease in what appears to be their natural setting as they prepare to entertain a crowd of spectators dressed, by comparison, like poverty-stricken beggars. For it is we, the modern-day arrivals, who seem to be out-of-time and out-of-place.

A boy in the doublet and hose of a page invites us to sit wherever we choose, and we choose to sit cross-legged on cushions at the very front, as near as we can get to the stage. We wait, and in due course, the audience having managed to settle itself and fallen silent, the silence is broken by a triumphant echoing trumpet fanfare introducing William Shakespeare's comedy, *The Taming of the Shrew*.

But when the play draws eventually to a close, and the cast has lined up to bow and curtsey, and we have clapped and clapped until our hands hurt, we are witnesses of an even more surprising transformation. Disappearing with alacrity, Petrucio

412

and Katherine and Bianca, and the entire retinue of their servants and companions, reappear a few minutes later minus the silks and satins, ruffs and swords. Instead we behold a bevy of unrecognisable young people scantily clad in bathing costumes and beach towels, jostling and shouting as they scamper pell-mell down to the swimming pool and throw themselves into it.

The last of the audience are trudging wearily up the steps, homeward-bound, but we, privileged by Robert Langley's Baker-connection, linger on, leaning over the parapet to watch enviously the splashing hilarious hurly-burly of bathers in the pool below. Can that laughing girl jumping in at the deep end actually be Katherine—Kate—who I saw with my own eyes less than half-an-hour earlier twitching angrily at the skirt of her long velvet gown when it snagged on a splinter of wood, and seeming, so excessive was her fury, not to care a jot that in tearing it free she ripped the gorgeous material? Her scornful rage, and the whole of the drama we have been transfixed by, was merely, after all, an extravagant pretence! Those god-like untouchable mesmerising stage-characters are able to discard their assumed personalities and in a trice revert to the jolly joking—though still glamorous—flesh-and-blood human beings we now see frolicking about in the water beneath us. How marvellous to be them! And I feel more sure than ever that the adult universe lying somewhere just ahead of me in an unknown future could be as marvellous as the lives led by these dazzling young men and women.

Much to our vexation we notice that David Cox has had the cheek to infiltrate the Shakespearean

Company of actors and actresses, and is engaged in showing off his diving prowess. I've often pondered on the oddity of names in general, and in particular it strikes me as most peculiar that there is a David Cox and also a David Wilcox in Newquay, unrelated by family but having practically identical names, and that both of them are terrible show-offs.

When we were younger David Wilcox had a really mean habit of swarming up to the top of the towering Bishop's Rock which stands mid-way between the Great Western Beach and Towan Beach, and from its dizzy pinnacle jeering at us Hallsmith children, calling out that we were cowardy-cowardy-custards for lacking the courage to follow him. We consider David Wilcox to be a swank-pot, and it's for this reason we've always avoided playing games with him, and why we won't invite him to tea. David *Cox*, who counts almost as a grown-up, has a very pretty sister called Celia. Neither she nor Wilfred Wilcox are swanky in the least; unlike their brothers. (I've never heard of anyone else with the name *Wilfred*, except for the penguin in the *Daily Mirror*'s 'Pip, Squeak and Wilfred' cartoon. I used to think it funny that Wilfred Wilcox had the name of a penguin).

'I wish we'd brought our bathing costumes along with us,' Pam says, yearningly.

Robert tells her to cheer up. We can come back, he says, next week. 'It'll be a lot better when this crowd has gone—we'll have the pool to ourselves. And the tide will be lower, too—it's a bit risky at the moment.'

So it is: downright dangerous, in fact. The bathers we are watching don't seem to realise the riskiness of chasing round and round the edges of the swimming pool while waves, enormous deep-sea rollers breaking on rocks a distance of only yards from them, fling up drenching showers of slippery spray.

But when we return next week, as Robert has promised we shall do, there'll be no need for us to worry. We shan't be in any danger, not with him in charge. Robert wouldn't allow us to bathe, I know, unless it was absolutely safe.

* * *

I am sitting, with Harvey curled up beside me, on the scrubby grass by my mother's basket-chair. Harvey has dozed off to sleep, clutching a half-eaten sponge finger. We've been down on the Great Western Beach with Mummy, and he's exhausted from playing football and racing about on the sands with me. Now it's teatime, and we are in what would be described as Mrs Mulroney's back garden if it had any flowers growing in it, which it hasn't. The long narrow strip of ground that runs from veranda to cliff-edge more resembles a field—and a neglected field, at that—than a garden, but Mrs Mulroney dispenses hospitality here under the drooping branches of a tamarisk tree as regally as though she were enthroned in the faded splendour of her drawing room.

For anyone possessing a sufficiently aristocratic Irish lineage, as does Mrs Mulroney, it may well seem to be not at all eccentric but perfectly rational to sit in the middle of an overgrown field and pour tea from a silver teapot into delicate porcelain cups and saucers nicely arranged on a lace tablecloth. Rex and Eve Dyer have never been either in awe of their grandmother or surprised by her behaviour, but to me the stiff-backed old lady is a somewhat formidable figure and everything about her I find interestingly unusual.

The cucumber sandwiches and sponge-fingers, carried out to us on a silver tray by Mrs Mulroney's maidservant, Mary, have mostly been consumed. With Harvey conveniently asleep, it's time for Mummy and her hostess to get down to the business of serious talking, which is the whole point of our visitation. Mummy is here to consult with Mrs Mulroney and to seek her advice on a matter that has exploded like a bombshell in the Hallsmith household.

Because of the secrecy with which our parents have attempted to muffle the bombshell's explosion inside Grosvenor House, the details filtering through to us children are few and foggy. That it has something to do with our father's employment by the Midland Bank is as much information as I have so far succeeded in acquiring, but I gather that a decision of some kind is going to have to be made, and be made, what's more, in a hurry: hence this visit to Mrs Mulroney.

My mother, who would have preferred to be unaccompanied on the visit, had no alternative but to bring me and Harvey with her. Pam has been taken by Robert Langley to bathe—just the two of them—in the Baker's Folly swimming pool; and my brother Jim, and Bradford Johns and Peter Mitchell, are spending the day climbing trees and running wild on Oliver Jenkins' estate; and it's Lucy's afternoon off.

Instead of the coded whispers our parents confer in at home, Mummy and Mrs Mulroney are discussing the problem quite openly, being either forgetful of me, or else assuming I'm stone deaf. There's nothing wrong with my ears, but unfortunately Mummy has her face turned away, and because of a slight breeze blowing in off the sea I can't catch more than occasional fragments of her side of the conversation. Mrs Mulroney, however, is facing in my direction and she speaks very loudly and very deliberately, in the manner of a magistrate pronouncing judgement, so I'm able to hear every word of her reply. She says:

'My dear Mrs Hallsmith, of course your husband has to accept this offer. I am astonished, frankly, that you should even hesitate. In my opinion—and you have asked for my opinion, have you not?—it is a heaven-sent opportunity for Mr Hallsmith and yourself to leave Newquay—an opportunity that must not, on any account, be missed. Of course, my dear—of *course* you must go!'

Go?—leave Newquay? A bombshell indeed! But why on earth should we—the Hallsmith family—be thinking of leaving Newquay? Go where? Why? I listen, keeping as quiet as a mouse so that Mummy won't be reminded of my presence; and I learn why.

Our father is the only cashier in the Newquay branch of the Midland Bank, (its only staff, according to him, since in Daddy's estimation the manager, Mr Oxley, doesn't signify), holding the fort, as it were, single-handed. And now, like a bolt from the blue, he has received the offer of a transfer to a much bigger branch in a much bigger town—a city, no less: Plymouth. His increase of

417

salary, although naturally welcome, is yet, in Mrs Mulroney's eyes, not the chief inducement to be considered.

'You have a daughter, Mrs Hallsmith—'

'Two daughters, Mrs Mulroney,' my mother murmurs. I catch the murmur, and am glad I haven't been altogether forgotten.

'It is to your elder daughter I am referring, Mrs Hallsmith—to your charmingly pretty daughter Pam. She is growing up, and will soon be of marriageable age. What, I ask you—and you should ask yourself, my dear—what will her prospects be if you were to remain in Newquay? Who is there for her to mix with in Newquay but shopkeepers and hoteliers?—a bunch of vulgarians! You must want better, surely, for your sweet girl than to have her marry some such low-class type of a person as that?' says Mrs Mulroney. 'And now you have been given the chance to move to Plymouth, to one of the chief ports of the Royal Navy, where your daughter will meet any number of suitable young men—young naval officers. For her sake, if not for his own, Mr Hallsmith—her father—ought to accept immediately, before it is withdrawn, this offer of promotion.'

I wait, expecting to hear my mother say that Bo'sun Hooper, who owned the Great Western Hotel, wasn't a low-class type of a person, a vulgarian. He was our very good friend. But Mummy says nothing.

Encouraged, it may be, by her silence, Mrs Mulroney proceeds to take my mother to task for laxity in the upbringing of her children. It is more than our patriotic, it is our Christian duty, she declares, to strive to maintain the fundamental

418

standards of a decent society when so much of the fabric of our civilisation has been destroyed by vandals in the Great War.

'Look at what happened in Russia! Let that be a warning to us!'

What happened in Russia? A warning of what? Mrs Mulroney goes on to speak of Bolshie behaviour, and how we want none of that sort of thing in this fair country of ours. It is we, she says, who must make a stand and stem the tide of degeneracy threatening to engulf us and all that we hold most sacred.

Who are *we*?—who is *us*? Wasn't Bo'sun Hooper one of us? The phrase *Bolshie behaviour* is by no means new to me. My father is fond of using it, but I've never thought of inquiring what precisely is implied by it, nor been aware before of its having a connection with Russia. Would Pam be able to explain this to me? Robert, more likely. I will ask him.

Mrs Mulroney confesses herself to be shocked that Lucy, our mother's maidservant, is allowed to address the children of Mr Hallsmith as Pam and Jim, Elspeth and Harvey, without the respectful prefix of a *Miss* or a *Master*. Is it any wonder that members of the lower orders are becoming Bolshie when they feel they have been given permission to communicate with their betters on an equal footing? If they are to be kept in their proper place, then it is up to us, their employers, to teach them what and where is their proper place, and to see they pay due heed to it.

Does this mean our mother is Bolshie?

Fearing, perhaps, that she has overstepped the mark and may have shaken her visitor's confidence

419

too severely, Mrs Mulroney softens her tone. There is no reason, she says, for Mr Hallsmith to feel disgraced by the menial position he is obliged to occupy as clerk in a bank. Many, alas, of our courageous defenders have been forced, as a consequence of the dreadful War, to earn their bread in circumstances unworthy of them. It does him, Mrs Mulroney assures my mother, no discredit.

'We understand! But you, my dear, you must never forget that your brave husband is, and will always be honoured as a true officer and a gentleman—God bless the man!'

Never forget . . . an officer and a gentleman . . . It could be my father uttering this admonition. Plainly he and Mrs Mulroney have much in common; or at any rate if nothing else they share a view of Daddy's rightful position in society, as well as of the rules by which that society ought properly to be governed.

But my mother, who is greeted with smiles by all the Newquay shopkeepers; who talks to Wilton's wife, Mrs Wilton, from whom she buys wallflowers in season, as easily, kindly, freely as one woman chats to another; who gives money—sixpences— and food and clothing to the tramps who come knocking at our back door, unemployed ex-servicemen, because they remind her, pityingly, of those wounded soldiers she cared for when she was Commandant of the King Edward's Convalescent Hospital in the Great War; who is worshipped by Lucy; is she, my mother—Mummy—in agreement with Mrs Mulroney's opinions and pronouncements? What does her silence indicate?

Mrs Mulroney tinkles a hand-bell; whereupon

Harvey stirs on his rug, and opens his eyes, and sits up. The half-eaten sponge-finger has fallen on to the grass. I tell him he can't eat it now.

'Oh no, Harvey—no! It's got ants, heaps of them—see!—crawling all over it—'

In the light of what I've been hearing, I study Mary with renewed attention when she trips out to fetch the silver tea-tray. And I can't—I really can't—imagine Lucy Coles wearing a similar frilly cap, or a little lace-edged apron in place of her big starched all-enveloping all-purpose one. Nor can I imagine Lucy calling our mother *Madam*. As for the description of *maidservant* given by Mrs Mulroney to Mary—that doesn't strike me as a fitting title for Lucy Coles, who is—well, I don't know, exactly. Who is she, if not a maidservant? Just our Lucy, I suppose. What else?

*   *   *

Following on Mummy's unsettling conversation with Mrs Mulroney, the remainder of the summer holidays of 1935 has a slightly worrying undercurrent of impermanence about it. Are we staying—or are we going?

If we do move to Plymouth, then my sister and I will be sent, we are reliably informed, to a real school. The main difference, as far as I can tell, between a real school and us having lessons with Miss Howard, is that we would be required to wear a uniform. As a matter of fact, although disliking the colour—brown—I have always rather envied and hankered after the blazer and the gymslip worn by pupils of St Kilda's, their uniform indicating membership of what I feel sure must be

421

a *real-school* world, although as an outsider I can only guess at its delights.

Wishing to overcome my ignorance and prepare myself for changes ahead, I have been reading books borrowed from Boots' Lending Library written by Angela Brazil, swapping tales of smuggling and pirates, and coral islands and kidnapping and the three musketeers—adventures that were formerly so engrossing—for accounts of hockey matches and dormitory feasts, and the heady prospect of mingling with lots and lots of girls the same age as me who will all, I am convinced, be my bosom friends.

The prevailing atmosphere of uncertainty as to whether we stay or whether we go doesn't affect the certainty of various dates already clearly marked on the calendar (distributed free to customers of Messrs John Julian Ltd., and advertising, as well as furniture bought and sold, the shop's furniture removal service) which hangs in our kitchen. One such important unalterable fixture is Miss Wendy Taylor's dance display, wherein I have been allotted the honour of a solo number.

On the morning before the Saturday afternoon when the display is due to take place in somebody's garden, it rains. This could be disastrous. But—providentially—the rain stops and the sun comes out just in time to avoid having to cancel the display. When it's my turn to present my own interpretation of *Mist*, the dampness of the setting, with drips pattering down from branches overhead at every puff of wind, seems to be entirely appropriate. Flimsily clad in a diaphanous grey tunic, and gracefully waving a long grey chiffon scarf, I drift and swirl to the accompaniment of Chopin's piano music issuing from a gramophone partially concealed behind the laurel bushes. And the sensation of wet grass under my bare feet is so delicious I could easily go on dancing, on and on for ever, in the middle of this audience of smiling applauding women (it's mostly women), perched in a circle on uncomfortable garden chairs.

'Oh, well done, Elspeth!' Miss Wendy Taylor whispers in my ear, embracing me, proud of me. It is a memorably happy occasion.

So also, for me—although not for the Twins—is the Junior Tennis Tournament, for which we have been practising all summer. Pam, at the last moment, scratches her name from the lists tacked up in the creosote-smelling pavilion of our Tennis Club, having ceased to be interested in taking part herself after Robert Langley sprains his ankle the day before the tournament and has to drop out of it.

Jim, unfortunately, draws a dud as a partner, a girl staying at the Bristol Hotel who can't play tennis for toffee-nuts. The result is, they lose every game of every match, and quickly too.

But I, on the contrary, with my partner, a visitor-boy called Graham, win the section for Under-14s. We owe our success, I must honestly admit, to my partner invariably yelling out, no matter if the ball is on his side of the court or mine: '*Leave it to me!*' I don't much care for Graham, who is extremely bossy, and looks like a midget bespectacled version of Dr Bell, but he does know how to play tennis, having had, he tells me, professional coaching. And a good many of my serves do—luckily—go over the net instead of into it, which helps.

423

Not all of this summer's holiday recollections are so pleasureable, though: for instance, there is the wound inflicted by our mother selling the doll's house that Lewarne Hosking gave me and Pam a few Christmases ago. She did it without asking us beforehand if she might. I try to find an excuse for her action. That our mother should launch a vigorous campaign of room-clearance in readiness for the family's probably imminent uprooting is perfectly sensible behaviour. But does the operation have to entail her getting rid of what she considers to be the clutter and rubbish of outgrown toys?

'Mummy says it took up an unnecessary amount of space, and we never nowadays play with it,' I report to Pam, '—which is understandable, she says, because for you and me, at our age, to enjoy playing with a doll's house would be ridiculous.'

'We can enjoy *having* it, can't we?—without actually *playing* with it,' my sister argues, angrily unforgiving. 'And anyway, it didn't belong to her. Lewarne gave it to us—it was ours. Mummy had no *right* to sell it.'

We feel the injustice, the unfairness, keenly. But we can't explain—we can't begin to explain—to our mother how deeply resented is her cheerful disposal of our treasured possession. She hasn't the least idea of how upset we are: we are *very* upset.

Blithely unconscious of the offence she has caused, and thereafter, in the belief that we will be pleased, compounding it, Mummy buys a brooch for each of her daughters with money from the sale of our doll's house. My brooch is meant to be the figure of a woman holding a tennis racquet, made of a dull greyish metal, picked out in green enamel—not even sparkly! It's ugly and awful, and I won't ever wear it.

But the event I shall least enjoy remembering is the Senior Tennis Tournament's prize-giving, the ceremony which every year traditionally closes the grass-court season.

News of our impending departure is by now fully out in the open, and it is no secret either that the Club's committee members, wanting to show appreciation of their Secretary's unflagging efforts in reviving the fortunes of Newquay's Lawn Tennis Club and putting it on the map, have had a whip-round and subscribed enough money to pay for, not something as banal as a chiming clock, but an extravagantly expensive, purpose-designed, eight-sided solid silver salver, raised on eight little exquisitely dainty shell-shaped feet: an object of beauty, to be marvelled at.

Throughout the whole afternoon it has lain exposed on the green baize cloth of the table, at the centre of the customary array of twinkling cups, for all the world to see and admire. Daddy himself has had ample opportunity to study the inscription engraved upon it, and as he reads it I watch his brow darkening, and fear that a storm is brewing.

When the finalists have fought to a finish their last victorious or defeated battles, and the cups been duly distributed, Mr Lodge—our own sweet smiling Mr Lodge—delivers a short address, in which he expresses the sincere gratitude of the Committee for Mr Hallsmith's dedicated work on behalf of the Club and the regret felt by all the Club's members at the loss of their excellent Secretary and his charming wife, Mrs Hallsmith; and in conclusion he desires to convey an assurance of the very many warm good wishes they will be taking with them to their new home. Having wound up his tribute thus satisfactorily, Mr Lodge, beaming, then hands over the wonderful salver to Daddy.

If our father, while listening to these kindly intended sentiments and well-chosen phrases, is grinding his teeth, none but his children will have guessed it. The scowl, the grimace, which is the nearest he can get to achieving a smile, would be interpreted by the assembled onlookers as an indication of modest embarrassment. He is known, Hallsmith, as a chap with not much ever to say for himself: a diffident sort of a chap—artistic.

Daddy is nodding his head, mumbling: 'Very kind of you—very kind!' More than this he's quite unable to utter, because he doesn't think it kind at all. He is absolutely furious; enraged, insulted. Mummy, however, is standing close by, and she, quick to save the situation, steps forward, covering any perceived awkwardness with just the right graciously delivered words of thanks, and a few affectionate memories, lightly related, with a joke or two thrown in. The danger—phew!—has been

426

averted: everybody is laughing, and clapping again.

Once we are back at home, the storm breaks. Why—*why* does the inscription include the name of *Mrs Hallsmith*? He, and he alone, has been the Honorary Secretary of Newquay Lawn Tennis Club—has slaved his guts out to make it what it is today. She—Janet—has had nothing to do with it—*nothing*!

'But Guthrie dear—Guth—'

It's no good. Mummy may indeed, as he bitterly declares, have had nothing whatever to do with his triumphs, his glowing success when Secretary of the Club, but there is not a single syllable she can now pronounce to repair the damage done to our father's self-esteem. His name, and only his name, should have been inscribed on the salver. They should have *known* that by adding her name the whole point of the exercise was rendered null and void.

At least (although Mummy is warned by some instinctive wisdom not to throw petrol on the flames by saying so) it could have been worse. The Committee did remember to make sure that Daddy's DSO was correctly engraved.

Wilton, sombre and silent, our father's indispensable staunch ally, without whom all the fine schemes to resurrect and glorify Newquay's Lawn Tennis Club would have been totally unavailing—he didn't get a silver salver, or even a vote of thanks. But a groundsman, naturally, doesn't deserve the same recognition as an Honorary Secretary. And anyway, what possible use would Mrs Wilton have had for a silver salver?

*　　　*　　　*

The summer holidays are finished and the winter term has begun. Jim is already back at Exeter School, and we shan't see Robert Langley again until next year, and then it won't be in Newquay. My sister Pam and I have had our last ever lessons with Miss Howard; have sat for the last time at a table with Mollie Purchase, and Kathleen and Miriam Kiley. Never again shall we cross the grocery store's backyard, sniffing its exotic spicy smells as we pass the piles of boxes and tea chests, to fumble our way up the dark little narrow boarded-in staircase, at the top of which Folly stands, waiting for us, barking, barking: that hateful dreaded noise.

This is the final week of September, 1935, and it is also the final week before the Hallsmith family leaves Newquay, the small seaside town on the north coast of Cornwall where I was born, for *ever*. What makes these few remaining September days preceding our departure so strangely unreal is that we are not spending them in Grosvenor House but camping out like gypsies in the Misses Clark-Ourry's Rose Café at Porth.

Once our parents had settled, with Mrs Mulroney's helpful advice, the major difficulty of deciding whether to stay or whether to go, they were then plagued by a multitude of lesser anxieties. Amongst them was the likelihood of me and Pam and Harvey getting thoroughly in the way, or of being perhaps worse than a nuisance, coming to actual harm (Harvey especially), while John Julian's removal men were trampling to and fro, stripping Grosvenor House of its beds and wardrobes, chests of drawers, carpets, mirrors,

428

cooking utensils—the lot. When fully loaded the couple of immensely tall top-heavy vans would be driven off to a distant address on the fringes of Dartmoor, in Devon, a different county entirely, and the furniture unloaded there into a new home that we children haven't yet seen. What our mother and father wanted to avoid at all costs—but how?—was having us three mixed up in the inevitable pandemonium of house clearance.

No sooner did the Clark-Ourry sisters hear of the vexatious problem than they offered to lend us their Rose Café. Because of Miss Isobel Clark-Ourry—lame, with a built-up boot, and always in poor health—suffering from a severe bout of bronchitis, the two old ladies had had to cut short their regular seasonal struggle to earn a precarious living by serving delicious cream teas to Porth visitors, and abandoning everything in haste—café, railway carriage, car park, sweetie kiosk—had had to retreat while it was still only August to their winter residence on Mount Wise. As temporary quarters we were more than welcome, they said, to make use of the café's facilities and their unoccupied bedrooms in the railway carriage for just as long as it suited us to do so.

At first our parents had flatly refused the offer. Good gracious, no! How very kind—but of course it was quite out of the question! Not, naturally, to Miss Veah and Miss Isobel Clark-Ourry, but to each other in private they pooh-poohed such a farcical proposal. Facilities indeed! That we, the Hallsmith family, should seek refuge for even a few days in that ramshackle old wreck of a boatshed masquerading as a café, or consider sleeping in a derelict railway carriage, was the height of absurdity—ridiculous! What *would* people *say*, for goodness sake?

The fact is they had pinned their hopes on being entrusted with the keys of the Hoskings' holiday bungalow, but as the date of our departure drew nearer that relied-upon plan—or hope—collapsed. Our warm-hearted generous friend, Lewarne Hosking, forgetful of a vaguely given promise, had continued to be absent on a second and prolonged honeymoon trip to Monte Carlo with his bride of a year, Nancy. The weeks went by, and then suddenly Enid, his crabby sister, without any prior explanation or warning, locked up the Porth bungalow and caught a train back to Liverpool. No alternative solution suggesting itself at this late stage, our parents were forced to swallow their pride and from sheer desperation agree to risk the stigma of extreme unorthodoxy.

Which is why—oh joy!—we are here!

Pam and I share the Misses Clark-Ourrys' cramped little sitting room, located beyond and two steps down from the miniscule kitchen. My sister sleeps on the saggy baggy sofa, and I improvise an Ali Baba type of bed by assembling a heap of cushions on the coconut-matting alongside her. Luckily the Miss Clark-Ourrys have a weakness for cushions, and so there is an ample supply of them available: cushions decorated with beads and tassels, covered in silk or satin or velvet, and as plump and sweetly scented as Miss Veah herself.

'What fun this is, children!' exclaims Mummy, gamely making the best of a situation she and Daddy view as unequivocally dire. Our father, incapable of pretending for a moment that he thinks it *fun*, has chosen not to join his wife and Harvey in their railway-compartment accommodation, and is stopping behind in Newquay, preserving his dignity by mounting guard, like a soldier on duty, over the chaotically emptying Grosvenor House. Dr and Mrs Mitchell, who live a mere quarter-mile or so further up Mount Wise, have invited him to be their guest, but Daddy elects to stick with grim determination to his solitary post.

Lucy has the worst of it. She is obliged to make do with a borrowed Li-Lo on the floor in a corner of the tearoom that has been cleared of tables and chairs.

'It's only for two or three nights, Lucy dear,' says Mummy, coaxing her. 'We just have to think of it—don't we?—as a sort of adventurous picnic. And the girls are too young to be left quite on their own—even though it's perfectly safe here,' she adds, reassuringly. 'Miss Veah Clark-Ourry told me that in all the years they've owned the boathouse—the café—they haven't ever been troubled by intruders—not once.'

This is Lucy's first awful humiliating experience of sleeping, like a wretched homeless vagabond, on the floor. She doesn't complain. She would do anything—go through fire—for our mother, but she is tight-lipped about her ordeal. Lucy has never cared for picnics.

When we've finished eating our supper—eggs and bacon and sausages, the same as we had for breakfast—I escort Mummy and Harvey across the road and along the path through the meadow to the railway carriage, which is raised up on stilts. I walk ahead of them, shining the torch that was one

431

of my birthday presents (from the Twins, actually: they each paid for half of it), to show the way. We climb the wooden steps, and Mummy lights the lamp in Miss Veah's tiny doll's house bedroom. Its cosiness is so entrancing I almost wish I was going to stay in the railway carriage too. But an enticement even greater is the prospect of walking back through the meadow by myself, illuminating with the beam of my torch the jungle of surrounding grasses, and knowing that Lucy has already drawn the curtains in the Rose Café, and lit the lamps, and will bring me and Pam mugs of cocoa after we've got undressed.

It's extraordinary for us to be lying in bed so near to the sea. We don't talk much. The tide has turned and is flooding up the estuary. It isn't high yet, but it will be soon. There's no wind at all. The night is so calm and so still we can hear the incoming waves lapping gently against the concrete jetty immediately beyond our door. Because the walls aren't built of bricks, as they would be in a proper house, but of planking, it feels as if, instead of being shut off from the waves, we are very close indeed to them: practically a part of the huge night outside.

*   *   *

As Mummy has said, we are only here for a few days. How many days, though—two or three? four? I don't ask. This brief pause between seasons, between the ending of summer and the beginning of winter, is an intermission curiously timeless, vague, suspended mysteriously, without boundaries, between our known past and our

432

unknown future. The air itself seems to be tinged with regret for something dear but indefinable that has gone, while promising simultaneously something just out of sight, unimaginably wonderful, yet to come.

Each early morning starts by being cool, verging on cold, a freshness that rapidly dissipates, so that presently, as the sun mounts higher in a blue sky, it's warm enough to bathe, to bask on the sand, to pretend, even, that it's an afternoon in August: warm enough—hot enough—to be summer. But then, too soon for summer, the sun dips down beyond the sea's horizon, and all at once the air has a chill sharp touch, and the stars appear prickly-bright, as if to warn in advance of the onset of frosty October evenings.

Our father has this year dedicated his annual fortnight's vacation to organising the removal of the Hallsmith family to a house rented by our parents in a moorland village some ten or so miles from the naval port and cathedral city of Plymouth, an undertaking that seems to necessitate him driving backwards and forwards a great deal, long exhausting trips which, although he would never admit to it, I think he enjoys. Mummy sometimes goes with him, sometimes not. However, when John Julian's vans eventually trundle out of Newquay she does insist on occupying the passenger seat of the Austin, in spite of Daddy declaring, irritably, that he's perfectly capable of overseeing the unloading of chairs and tables without the benefit of her presence. But it's essential, she tells him, for her to be there too, so as to make sure the various pieces of furniture, on their arrival, are deposited in the right rooms.

The following day they drive over again, and Harvey goes with them, sitting on Mummy's knee, Lucy having been given a lift into Newquay to save her catching the bus, and dropped off at the now empty Grosvenor House where, by arrangement, her sister Lily will join her and help in the task of cleaning the newly vacated premises from top to bottom. Lily, stout and strong, whose wedding to Albert I once witnessed, has a reputation for being good at scrubbing floors, and at doing what is generally referred to as the rough work.

They depart, and we are left on our own, the two of us, me and Pam, in charge of the Rose Café and each other, unsupervised and free to pass the hours from dawn to dusk in whatever way we fancy. Lucy will be back to cook us our supper, probably catching the last bus out from Newquay, and our father will deliver Mummy by car, and a sleepy Harvey, sometime later: they can't say exactly when. Meanwhile the day, and Porth, belong to us alone. The holiday season has ended, and Porth, as empty of its visitors as Grosvenor House of its furnishings, is all ours.

We spend the morning apart. I leave Pam dangling her legs idly over the edge of the wharf in dreamy contemplation of the outgoing tide. She has equipped herself with sketchpad and paintbox, it being her intention, she says, later—no hurry— to paint a picture of the Rose Café.

As for me, I have my own ritual of farewell to conduct. My aim is to revisit systematically every nook and cranny, every beach and inlet of a Porth made familiar by years of Sunday outings.

Carefully, solemnly, I descend and ascend the well-remembered tracks leading from grassy cliff-tops—cliffs too low almost to be described as cliffs—down to our favourite picnicking sites. The care taken is quite unnecessary: they were easy enough tracks to negotiate when laden, as we used to be, with baskets and bags and, more recently, with a baby, and all I'm carrying today is a bathing costume and a towel; but this goodbye tour must not be rushed.

I've compiled a list, a mental inventory, and every item on it must be ticked off, one by one. No rushing, no skimping: it's got to be thorough. Besides reminding myself of each separate cove, I have to cross, by the draughty unsteady footbridge, the gap dividing mainland and island, allowing a full five minutes to linger, leaning on its rail, for the fascination of watching waves hustle and crowd into the constricted passageway from opposite entrances, and their tumultous collision.

Next, I shall station myself at the furthest highest point of the island in order to count the number of brown heads bobbing about in the green deep-water swells of the seals' colony. Then I must bathe; and after bathing, wait until the tide will have ebbed sufficiently far out for me to be able to scramble over the clutter of slippery wet rocks underneath the bridge, to emerge, like an explorer discovering a new continent, on to the clean-washed untrodden uninhabited beach beyond.

There are people who collect butterflies, and others who collect—as does my brother Jim—stamps. I am collecting a place, attempting by a concentration of memory, to capture somewhere I love—Porth—and so to preserve it inside my head for ever.

This is how I occupy the morning, retracing my

steps only when alerted by pangs of hunger to the need for food.

Pam shows me her painting of the Rose Café and a sketch of the railway carriage, and her drawings of seagulls posing atop the mushroom-shaped bollards of the old wharf. We sit on the sun-warmed concrete of its cracked and broken surface, eating the sandwiches that Lucy prepared hours earlier for our lunch; and as the hot still afternoon, this ultimate golden gift of late September, glides effortlessly by, we let it go, content to do nothing except, perhaps, to read a little, doze a little, hardly bothering ourselves to talk but lazily glad—or at any rate I am, and I feel Pam is as well—to be here, outside the Rose Café, we two together, and once again a pair of sisters. If we don't say much it's because words are simply not required.

Lucy does travel back to Porth on the six o'clock bus, as expected. She brings us a message. Mummy and Harvey won't, after all, be joining us for supper. They are to stay tonight, apparently, with Dr and Mrs Mitchell. And it turns out to be just as well they have decided to accept the Mitchells' hospitality and stop on in Newquay, for as darkness falls the weather changes. Thick clouds gather, obliterating the stars, and a gale-force wind comes whistling in with the tide.

Every so often through the night we are wakened by the sound of torrential rain drumming on the corrugated roof of our annexe. We lie and listen to the intermittent slosh of waves breaking against the end of the wharf, and the splatter of pebbles cast up by flying spray, landing, like a volley of bullets, on the concrete immediately outside our door.

The noise is stupendous, and all the more deafening for being in such contrast to the preceding days of quiet serenity. For me and Pam, knowing that we are safe ashore, and not aboard a sinking ship in danger of drowning, the unleashed fury of the elements is exciting rather than alarming; but for country-bred Lucy Coles, alone on her Li-Lo in a corner of the big tearoom, the racket created by raging winds and sea so close at hand must be terrifying.

With dawn, and an outgoing tide, the extreme violence of the weather has a good deal abated, although the skies remain dark and threatening and the rain continues to fall, with occasional lulls, throughout the morning and afternoon. It's amazing to recall that only yesterday we sat sunning ourselves on a wharf now strewn with sand and stones, and branches torn from the tamarisk tree which overhangs the lean-to wherein is housed the waitresses' primitive lavatory.

We don't actually care, my sister and I, how long we may find ourselves marooned here. Snuggled down on sofa and cushions, devouring cream toffees from a large tin given to us by Miss Isobel Clark-Ourry for a holiday treat, and well supplied with a selection of Edwardian romances in faded red cloth bindings, our situation as castaways could hardly be bettered. The novels are the result of a hasty splashy dash between one drenching downpour and the next to her sweetie kiosk standing in what has become overnight a flooded car-park. Behind Miss Isobel's rows of glass jars containing bulls' eyes and acid drops are the few dimly lit mouldy shelves, labelled, rather grandiosely, *Lending Library: 2d. per Volume*, from which we have borrowed enough reading material to keep us entertained for weeks. With toffees to suck, and books to read, and Lucy's devotedly regular mugfuls of cocoa to drink, we are in a sort of heaven, and our sense of luxurious comfort is agreeably increased by the buffeting of the storm outside.

As a consequence of this happy state of affairs we feel quite sorry when, at teatime, the Austin appears with a squeal of brakes on the wharf of the Rose Café. Here is our father, arriving in a tremendous hurry, to fetch us back from Porth. The Mitchells, he says, have kindly offered to put us up—we two Hallsmith girls—in addition to Mummy and Harvey, for our final night in Newquay, Cornwall.

Daddy is at his most impatient. Why, he wants to know, are we so totally unprepared? We should have had the common sense to be expecting him: to have everything packed and be waiting to leave. 'Chuck all your stuff in the car—never mind how— just get it *in*! Come on, come *on*—'

We scurry about, obeying commands. And as to any twinges of disappointment my sister Pam and I may secretly suffer at having what was a short but blissful Robinson Crusoe chapter in our lives brought to this abrupt conclusion, it is a disappointment Lucy Coles does not share with us. Lucy is unrelievedly thankful to be rescued.

Driving away from Porth, on the stretch of road that skirts the wide head of the estuary, I screw myself round in my seat to take a last look at the Rose Café; but it has already vanished, the deepening dusk and a renewed onslaught of rain combining to blot it from sight.

*   *   *

When first I heard that our parents had made up their minds definitely to accept the Midland Bank's offer of a transfer from Newquay to Plymouth, I reminded them—warned them: 'If ever we aren't able to find something, Lucy always knows where it is. We tell her, and she always finds it—' For I had just learned that in leaving Newquay, we shall be leaving Lucy too. Such a parting is almost inconceivable. How are we to manage in the future without Lucy? How shall *I* manage without her?

I meant—and mean—of course, much more than my shocked immediate outburst implied. A declaration of the Hallsmith family's dependence for years and years, for as long ago as I can remember, on Lucy Coles infallibly finding for us the odds and ends we daily, carelessly mislay, although true, is only a fraction of what I really mean. But how can I express in words the immensity of the loss I have begun to realise will be mine? Lucy herself I shall be losing—my Lucy, yes!—but what else with her? The rocks, the sands of the Great Western Beach, that playground of ours we have always taken for granted, will be gone for ever; and the sea—the *sea*! Most of all, I shall miss the sea.

Goodbye, my childhood!

AFTERWORD

O my parents, my poor tragic parents—my good and beautiful, brave, dramatic, unperceptive mother; my disappointed, embittered, angry, lonely, talented father: locked, both of them, inside a prison they had not deserved, for reasons they didn't understand, by conventions they took to be immutable laws.

I see them now as they were in my childhood: blindly struggling, trapped by social circumstances beyond their control, governed by inherited prejudices not worthy of them.

How I wish I could have saved you, set you free, given you the happiness you once expected, all the success you had hoped and longed for, and never managed to make your own.

Forgive me, my father, my mother. I have written this memoir, however much it may seem to be otherwise, out of great pity, and with great love.

A NOTE ON THE AUTHOR

Emma Smith was born Elspeth Hallsmith in 1923 in Newquay, Cornwall, where until the age of twelve, she lived with her mother and father, an elder brother and sister, and a younger brother. During the Second World War, having completed a secretarial training course, she was taken on in 1942 by the Records Department of the War Office; a job she left the following year so as to join a scheme for employing girls on the Grand Union Canal. Their strenuous occupation, requiring them to carry steel and coal cargoes in pairs of narrowboats between London, Birmingham and Coventry docks, provided her with the necessary material for *Maidens' Trip* (1948). Her first book, it won the John Llewellyn Rhys Memorial Prize. The winter of 1946–7 had been spent with a documentary film unit in India and the diary she kept on that trip was put to good fictional use in 1948, when, alone in Paris for the whole hot summer, she either sat in her little hotel room or by the banks of the Seine, writing *The Far Cry*. Published in 1949, it was awarded the James Tait Black Memorial Prize. In 1951 Emma Smith married Richard Stewart-Jones. After her husband's death in 1957 she went to live, with her two young children, amongst the sheep-farming hills of Wales, where she proceeded to write and have published four successful children's books including *No Way of Telling*, runner-up for the Carnegie gold medal, a number of short stories and, in 1978, her novel *The Opportunity of a Lifetime*. Since 1980 she has lived in the London district of Putney.